D1610150

Lincolnshire
COUNTY COUNCIL

COMMUNITIES, CULTURAL SERVICES
and ADULT EDUCATION

**This book should be returned on or before
the last date shown below.**

SE3

SE3 11/03   BRACEBRIDGE   1 8 AUG 2018

13. APR 11.   -- OCT 2002   1 8 OCT 2018

13. JUL   Tel: 01522 520649

26.   Netherham Library

21.   1 c FEB 2014
          Tel: 01

KIRTON LIBRARY
TEL: 01522 782010
          16. SEP 14,
17. OCT   Scotter Library

          2 7 JUL 2012

          Tel: 01522

To renew or order library books please telephone 01522 782010
or visit www.lincolnshire.gov.uk
You will require a Personal Identification Number.
Ask any member of staff for this.

04670178

BRITISH & ALLIED AIRCRAFT MANUFACTURERS
OF THE FIRST WORLD WAR

TERRY C. TREADWELL

AMBERLEY

First published 2011

Amberley Publishing Plc
Cirencester Road, Chalford,
Stroud, Gloucestershire, GL6 8PE

www.amberley-books.com

Copyright © Terry C. Treadwell 2011

The right of Terry C. Treadwell to be identified as the Author
of this work has been asserted in accordance with the
Copyrights, Designs and Patents Act 1988.

All rights reserved. No part of this book may be reprinted
or reproduced or utilised in any form or by any electronic,
mechanical or other means, now known or hereafter invented,
including photocopying and recording, or in any information
storage or retrieval system, without the permission in writing
from the Publishers.

British Library Cataloguing in Publication Data.
A catalogue record for this book is available from the British Library.

ISBN 978 1 4456 0101 4

Typeset in 10pt on 12pt Sabon.
Typesetting and Origination by Amberley Publishing.
Printed in the UK.

Contents

Introduction

At the turn of the twentieth century aircraft manufacturers, if you could really call them that, were in their infancy and almost all aircraft being built or developed were either in sheds in someone's back yard, or if the manufacturers were wealthy enough, in workshops. The pilots themselves had no training in these formative years as every day and every attempt to fly was a learning curve for these men. Where there were schools to teach people to fly, the instructors themselves were barely capable of flying the aircraft. It was against this kind of background that aviation struggled to find a place in the military machine, a military full of prejudice against change, whose answer to most problems in battle was 'a damn good cavalry charge and a taste of cold steel'. This, to their traditional and stubborn way of thinking, would be sufficient to rout the enemy.

In September 1910, three officers from the Royal Field Artillery, Captain Bertram Dickinson and Lieutenants Lancelot Dwarris Louis Gibbs and Robert Lorraine, took their aircraft to the army's autumn manoeuvres on Salisbury Plain. Like all flyers at the time, the three officers had learned to fly at their own expense and had purchased their own aircraft. This of course meant that only the very wealthy could afford to learn to fly, thus creating an elitist group of people. Their low-level flights across the heads of the cavalry units caused a great deal of displeasure and anger from the vast majority of the cavalry officers there, but fortunately there were those in the War Office whose eyes were not so blinkered. The trials they carried out proved even to the most sceptical of senior army officers present that there was tremendous value to be had using the aircraft as a reconnaissance device. Earlier in the year the War Office had placed a large shed at Larkhill on Salisbury Plain at the disposal of the Hon. Charles Rolls, who had offered to instruct army officers in the art of flying. Unfortunately, during a flying meeting at Bournemouth on 12 July, Charles Rolls was killed when his aircraft crashed on the airfield there. The programme of flying training was then handed over to Captain Robert Fulton, who had learned to fly in France, and he set about setting up a school. The Committee of Imperial Defence suddenly and inexplicably stated that:

> Experiments with aeroplanes should be discontinued, but that advantage should be taken of private enterprise in this branch of aeronautics.

Astonishingly, one month later the War Office issued an Army Order creating the Air Battalion of the Royal Engineers, and placed it under the command of Brevet Major Sir Alexander Bannerman with Captain Philip William Lilian Broke-Smith as his adjutant. This order seems to have gone against the advice of the Committee of Imperial Defence.

The new unit was divided into two sections: the first, No. 1 Company, was the Airship section; the second section, No. 2 Company, flew the aircraft that were already based at Larkhill. Among the commanders of the company was Captain Henry Robert Moore Brooke-Popham of the Oxfordshire & Buckinghamshire Light Infantry; Brooke-Popham was later to become Air Chief Marshal Sir Robert Brooke-Popham, RAF. In one of his many lectures in support of aviation he said:

> I see no reason why aviators should not shoot at one another while flying.

Brooke-Popham carried out a number of experiments using pistols, rifles and, it is said, attempted to install a machine gun on one of the aircraft.

Another of the advocates for aviation was Captain Bertram Dickinson, who, in a memorandum to the sub-committee of the Committee of Imperial Defence, stated:

> In the case of a European war between two countries who were equipped with large corps of aeroplanes, both sides would try to obtain information about the other side in order to hinder or prevent the enemy from obtaining information. This would inevitably lead to war in the air by armed aeroplanes against each other. This fight for supremacy in the air in future wars will be of the greatest importance ...

The report struck home, and almost immediately the sub-committee recommended the formation of an aerial service to be known as the Royal Flying Corps (RFC); it was to consist of a Naval Wing (later to become the Royal Naval Air Service, RNAS), a Military Wing and a Central Flying School. On 13 April 1912, the organisation was formed by Royal Warrant. No. 2 Aeroplane Company of the Air Battalion became No. 3 Squadron RFC, the remainder of the pilots at Farnborough and Larkhill became the nucleus of No. 2 Squadron RFC and No. 1 (Airship) Company became No. 1 Squadron RFC.

In August 1912, the Military Aeroplane Competition was held at Larkhill to select an aircraft to be used by the RFC. The winner of the competition was the Cody biplane, but there was no way that the aircraft could be construed as a military machine. The nearest model to that was the B.E. (British Experimental) 2, designed by Geoffrey de Havilland, which was the one selected. Thirty-two aircraft entered the competition and all were allotted consecutive serial numbers.

No. 1 Hanriot monoplane powered by a 100-hp Gnome engine
No. 2 Hanriot monoplane powered by a 100-hp Gnome engine
No. 3 Vickers No. 6 monoplane powered by a 70-hp Viale engine
No. 4 Blériot XI-2 monoplane powered by a 70-hp Gnome engine
No. 5 Blériot XXI monoplane powered by a 70-hp Gnome engine
No. 6 Avro Type G biplane powered by a 60-hp Green engine
No. 7 Avro Type G biplane powered by a 60-hp Green engine
No. 8 Breguet U2 biplane powered by a 110-hp Canton-Unne engine
No. 9 Breguet U2 biplane powered by a 110-hp Canton-Unne engine
No. 10 Coventry Ordnance Works biplane powered by a 100-hp Gnome engine
No. 11 Coventry Ordnance Works biplane powered by a 110-hp Chenu engine
No. 12 Bristol G.E.2 biplane powered by a 100-hp Gnome engine
No. 13 Bristol G.E.2 biplane powered by a 70-hp Daimler-Mercedes engine
No. 14 Bristol-Coanda monoplane powered by an 80-hp Gnome engine
No. 15 Bristol-Coanda monoplane powered by an 80-hp Gnome engine
No. 16 Flanders biplane powered by a 100-hp ABC engine
No. 17 Martin-Hanasyde monoplane powered by a 75-hp Chenu engine
No. 18 Aerial Wheel powered by a 50-hp NEC engine
No. 19 Mersey monoplane powered by a 45-hp Isaacson engine

No. 20 British Deperdussin monoplane powered by a 100-hp Anzani engine
No. 21 British Deperdussin monoplane powered by a 100-hp Gnome engine
No. 22 Maurice Farman biplane powered by a 70-hp Renault engine
No. 23 D.F.W Mars monoplane powered by a 100-hp Mercedes engine
No. 24 Lohner biplane powered by a 120-hp Austro-Daimler engine
No. 25 Harper monoplane powered by a 60-hp Green engine
No. 26 French Deperdussin monoplane powered by a 100-hp Gnome engine
No. 27 French Deperdussin monoplane powered by a 100-hp Gnome engine
No. 28 Handley Page Type F monoplane powered by a 70-hp Gnome engine
No. 29 Piggot biplane powered by a 35-hp Anzani
No. 30 Cody IV monoplane powered by a 120-hp Austro-Daimler engine
No. 31 Cody V biplane powered by a 120-hp Austro-Daimler engine
No. 32 Borel monoplane powered by an 80-hp Gnome

One of the aircraft entered in the trials was No. 18 – The Aerial Wheel. Even by the standards of the day, this was a truly eccentric piece of machinery. Developed by a man with the name of George Sturgess, it was originally known as the Sturgess Flying Wheel and had been designed, Sturgess said, to enable it to land on uneven ground safely. Powered by a 50-hp NEC engine, the 'aircraft' was a monoplane with a canard wing projecting in front, much like the Wright brothers' design, the landing gear consisted of a single wheel with outboard skids. Although present at the Military Trials, the aircraft never appeared and took no part in the competition. The first anyone saw of the 'aircraft' was in June 1913, when a photograph was published in *The Aeroplane*. From its construction, it was obvious that had anyone attempted to fly the aircraft it would have been extremely dangerous to anybody in a close proximity.

Of the thirty-two entrants, only twenty-four actually turned up at Larkhill, and of those, only twenty actually entered the competition. The general public were kept up to date with the trials through the magazines *Flight* and *The Aeroplane*, but it has to be realised that no one at the time had any real idea of what they were looking for in these aircraft. The level of expertise in flying these aircraft was measured by the fact that if you could take off and land without crashing, you were an expert! This was the first time ever that aircraft were being considered as a weapon of war.

The Royal Flying Corps suffered a serious setback just two weeks after the trials when the Military Wing of the RFC lost four of its pilots during training. The aircraft they were flying were monoplanes, and the War Office immediately issued an order that no more flying was to be carried out in these aircraft. The Admiralty, however, a law unto itself, refused to issue such an order to their pilots, who continued to fly and train in monoplanes.

The tragic accidents brought all the sceptics and critics out of the woodwork, and none was more venomous than C. C. Grey, the editor of *The Aeroplane*. Grey, for reasons best known only to himself, had an intense hatred for the Royal Aircraft Factory and anyone associated with it. Geoffrey de Havilland was their chief designer at the time, and was often targeted by Grey. He would write venomous accounts of their aircraft and employees, knowing full well they had no chance to reply and rebuff his statements and accusations.

De Havilland aircraft appeared prominently during the First World War, but in fact the De Havilland Company did not come into existence until after the war. The Airco Co. Ltd actually built the aircraft designed by Geoffrey de Havilland, and were always referred to as De Havilland aircraft.

With war clouds looming in Europe, the War Office realised that they were going to need a lot more aeroplanes than they had at first envisaged. Nos 2 and 3 Squadrons, RFC, had twenty-two B.E.2as, six Henry Farman F.20s and five Blériot XI monoplanes between them by 31 July 1914, and all the training up to this point had been for reconnaissance purposes. None of the pilots had been trained as fighter pilots, and their observers were not versed in using the machine gun as a defensive weapon. All the aircraft were of flimsy construction and not designed for combat. All of a sudden, the realisation of the enormity of the task that lay before them caused the War Office to rapidly re-think their strategy and order additional aircraft to be built.

Fortunately, unlike the German Empire, there were no problems within the country with regard to sovereignty. There were no separate principalities or dukedoms to interfere with the government, except for the normal political wrangling and in-fighting that is prevalent universally. Like most countries, Britain, too, suffered from increasing bureaucracy, the majority of which came from empire-building, muscle-flexing groups who felt it necessary to be intransigent for reasons best known only to themselves, and all under the umbrella of patriotism.

With the demand for aircraft soon outstripping the production lines, the War Office turned to French aircraft manufacturers like Morane-Saulnier, the Farman Brothers, Caudron, Breguet, Blériot and Nieuport to help fill the gaps.

Soon designs were flooding into the War Office, and within months contracts had been issued to some of the major British and French manufacturers; it is these manufacturers and their aircraft that this book concentrates on. There were of course a number of smaller firms, but although their contribution to aviation was significant, they did not produce enough different types of aircraft to be considered as serious manufacturers. The following companies, however, did produce aircraft that made a major contribution to the war in the air. The aircraft described in this book are the military aircraft that were built by the manufacturers and used during the First World War.

The following is a list of British aircraft manufacturers that designed, constructed or assembled aircraft either under licence or subsidiaries of other major aircraft companies:

The Aeronautical Syndicate, Ltd, Hendon
The Aircraft Manufacturing Co. Ltd (AIRCO), Hendon
The Alliance Aeroplane Co. Ltd, London
Sir W. G. Armstrong, Whitworth & Co. Ltd, Newcastle upon Tyne
Royal Aircraft Factory, Farnborough
The Austin Motor Co. Ltd, Birmingham
Barclay, Curle & Co. Ltd, Glasgow, Scotland
William Beardmore & Co. Ltd, Dumbartonshire, Scotland
Beatty School of Flying, Hendon and Cricklewood
F. W. Berwick & Co. Ltd, London
The Birmingham Carriage Co. Ltd, Birmingham
Blackburn Aeroplane & Motor Co. Ltd, Leeds
The Blair Atholl Aeroplane Syndicate Ltd, London
Blériot Aeronautics, Hendon
L. Blériot (Aeronautics) Ltd, Brooklands
Blériot & SPAD Ltd, Addlestone, Surrey
Boulton & Paul Ltd, Norwich
Breguet Aeroplanes, London
The British Caudron Co. Ltd, Cricklewood
The British & Colonial Aeroplane Co. Ltd, Bristol
The British Deperdussin Aeroplane Co. Ltd, London
The Brush Electrical Engineering Co. Ltd, Loughborough
Clayton & Shuttleworth Ltd, Lincoln
S. F. Cody, Farnborough, Hants
The Coventry Ordnance Works, Coventry
Cubitt Ltd, Croydon
The Daimler Co. Ltd, Coventry

A. Darracq & Co., London
The Darracq Motor Engineering Co. Ltd, London
William Denny & Bros, Dumbarton, Scotland
Dudbridge Iron Works Ltd, Stroud, Gloucestershire
The Eastbourne Aviation Co. Ltd, Eastbourne
The Fairey Aviation Co. Ltd, Hayes, Middlesex
Richard Garrett & Sons, Leiston, Suffolk
The Glendower Aircraft Co. Ltd, London
The Gloucestershire Aircraft Co. Ltd, Cheltenham
The Gosport Aviation Co. Ltd, Gosport
The Grahame-White Aviation Co. Ltd, Hendon
Handley Page Ltd, Barking, Essex
Harland & Wolff Ltd, Belfast
Harris Lebus, Ltd, London
The Henderson Scottish Aviation Factory, Aberdeen, Scotland
Hewlett & Blondeau Ltd, London
Hooper & Co. Ltd, London
R. L. Howard-Flanders Ltd, Richmond, Surrey
Howard T. Wright, London
Humber Ltd, Coventry
The Joucques Aviation Co., London
The Kingsbury Aviation Co. Ltd, London
Mann, Egerton & Co. Ltd, Norwich
Marsh, Jones & Cribb Ltd, Leeds
Marshall Sons & Co. Ltd, Gainsborough
Martin & Handasyde, Brooklands, Surrey
The Metropolitan Carriage, Wagon & Finance Co., Birmingham
Morgan & Co., Leighton Buzzard
D. Napier & Son, London
National Aircraft Company No. 1, Surrey
National Aircraft Company No. 2, Stockport, Cheshire
National Aircraft Company No. 3, Liverpool
Nieuport & General Aircraft Co. Ltd, Cricklewood
Northern Aircraft Repairs Depot, Coal Aston
Palladium Autocars Ltd, London
Parnall & Sons Ltd, Bristol
The Phoenix Dynamo Manufacturing Co. Ltd, Bradford
Piggott Brothers & Co. Ltd, London
Planes Ltd, Freshfield, Lancashire
Portholme Aerodrome Ltd, Huntingdon
Ransome, Sims & Jefferies, Ipswich
Robey & Co. Ltd, London
A. V. Roe & Co. Ltd, Manchester and Hamble
Royal Aircraft Factory, Farnborough, Hampshire
Ruston, Proctor & Co. Ltd, Lincoln
Frederick Sage & Co., Peterborough
Angus Sanderson & Co., Newcastle upon Tyne
S. E. Saunders Ltd, East Cowes, Isle of Wight
Savages Ltd, Kings Lynn, Norfolk
Short Brothers, Rochester
The Siddeley-Deasy Motor Car Co. Ltd, Coventry
The Sopwith Aviation Co. Ltd, Kingston-on-Thames
Standard Motor Co. Ltd, Coventry
Alexander Stephen & Sons, Glasgow, Scotland

The Sunbeam Motor Car Co. Ltd, Wolverhampton
Vickers Ltd, London
Vulcan Motor & Engineering Co. Ltd, Southport
Waring & Gillow Ltd, London
G. & J. Weir Ltd, Glasgow, Scotland
Wells Aviation Co. Ltd, London
Westland Aircraft Works, Yeovil, Somerset
Weston Hurlin & Co, London
Whitehead Aircraft Ltd, Richmond, Surrey
Wight, J. Samuel and Co. Ltd
Wolseley Motors Ltd, Birmingham

The following aircraft companies are those selected for the text.

Airco – Aircraft Manufacturing Company
A. V. Roe & Company Ltd (AVRO)
Armstrong Whitworth & Company Ltd
Blackburn Aircraft Company Ltd
Blériot Aéronautique
Société des Avions Louis Breguet
British & Colonial Aeroplane Company – Bristol
Caudron Aircraft Company
Curtiss Aeroplane and Motor Corporation
Fairey Aircraft Company Ltd
Farman, Henry
Farman, Maurice
Felixstowe
Franco-British Aviation
Handley Page
Martinsyde
Morane-Saulnier Company
Nieuport
Norman Thompson Flight Company
Royal Aircraft Factory
Salmson-Moineau
Short Brothers
Sopwith Aircraft Company
SPAD (Société Anonyme pour l'Aviation et ses Derives)
Tellier
Vickers (Aviation) Ltd
Voisin
Wight, J. Samuel Co. Ltd

The Aircraft Company Ltd (Airco)

In the summer of 1911, a British entrepreneur businessman by the name of George Holt Thomas acquired the manufacturing rights from the Maurice and Henry Farman Aircraft Company to build their aircraft. At the same time, he negotiated the rights to build the French Le Rhône and Gnome engines. Within nine months he had created the Aircraft Manufacturing Company Ltd (AMC), based at Hendon, London, and combined it with his other two companies, the Aeroplane Supply Company and Airships Ltd, with a capital of just £14,700.

The formation of the Royal Flying Corps (RFC) on 13 April 1912 opened the doors to aircraft manufacturers to submit their designs to the War Office. In the summer of 1912 a competition known as the 'Military Trials' was held, and among the companies who submitted aircraft was the AMC. The aircraft they entered was the Maurice Farman 70-hp biplane. As agents for the company, if they were successful, they would have the manufacturing rights to build them in Britain. The aircraft performed reasonably well in all the tests, unlike the majority of the others who performed well in some tests and failed miserably in others. The company was awarded a £100 consolation prize, but did not get the contract to build aircraft for the RFC. The winner of the competition was the Cody *Cathedral*.

For the next two years Holt Thomas acted just as an agent for the Farmans, and then he was approached by Geoffrey de Havilland with the suggestion that Airco, as it had now become known, should build their own aircraft. Holt Thomas had met Geoffrey de Havilland some time earlier, and was quick to spot the potential in the man who had spent the previous three years as a test pilot and designer with the Royal Aircraft Factory. He offered de Havilland a job as a designer at a salary of £600 per year plus commission on every aircraft sold, and instructed him to create his own design department. Geoffrey de Havilland had already distinguished himself by designing the B.E. (British Experimental) series of aircraft, and was in the process of putting together a team when war was declared and he was immediately called up. Geoffrey de Havilland, who held the rank of lieutenant in the RFC reserve, was immediately posted to Montrose in Scotland.

Holt Thomas was not without influence, and after a great deal of badgering and a certain amount of common sense on the part of the War Ministry, de Havilland was returned to Airco. Just before the war de Havilland had been working on the design of a tractor biplane, but when he submitted the idea to the War Office they turned it down, stating that they were looking for a pusher biplane which would give the gunner a clear, uninterrupted forward view. At the beginning of 1915, the first of the two-seater models designed by de Havilland appeared – the Airco D.H.1. Initially it had been intended to have the aircraft powered by a 100-hp Green engine, but the Green Engine Factory were already at full stretch providing engines for the Royal Aircraft

Factory's F.E.2a. The company turned to the French engine manufacturer Renault, and this of course meant that the D.H.1 had to be re-designed to accommodate the 70-hp engine.

The D.H.1 was mostly put through its paces by its designer, Geoffrey de Havilland. The War Office was impressed by the aircraft, despite it being underpowered, and placed an order for forty-nine models to be built. This initially caused a problem for Airco, as it was at full stretch, committed to building Maurice and Henry Farman aircraft. The answer was to bring in a sub-contractor, Savages Ltd of Kings Lynn. Why this firm was chosen is a mystery, as they had never built any aircraft and were predominantly involved in building fairground equipment. Maybe it was because they were capable of building complicated machinery that they were chosen, but because of their inexperience, production of the D.H.1 was delayed.

In the meantime, Geoffrey de Havilland was involved in designing the next generation: the D.H.2. The 100-hp Green engine in the F.E.2a had been replaced by the more powerful 120-hp Beardmore engine, giving it almost twice the power of the D.H.1. At the end of 1915, the first five D.H.1s off the production line had been allocated to training units. The remainder of the first production batch were fitted with the 120-hp Beardmore engine, which brought them into line with the F.E.2a. This model was renamed the D.H.1a.

Six D.H.1a aircraft from the first batch saw service in the Middle East, and a further twenty-four were assigned to Home Defence units. The second batch of forty-nine were again built by Savages Ltd, but only seventy-three of the total number built saw service with RFC units.

The development of the second of de Havilland's designs, the D.H.2, produced a single-seat fighter powered by a 100-hp Gnome Monosoupape rotary, air-cooled engine. The simple construction produced a two-bay biplane with unstaggered wings, a skeletal tubular steel airframe and a steerable tailskid. The light, immensely strong structure of the aircraft lent itself to the aerobatic conditions it would be subjected to during combat. It was fitted with a .303 Lewis machine gun that could be moved onto swivels fitted either side of the cockpit. Initially there were problems for the pilot moving the weapon under combat conditions while also trying to fly the aircraft. Pilots soon learned to aim the aircraft at their target, enabling them to use the machine gun as a fixed weapon.

The flight trials of the D.H.2 impressed the War Office to the extent that they immediately placed an order, and with this in place the factory at Hendon undertook to manufacture the aircraft there. This meant that the Savages Company in Kings Lynn were no longer used as sub-contractors and Airco ceased making Farman aircraft.

A small number of D.H.2s that came off the production line were fitted with the 110-hp Le Rhône rotary engine, but it made little difference to the aircraft's performance.

The first squadron to be equipped with the aircraft was No. 24 Squadron, RFC, commanded by Major Lanoe G. Hawker, which received twelve D.H.2s. Just one month after receiving the aircraft and carrying out familiarisation flights, the squadron was posted to Saint-Omer, France. Within a short time two more squadrons, No. 29 and No. 32, were equipped with the D.H.2, and they too joined No. 24 at Saint-Omer. All three squadrons were involved in the Battle of the Somme and acquitted themselves very well against the German E.I. Fokkers and Halberstadts, which up to this point had faced very little strong opposition. Throughout the early part of the war and indeed into the middle of the war, the D.H.2 was one of the aerial mainstays of the British Expeditionary Force (BEF) in France.

It was in his D.H.2 that Major Lanoe Hawker died when he and the legendary Manfred von Richthofen – the Red Baron – met in the skies over France. Their aerial duel was perhaps the longest single-combat fight of the First World War. It was a D.H.2, flown by Captain R. M. S. Saundby, which attacked and destroyed the Zeppelin L.48 over Suffolk.

In 1917, thirty-two D.H.2s of No. 17, No. 47 and No. 111 Squadrons were dispatched to Palestine and Macedonia. Right up until September 1918, the D.H.2 fought in almost all the theatres of war and with distinction.

At the beginning of 1916, the third of Geoffrey de Havilland's designs appeared: the D.H.3. This was a large two-bay aircraft, designed primarily as a reconnaissance/bomber, and was completely different in appearance to the previous two models. The slim, tapered fuselage was built of spruce and covered in plywood. It had a four-wheel undercarriage, two under the nose and two under the pilot's cockpit. Like the previous models it was of the pusher-type, with two 120-hp Beardmore engines mounted in nacelles between the mainplanes.

The prototype carried out flight tests to the satisfaction of the War Office, but only the one was built. A second prototype with a number of minor modifications was built, powered by two 160-hp Beardmore engines. It was given the designation of D.H.3A, and almost immediately the War Office ordered fifty of the aircraft to be built. Before the first of the aircraft came off the production line, the order was cancelled because the War Office deemed that a twin-engined bomber was both unnecessary and impracticable. This was to be proved extremely short-sighted, as within a year London was experiencing bombing raids.

In August 1916, one of the most outstanding aircraft of the First World War took to the air at Hendon on its first test flight, with test pilot/designer Geoffrey de Havilland at the controls: the Airco De Havilland 4 or D.H.4, as it was more popularly known. The fuselage was constructed from spruce and ash with a plywood covering. There were two cockpits; the rear observer's cockpit had a Scarff ring fitted, on which was mounted either a single or twin Lewis machine guns. In front of the pilot was mounted a single, synchronised forward-firing Vickers machine gun. Two 230-lb bombs or four 112-lb bombs were mounted in racks under both the fuselage and the wings. The fin and rudder were the standard shape, and the undercarriage suspension consisted of two 6 ft 9 in (2.0 m) rubber cords wound into nine turns for each of the wheels.

A 230-hp B.H.P 6-cylinder, water-cooled engine powered the prototype, producing a surprising turn of speed of 106 mph. The aircraft was sent to the CFS (Central Flying School) Testing Flight for evaluation, and the report that came back was nothing less than 'highly commended'. In the meantime, Geoffrey de Havilland was building the second prototype with a number of modifications. The B.H.P. engine had been larger than anticipated and had extended and raised the nose of the aircraft, reducing the pilot's forward visibility. By installing the new 250-hp Rolls-Royce engine, the nose was lowered by 3 in, which although a relatively small amount, improved the pilot's visibility considerably.

Captain R. H. Mayo, who had demonstrated the aircraft to a number of squadron commanders who also flew the aircraft, had flown the first prototype to France. On his return, Major-General Trenchard wrote to the Director of Air Organisation, Major-General Sefton Brancker, with his suggestion for the role of the D.H.4. Brancker's reply showed that he had a real grasp of what was required:

It is now necessary to come to some decision as to the exact role of the De Havilland 4. It was designed as a bomber, and it is intended to equip it, if employed as such, with a gyroscopic sight fitted in the rear seat and used by the passenger looking through the floor. Very accurate results have been obtained lately with this sight in the hands of the passenger, his pilot being directed over the target by an automatic indicator.

If this is agreed to, it would be possible to standardise on R.E.8 (first with the R.A.F.4a and eventually with the Hispano-Suiza), and on the de Havilland 4 (first with the Rolls-Royce and eventually with the B.H.P. engine), for all work other than that of fighting pure and simple and of long range bombing.

I would be glad of your opinion on this suggested policy that would eventually eliminate all B.E.2s, R.E.7s, Armstrong Whitworth 160-hp Beardmore, and

Martinsydes from the programme sent over to you under this office No.87/Aeros/597 (A.O.1) dated 17th October 1916.

The reply supported all of the proposals, and asked that arrangements be made to equip seven squadrons with the D.H.4 for use in France. An immediate order for fifty of the aircraft was made, followed three months later by a second order for a further 690 of the aircraft. The production lines at Airco went into top gear immediately.

The first production D.H.4s were delivered to No. 55 Squadron, RFC on 6 March 1917 and had their first operational flight one month later at Valenciennes. They were used on a number of bombing missions and high-altitude photo-reconnaissance flights. There were several problems that caused some concern among the crews that flew the aircraft. One of the major ones was that during combat, if an enemy aircraft surprised them, communication was impossible. This was because the two cockpits were so far apart; communication between the two was by means of a tube called the Gosport Tube, which, with the wind and engine noise and the heat of battle, was useless. This prevented the pilot from taking any avoiding action, unless, of course, he managed to get sight of the enemy aircraft. There was also another problem, and that was the 60-gallon fuel tank mounted between the two cockpits. If that was hit, the aircraft would explode into a ball of fire, earning itself the nickname of the 'The Flaming Coffin'. That aside, the aircraft was praised by almost everybody who flew it.

Improvements to engine manufacture were ongoing, and Rolls-Royce was no exception. Their only problem was that they could not keep up with the demand, and their cause was not helped by the government's intransigence in denying them permission extend their factory and build a special repair shop. The development of the Eagle series of engines by Rolls-Royce produced the 375-hp Eagle VIII. This powerful engine drove a much larger propeller that, in turn, required a much taller undercarriage and a sturdier airframe.

The RNAS took a strong interest in the D.H.4 after it had been lent one fitted with the 375-hp Rolls-Royce Eagle VIII engine, and subsequently ordered fifty of the aircraft. The one aircraft that they had been lent was assigned to No. 2 Squadron, RNAS in Dunkerque, where it operated until the end of the war.

Westland at Yeovil built the RNAS D.H.4s because the Hendon factory could no longer keep up with the demand for the aircraft. A number of other manufacturers were sub-contracted to build the D.H.4; they were F. W. Berwick of London; the Vulcan Motor & Engineering Co. of Lancashire; Palladium Autocars Ltd of London; Waring and Gillow Ltd of London and later the Atlantic Aircraft Corp., New Jersey, USA; Boeing Airplane Corp., Seattle, USA; the Dayton-Wright Airplane Co., Dayton, USA; the Fisher Body Corp., USA and the Standard Aircraft Corp. New Jersey, USA.

Slowly but surely, the RFC squadrons in France started to receive the D.H.4 as replacements for the D.H.2 and F.E.2bs. Almost all of the delays were the result of engine manufacturers not being able to deliver their engines on time, and when they did, Airco discovered that some of the engines had had modifications made which resulted in them having to alter the aircraft's airframes to accommodate them. Incredibly, even with all these delays, the government, in its infinite wisdom, decided to supply the Russian Government with fifty D.H.4s. These models were to be fitted with the Fiat A.12 engine. Fortunately, the Russian winter had set in and the Bolshevik revolution was about to break out, so it was impossible to deliver the aircraft. They were immediately, and gratefully, snatched up by the RFC to supplement their already stretched bomber force. The British government agreed with the Russians to replace the aircraft with an additional twenty-five in the spring of 1918, but because of the outcome of the revolution in Russia this never happened.

A variety of engines were used in the D.H.4, the most successful being the Rolls-Royce Eagle VIII that was installed in aircraft being used for special photo-reconnaissance missions. However, the majority of aircraft from both sides suffered from the delays in the deliveries of the engines which caused serious delays in their development.

In the United States, a total of 4,587 D.H.4s with Liberty engines were built, which was more than three times that of the British factories. Of this total, 1,885 were shipped to France but the Armistice intervened before any more could be sent and the majority of the remaining aircraft were sold off to Latin American countries.

The RFC struggled to come to terms with the interruptor gear fitted on the German aircraft, and relied heavily on the pusher type like the D.H.2 which gave the observer the forward firing position. The realisation that the German aircraft performance was substantially better than the Allied models forced Geoffrey de Havilland to look at an idea put forward by Constantine Constantinesco, who claimed to have perfected an interruptor mechanism. The mechanism worked, and de Havilland got to work designing a single-bay biplane with a tractor engine upon which this mechanism could be fitted.

In an effort to enhance the performance of the aircraft and increase the pilot's all-round view, de Havilland designed the aircraft to have a 27-inch backward stagger on the upper wing, which brought the cockpit in front of the upper wing's leading edge. Although under normal test conditions this was acceptable, under combat conditions the pilot had no view above or behind and this was one of the reasons why the aircraft was later relegated to low-level duties.

Like the D.H.4, the wooden box-girder fuselage, rounded on top with flat sides, was strengthened with plywood. The single Vickers machine gun was mounted on top of the front section and offset to the portside of the fuselage, and synchronised to fire through the propeller. It was powered by a 110-hp Le Rhône rotary engine, giving it a top speed of 109 mph.

The prototype was flown by Major Mills first to No. 1 Aircraft Depot, and then to No. 2 Aircraft Depot before going to No. 24 Squadron, RFC, where flight evaluation was carried out. In a letter to the Director of Aircraft Equipment, Brigadier-General Brooke-Popham said:

> Reference the D.H.5 it is not considered that any alterations require to be made to this machine before fitting the gun. This gun should be mounted on the machine to fire through the propeller and be movable in a vertical plane so as to give an elevation of from 0 to 45 degrees. Movement in horizontal plane is not necessary. Arrangements to be made for 500 rounds of ammunition in a disintegrating belt, and an improvement which should be considered in future types of this machine is doing away with the centre section entirely so as to allow the pilot a good view to the rear.

In a reply the War Office agreed with the recommendations, and said that it was carrying out an experiment to do away with the centre section of the top plane.

However, initial tests discovered that the D.H.5s fitted with the 110-hp Le Rhône engine vibrated so badly that the pilot was unable to read his instruments. At first the blame was laid squarely at the feet of the engine, but after other engines had been tried to no avail, it was discovered that it was in fact the engine bearer plate that was the problem. A relatively simple modification that strengthened the plate solved the problem. Other problems appeared, this time with the Constantinesco interruptor gear. So many, in fact, that both No. 24 and No. 32 Squadron were out of action. Other squadrons that had the D.H.5 on their strength also suffered from this problem, rendering their aircraft non-operational.

Over 550 of the aircraft were built: 200 by Airco, the remaining 350 by three sub-contractors: the Darracq Motor Engineering Co. Ltd of London; Messrs March, Jones & Cribb of Leeds and the British Caudron Co. Ltd, London.

Despite all the favourable reports on its handling qualities by front-line pilots, at heights above 10,000 feet it was no match for the faster, more agile German Fokker fighters. After a number of losses, the aircraft was relegated to ground attack duties.

It was here that the D.H.5 really excelled itself, and during the Battles of Ypres and Cambrai it proved to be an invaluable asset to the advancing Allied troops when it carried out low-level strafing and bombing runs on enemy positions.

As the demand for pilots and observers increased almost daily, there was a need for training aircraft. What was required was a cheap practical aircraft upon which to train pilots and observers. The aircraft had to have no refinements and would carry no weapons, but needed to be of a rugged construction. The need had come about in June 1916, after Field Marshal Sir Douglas Haig had requested the War Office to authorise the creation of another fifty squadrons for the RFC. Within months the Army Council had met, and approved the expansion of the RFC to 106 operational squadrons and ninety-five training squadrons. It was with this need in mind that Geoffrey de Havilland came up with the D.H.6.

The aircraft was designed for ease of manufacture, maintenance and repair. Instead of the two tandem cockpits there was one communal cockpit, which made it much easier for the tutor to instruct his pupil. The dual controls could be disengaged by the instructor in the case of an emergency, by means of a handle alongside his cockpit position.

The aircraft had a two-bay wing arrangement that had been designed for low speed and good handling, a robust fin and horn-balanced rudder and was powered by a 90-hp R.A.F.1a engine. The prototype was built in October 1916, and after flight trials was immediately accepted by the War Office. An initial 200 were ordered in January 1917, but these were to be built by the Graham-White Aviation Company because the Airco Company was already heavily committed to the production of the D.H.4 and D.H.5. Then in April a further 500 were ordered, so other manufacturers had to be brought in to assist. Among these were: the Gloucestershire Aircraft Company, Kingsbury Aviation Co., Harland & Wolff and Canadian Aeroplanes, who built the aircraft as a standby for the Curtiss JN-3 which was being used as a trainer by the Canadian Flying Corps. This was the first British-designed aircraft to be built in Canada.

The aircraft acquired a number of nicknames, among which were the Dung Hunter (Australian), SkyHook, Clutching Hand, the Crab and the Clockwork Mouse. These were the more printable nicknames.

By the end of 1917 the RFC's standard trainer was the Avro 504K, and more than 300 D.H.6s had been transferred to the RNAS to be used for anti-submarine duties. Some were given to the United States Navy in southern Ireland for similar duties. Problems were discovered after flying the aircraft on long patrols, something they had never done before. One of the aircraft was returned to Airco for trials and modifications were made. A large number of the aircraft were modified, giving them the designation D.H.6A.

The aircraft was ideal for flying over long stretches of water, as on a number of occasions the aircraft had been forced to ditch and was able to stay afloat for more than 10 hours. Trials were carried out using flotation gear, but it was deemed to be unnecessary.

Despite its shortcomings and list of derogatory nicknames, by the end of the war the RAF (as it had now become) still had over 1,000 of the aircraft operational. The following year the surplus (which was the majority of them) was sold off at an auction at Hendon, and they were sold for between £60 and £100 depending on condition.

There was a design for the D.H.7, a single-seat fighter with a tractor Rolls-Royce engine, but because of the non-availability of the engine, the project was cancelled. A new design quickly followed: the Airco D.H.8. Like the D.H.7, this was a design for a single-seat fighter, but fitted with a pusher engine and with a 1½ pounder cannon mounted in the nose. Like the D.H.7, it was the non-availability of the engine that prevented it from going any further than the design stage.

By the middle of 1917 the RFC had a need for a fast reconnaissance/bomber capable of carrying large loads over greater distances. Up to this point the D.H.4 was fulfilling this role, but as the Allies progressed so did their needs. Structurally, the D.H.9 was very similar to the D.H.4, but that is where the resemblance ended. In the D.H.4 there had been a problem with communication between the pilot and the observer because the two cockpits were so far apart, but in the design of the D.H.9 the cockpits were almost back-to-back.

The prototype was powered by a 230-hp B.H.P Galloway-built engine called the Adriatic, and after flight trials the War Office was so impressed that contracts were issued and the aircraft was put into immediate production in place of the D.H.4. The need for this aircraft was great, and the production rate was put at a staggering one every 40 minutes. The production models were powered by the 300-hp Siddeley Puma engine, which produced problems right from the start. In the end the engine had to be de-rated to 230-hp, which greatly underpowered the D.H.9 and subsequently affected the aircraft's performance: carrying a full military payload the aircraft could barely make 13,000 feet. The problem was highlighted on 31 July 1918 when ten D.H.9s out of twelve on a bombing mission over Germany were lost – some to engine failure, others to being shot down by faster German fighters.

During 848 sorties flown by Nos 99 and 104 Squadrons RFC, 123 engine failures were recorded. The aircraft fared much better in the Middle East, where the opposition was not so strong and the long range of the aircraft proved to be invaluable.

Back in Europe the D.H.9 was relegated to coastal defence duties, despite a variety of engines being tested to see if they could improve the aircraft's performance – which they couldn't. It wasn't until after the war that improvements to the manufacture of engines showed that the D.H.9 had been capable of a lot more than it was able to deliver during the war.

The Westland-built D.H.9A, on the other hand, proved to be a worthy adversary. Developed from the D.H.9, the D.H.9A had a 375-hp Rolls-Royce Eagle VIII engine fitted at the behest of the Technical Department of the War Office. To accommodate this larger engine the mainplanes and ailerons were enlarged and the fuselage strengthened, but the undercarriage and tail section remained the same as the D.H.9. Harry Hawker, who later created his own aircraft company, carried out a number of the initial flight tests.

With the tests completed, a number of the aircraft were assigned to No. 110 Squadron, RAF, who used them to carry out bombing raids on Coblenz, Frankfurt and a number of other German manufacturing cities. One of the aircraft had been paid for by the Nizam of Hyderabad, commemorated by an inscription painted on the side of the aircraft.

By the middle of 1918, the conversion to the Packhard Motor Company-built Liberty engine had been completed and the aircraft was sent to Martlesham Heath for evaluation, while at the same time the Americans were promising deliveries of the engine. Twelve of the engines were already in Britain, and tests with the Liberty engine-powered D.H.9A had been extremely encouraging. A number of different sub-contractors had to be brought in because Airco were heavily committed to the design and development of a new day bomber, the D.H.10. Among the sub-contractors were the Vulcan Motor and Engineering Co.; The Westland Aircraft Works; Mann, Egerton Co.; the Whitehead Aircraft Co. and F. W. Berwick.

The deliveries of the American Liberty engines started to come in, but in July 1918 they stopped abruptly after 1,050 had been delivered. Winston Churchill, who was Minister for Munitions at the time, immediately contacted the US Under-Secretary for Aviation, Mr Ryan. Ryan informed Churchill that the US Navy had staked a priority claim on all the Liberty engines that were currently under construction. This was devastating news to Airco, as they now had to find a replacement engine rapidly. The one that sprang to mind was the Rolls-Royce Eagle VIII, which was currently under evaluation in a Westland-built D.H.9A.

Enquiries were also made of the 500-hp Galloway Atlantic engine that was currently under evaluation. Seventy-two of these engines were ordered in September 1918 with a possible increase to 1,000, but only one was ever fitted into a D.H.9A, which was re-designated the D.H.15.

The successes being experienced by German bomber crews over London forced the War Office to think of using a medium bomber for retaliatory strikes. The unsuccessful D.H.3 was one of the bombers that came into mind. Airco produced a design based on the D.H.3, but in a somewhat larger version. The design was accepted and construction began in August 1917. Powered by two 230-hp B.H.P. water-cooled engines, which were mounted between the two mainplanes, the D.H.10 retained the plywood-covered, box-like fuselage of the D.H.3. It carried a crew of three with front and rear gunner cockpits, on which the guns were mounted on Scarff rings, but unusually it had dual controls fitted in the rear cockpit.

The first prototypes were given the name 'Amiens' by the Air Board, making them Amiens Mk I and Mk II. Flight tests and evaluations were quickly carried out, and orders for 1,295 aircraft were placed with Airco as the main contractor and six other subcontractors: the Alliance Aeroplane Co., London; the Daimler Co. Ltd, Coventry; the Siddeley-Deasey Motor Car Co. Ltd, Coventry; National Aircraft Factory No. 2, Stockport; Mann-Egerton Co. Ltd, Norwich; and the Birmingham Carriage Co., Birmingham.

The production lines started to gear up, but the war ended before they could get into mass production. Only eight were supplied to the RFC, but after the war the D.H.10 saw a great deal of service as a mail carrier and, after some modifications, a passenger aircraft.

While the development of the D.H.10 was taking place, Airco were also working on another long-distance bomber: the D.H.11. Structurally it was almost identical to the D.H.10, using spruce for the main airframe and steel tubing for the engine mountings, but that's where the similarity ended. The fuselage was 4 feet wide and 6 feet deep, which enabled the fuel tanks, containing 170 gallons, to be fitted and still leave enough room for a walkway beneath. This enabled the rear gunner to have access through to the front gunner, as the pilot's position was set to the starboard side of the aircraft. To gain access to the aircraft, a trapdoor was fitted between the spars of the lower wing, opening directly on to the walkway.

The D.H.11 was powered by two 320-hp A.B.C. Dragonfly radial engines that were housed in nacelles directly mounted to the lower mainplane. Armament consisted of two Lewis machine guns mounted on Scarff rings: one in the rear cockpit, the other in the front cockpit. Provision was made to carry 1,000 lbs of bombs internally. Only one prototype was built, and because of problems with the unreliable Dragonfly engines and the end of the war, the aircraft never went into production.

The D.H.11 was in fact the last of the Airco aircraft designed by de Havilland built during the First World War. The de Havilland Company went on to bigger and better things, and took the development of aircraft way beyond anyone's dreams and the period covered by this book

SPECIFICATIONS

Airco D.H.1/1a

Wingspan:	41 ft 0 in (12.4 m)
Length:	28 ft 11¼ in (8.8 m)
Height:	11 ft 2 in (3.4 m)
Weight Empty:	1,356 lb (615 kg) (D.H.1)
	1,610 lb (730 kg) (D.H.1a)
Weight Loaded:	2,044 lb (927 kg) (D.H.1)
	2,340 lb (1,061 kg) (D.H.1a)
Maximum Speed:	80 mph (132 km/h) (D.H.1)
	90 mph (144 km/h) (D.H.1a)

Ceiling:	13,500 ft (4,114 m)
Duration:	4 hours
Engine:	One 70-hp Renault (D.H.1)
	One 120-hp Austro-Daimler (D.H.1a)

Airco D.H.2

Wingspan:	28 ft 3 in (8.6 m)
Length:	25 ft 2½ in (7.6 m)
Height:	9 ft 6½ in (2.8 m)
Weight Empty:	934lb (423 kg) – Monosoupape engine
	1,004 lb (455 kg) – Le Rhône engine
Weight Loaded:	1,441 lb (653 kg) – Monosoupape engine
	1,547 lb (702 kg) – Le Rhône engine
Maximum Speed:	93 mph (144 km/h) – Monosoupape engine
	92 mph (143 km/h) – Le Rhône engine
Ceiling:	14,000 ft (4,270 m)
Duration:	2½ hours
Engine:	One 100-hp Gnome Monosoupape
	One 110-hp Le Rhône 9J
	One 110-hp Clerget 9Z
Armament:	One .303 Lewis machine gun
	Six le Prieur rockets

Airco D.H.3

Wingspan:	60 ft 10 in (18.4 m)
Length:	36 ft 10 in (11.2 m)
Height:	14 ft 6 in (4.4 m)
Weight Empty:	3,980 lb (1,805 kg)
Weight Loaded:	5,810 lb (2,635 kg)
Maximum Speed:	95 mph (148 km/h)
Ceiling:	14,000 ft (4,270 m)
Duration:	8 hours
Engine:	Two 120-hp Beardmores (D.H.3)
	Two 160-hp Beardmores (D.H.3a)
Armament:	Two .303 Lewis machine guns and 680 lb bombs

Airco D.H.4

Wingspan:	42 ft 4½ in (12.9 m)
Length:	30 ft 8 in (9.3 m)
Height:	10 ft 1 in (3.0 m)
Weight Empty:	2,197 lb (996 kg) – BHP engine
	2,230 lb (1,011 kg) – Siddeley Puma engine
	2,209 lb (1,002 kg) – Galloway Adriatic
	2,303 lb (1,044 kg) – Rolls-Royce III engine
	2,387 lb (1,082 kg) – Eagle VIII engine
	2,304 lb (1,044 kg) – R.A.F.3A engine
	2,306 lb (1,045 kg) – Fiat A.12 engine
	2,391 lb (1,084 kg) – Liberty 12 engine
Weight Loaded:	3,386 lb (1,535 kg) – BHP engine
	3,344 lb (1,516 kg) – Siddeley Puma engine
	3,641 lb (1,651 kg) – Galloway Adriatic

	3,313 lb (1,502 kg) – Rolls-Royce III engine
	3,472 lb (1,574 kg) – Eagle VIII engine
	3,340 lb (1,515 kg) – R.A.F.3A engine
	3,360 lb (1,524 kg) – Fiat A.12 engine
	3,297 lb (1,949 kg) – Liberty 12 engine
Maximum Speed:	108 mph (173 km/h) – B.H.P.
	106 mph (171 km/h) – Siddeley Puma
	119 mph (191 km/h) – Rolls-Royce III
	143 mph (230 km/h) – Eagle VIII
	122 mph (196 km/h) – R.A.F 3A
	114 mph (183 km/h) – Fiat A.12
	124 mph (199 km/h) – Liberty 12
Ceiling:	17,500 ft (5,334 m) – B.H.P.
	17,400 ft (5,324 m) – Siddeley Puma
	16,000 ft (4,876 m) – Rolls-Royce III
	22,000 ft (6,705 m) – Eagle VIII
	18,500 ft (5,638 m) – R.A.F. 3A
	17,000 ft (5,181 m) – Fiat A.12
	17,500 ft (5,334 m) – Liberty 12
Engine:	200-hp B.H.P.
	230-hp Siddeley Puma
	230-hp Galloway Adriatic
	200-hp R.A.F. 3A
	260-hp Fiat A.12
	250-hp Rolls-Royce Mk I, II, III, IV
	275-hp Rolls-Royce Mk I, II, III
	375-hp Rolls-Royce VIII
Duration:	Between 3 and 4½ hours
Armament:	One .303 Vickers machine gun mounted on top of the engine
	Two .303 Lewis machine guns in the observer's cockpit
	Two 230 lb or four 112 lb bombs

Airco D.H.5

Wingspan:	25 ft 8 in (7.8 m)
Length:	22 ft 0 in (6.7 m)
Height:	9 ft 1½ in (2.7 m)
Weight Empty:	1,010 lb (458 kg)
Weight Loaded:	1,492 lb (676 kg)
Maximum Speed:	102 mph (164 km/h)
Ceiling:	16,000 ft (4,876 m)
Duration:	2½ hours
Engine:	One 110-hp Le Rhône 9J
	One 110-hp Clerget 9Z
	One 100-hp Gnome Monosoupape
Armament:	One .303 Vickers machine gun
	Four 250 lb bombs

Airco D.H.6

Wingspan:	35 ft 11¼ in (10.9 m)
Length:	27 ft 3½ in (8.2 m)
Height:	10 ft 9½ in (3.2 m)
Weight Empty:	1,460 lb (662 kg)

Weight Loaded:	2,027 lb (919 kg)
Maximum Speed:	66 mph (106 km/h)
Ceiling:	16,000 ft (4,876 m)
Duration:	2½ hours
Engine:	One R.A.F.1a
Armament:	One .303 Vickers machine gun in rear cockpit
	Four 250 lb bombs

Airco D.H.9

Wingspan:	42 ft 4½ in (12.9 m)
Length:	30 ft 5 in (9.2 m) – Powered by Puma engine
	30 ft 0 in (9.1 m) – Powered by Fiat engine
	30 ft 9½ in (9.3 m) – Powered by Lion engine
	30 ft 0 in (9.1 m) – Powered by Liberty engine
Height:	11 ft 3½ in (3.4 m) – Powered by Puma engine
	11 ft 2 in (3.3 m) – Powered by Fiat engine
	11 ft 7½ in (3.5 m) – Powered by Lion engine
	11 ft 2 in (3.3 m) – Powered by Liberty engine
Weight Empty:	2,230 lb (1,011 kg) – Siddeley Puma engine
	2,460 lb (1,115 kg) – Fiat engine
	2,544 lb (1,153 kg) – Lion engine
	2,460 lb (1,115 kg) – Liberty 12 engine
Weight Loaded:	3,325 lb (1,508 kg) – Puma engine
	3,600 lb (1,632 kg) – Fiat A.12 engine
	3,667 lb (1,663 kg) – Lion
	4,645 lb (2,106 kg) – Liberty 12 engine
Maximum Speed:	104 mph (167 km/h) – Siddeley Puma
	117 mph (188 km/h) – Fiat A.12
	138 mph (222 km/h) – Lion
	114 mph (183 km/h) – Liberty 12
Ceiling:	15,500 ft (4,724 m) – Siddeley Puma
	17,500 ft (5,334 m) – Fiat A.12
	23,000 ft (7,010 m) – Lion
	17,500 ft (5,334 m) – Liberty 12
Engine:	230-hp B.H.P.
	230-hp Siddeley Puma
	290-hp Siddeley Puma
	250-hp Fiat A-12
	300-hp A.D.C. Nimbus
	300-hp Hispano-Suiza 8Fb
	430-hp Napier Lion
	435-hp Liberty 12A
	465-hp Wright Whirlwind R-975
	200-hp Wolseley Viper
	450-hp Bristol Jupiter VI
	480-hp Bristol Jupiter VIII
Duration:	Between 4½ hours
Armament:	One .303 Vickers machine gun mounted on top of the engine
	One .303 Lewis machine gun in observer's cockpit
	Two 230 lb or four 112 lb bombs

Airco D.H.10

Wingspan:	62 ft 9 in (19.1 m) – two prototypes
	65 ft 6 in (19.9 m) – production models
Length:	38 ft 10¼ in (11.8 m) – two prototypes
	39 ft 6 in (12.0 m) – production models
Height:	14 ft 6 in (4.4 m)
Weight Empty:	5,004 lb (2,270 kg) – two prototypes
	5,600 lb (2,540 kg) – production models
Weight Loaded:	6,950 lb (3,152 kg) – two prototypes
	9,000 lb (4,082 kg) – production models
Maximum Speed:	100 mph (160 km/h) – two prototypes
	112 mph (180 km/h) – production models
	106 mph (171 km/h) – Siddeley Puma
Ceiling:	15,000 ft (4,572 m) – two prototypes
	16,500 ft (5,029 m) – production models
Engine:	200-hp B.H.P.
	Two 230-hp Siddeley Puma
	Two 360-hp Rolls-Royce Eagle VIII
	Two 375-hp Rolls-Royce Eagle VIII
	Two 396-hp Liberty 12
	Two 405-hp Liberty 12
Duration:	Between 3 and 5½ hours
Armament:	Three .303 Vickers machine gun, one in the bow cockpit, one in observer's cockpit and one firing behind under the tail section
	Six 230 lb bombs

Airco D.H.11

Wingspan:	60 ft 2 in (18.3 m)
Length:	45 ft 3 in (13.7 m)
Height:	13 ft 6 in (4.1 m)
Weight Empty:	3,795 lb (1,721 kg)
Weight Loaded:	7,027 lb (3,187 kg)
Maximum Speed:	117 mph (188 km/h)
Ceiling:	16,000 ft (4,876 m)
Duration:	3¼ hours
Engine:	Two 320-hp A.B.C. Dragonfly
Armament:	Two .303 Vickers machine gun in rear and front cockpits
	1,000 lb bombs

A. V. Roe (Avro)

Alliott Verdon Roe's first excursion into the world of aviation took place at the Alexandra Palace Exhibition in April 1907, when his canard biplane won him £75. Based on the Wright design, the three-bay biplane was powered by a 90-hp J.A.P. (J. A. Prestwich) air-cooled motorcycle engine, which drove a two-bladed pusher propeller. The Roe I biplane, as it was known, was built in the stables behind his brother's surgery, and when finished was taken to Brooklands in September 1907 to take part in a flying competition there. A £2,500 prize had been offered to the first pilot who could an aircraft around the Brooklands racetrack unaided and non-stop. The prize was never awarded.

A. V. Roe discovered that his aircraft was fine during taxiing, but there was insufficient power for the aircraft to take off under its own steam. This was achieved, however, when one of the car drivers who were on the track at the time towed the aircraft into the air. This happened on a number of occasions, but until Roe devised a quick release device there were one or two accidents that resulted in damage to the aircraft. In May 1908, the arrival of a 24-hp Antoinette eight-cylinder engine solved the problem and the following month he managed to take the aircraft off the ground under its own power. The first flight was only in hops, at a height of no more than six feet. Roe kept the secret of his flight to himself for two years before he let the information out. The fact that he was the first man in Britain to fly an aircraft did not seem to bother Roe, but when the Royal Aero Club learned of his achievement they denied his claim on the grounds that he had not stayed airborne for sufficient distance to qualify. The fact still remains that he was the first, albeit not officially.

The results from his first aircraft spurred Roe on and he went into partnership with J. A. Prestwich (J.A.P.), the engine designer, to build his next aircraft, the Roe I Triplane. It was powered by the same 9-hp J.A.P. engine that had powered his first aircraft, and was an elegant version of the French Voisin II. The fuselage was of a triangular construction, consisting of three deal longerons with spruce cross struts. Control of the aircraft was by a single lever which moved fore and aft to control the pitching of the aircraft, but when moved from side to side warped the central mainplane by means of push rods. There were no movable surfaces like ailerons and rudder. For ease of travel, the outer 6 feet of wing panel folded back. The fuel tank and the pilot's seat were suspended on rubber webbing, the webbing having been made at H. V. Roe's (A. V.'s brother) Bulls Eye Braces factory. It was this that gave Avro aircraft their name, 'Bulls Eye Avroplane', a feature which became part of the Avro trademark for many years.

Roe built the aircraft in two rented railway arches at Lea Marshes, Essex, where the first flying trials took place. The initial flights in June 1909 suffered a variety of setbacks from accidents, all of which were directly attributed to either pilot error or lack of power. Encouraged by the results of the tests, he sustained a flight distance of 900 feet at a height of 10 feet on 23 July 1909, becoming the first British pilot to fly a British-designed aircraft powered by a British-designed and built engine.

Roe entered his aircraft in the Blackpool Race Meeting in October 1909, but incessant rain badly affected the oilpaper covering his aircraft to the extent that it never flew. The aircraft was placed in storage, where it stayed for eleven years before being given to the Science Museum. Using the knowledge gained from the first of the Triplanes, A. V. Roe designed and built a second Roe I Triplane; this time it was fitted with a 20-hp J.A.P. engine. It was based on the first model, but there were a number of noticeable differences. The fuselage was tapered on the second model and had a long tailskid in place of the tail wheel. The undercarriage was strengthened with extra struts, and a larger cigar-shaped fuel tank was mounted on the struts in front of the pilot.

In the meantime Roe had moved from Lea Marshes to the Old Deer Park, Richmond, Surrey, and then a few weeks later to Wembley Park, Middlesex. It was here on 6 December 1909 that he made the first of a number of successful flights. At the beginning of January 1910, with financial backing from his surgeon brother, Dr H. V. Roe, A. V. Roe formed his new firm, A. V. Roe & Company, at Manchester. The company had workshops within another factory, Everard & Company, which was owned by A. V. Roe's brother, H. V. Roe. For the next two months A. V. Roe carried out flight tests at his new base, then in March 1910 the owners of Brooklands converted the centre of the racetrack into an airfield. Roe immediately moved his entire operation back to Brooklands, where he constructed his latest aircraft, the Roe II Triplane.

This was the first aircraft to be built by the company, and was given the name *Mercury*. It was a single-seat triplane powered by a 35-hp Green water-cooled, four cylinder engine. The engine's radiators were mounted flush along the side of the front section of the triangular-shaped fuselage, which was constructed from ash, with silver spruce struts and spars, all covered in Pegamoid fabric. The three wings were of equal length, as was the triplane tail section, from which control of climbing and diving by means of pivoting the entire section, which was in turn linked to the centre mainplane variable incidence gear, was carried out. Control of the mainplane was by a single control stick in the pilot's cockpit. The two-wheeled undercarriage was secured to the axle by means of rubber shock absorber cord, which in turn was fixed to a rigid, tubular steel triangulated structure.

On 4 March 1910, the aircraft appeared in public for the first time at a model aircraft show at White City, Manchester and was the star of the show. When the Prince and Princess of Wales visited the show, A. V. Roe showed them around the machine himself. Priced at £550, including flight instruction, an order was received while at the show, from Sir Walter Windham, MP, who also manufactured car bodies. The show aircraft was retained by the company for training and experimental purposes. During a flight training session, a student pilot crashed the aircraft on landing, resulting in a number of modifications being made.

The centre of gravity (CG) was corrected by moving the pilot's seat forward, the wing warping control was abandoned and large unbalanced ailerons were fitted to the upper wing. The work was completed in ten days, and tests carried out proved to be more than satisfactory.

At the beginning of May, Sir Walter Windham's aircraft was ready and after some initial instruction he took control of his aircraft. The taxiing trials were successful, and Sir Walter took to the air a couple of days later. Not much is known about what happened to the aircraft, but it is known that on one of his landings the ground turned out to be too soft and the aircraft flipped on to its back.

In the meantime, Roe had been working on his next project, the Roe III Triplane. This model still retained the triangular-shaped fuselage but was a two-seat aircraft.

The controls were different for this aircraft: the lifting tail remained, but a tail elevator was installed which controlled the climbing and diving aspects. Lateral control was made by means of 5 ft by 2 ft ailerons fitted to the rear spar on the upper wing. The undercarriage was strengthened by means of a four-wheeled 'Farman type' unit with twin skids. A 35-hp J.A.P. V-8 cylinder air-cooled engine powered the aircraft.

The initial taxiing trials were made at Brooklands, after which short hops were made. These were followed by longer and longer flights, but they rarely exceeded 20 minutes. This was because the engine tended to overheat, and when it did so it ejected hot sooty oil from scavenger holes situated in the base of the engine's cylinder walls. Carburettor fires were a constant worry, but modifications slowly but surely overcame the problem.

Another of the aircraft was constructed; this time it was powered by a 35-hp Green four cylinder, water-cooled engine. Modifications were made to the positioning of the ailerons, and these were fitted to the rear spar of the centre wing. The results from the tests were extremely encouraging and full of confidence, Roe decided to take his Roe II 'Mercury' Triplane and his latest venture, the Roe III Triplane, to the Blackpool Flying Meeting on 1 August 1910 by railway. Fate once again took a hand. The first time, it was the rain that dashed his hopes; this time it was sparks from the engine from the LNWR (London & North Western Railway) as it struggled up a steep incline near Wigan that set the carriage containing the dismantled aircraft alight. Both the carriage and the aircraft were reduced to ashes.

Not to be deterred, Roe had spare parts shipped up to Blackpool and a brand new 35-hp Green engine sent direct from the factory. Roe, together with his mechanic Howard Pixton, started work constructing another Roe III Triplane on 28 July. Five days later, on 1 August, the aircraft took to the air. The fuselage was just a skeletal one, as there had been no time to cover it. The first flights were relatively successful, but a number of minor mishaps caused repairs to be made before Roe took to the air again, this time with a passenger. He was awarded the princely sum of £50 for this achievement, but what was even more rewarding was the purchase of one of his aeroplanes by a J. V. Martin from the Harvard University Aeronautical Society, USA.

Within three weeks, the aircraft had been built, crated and dispatched to Boston, USA, aboard the Cunard ship *Ivernia*. A. V. Roe was invited to attend the Boston Aviation Meeting, so, together with his mechanics Pixton and Halstead, he dismantled the repaired Blackpool-built Roe III Triplane, crated and shipped it and themselves aboard the White Star liner *Cymric* to Boston. After re-assembling the aircraft on their arrival, the team carried out a number of flight tests but the results were less than encouraging and after a month they returned to England. The Harvard University Aeronautical Society's Roe III Triplane, which although assembled, was untried in the air by the time Roe and his team had left.

With the information gathered from the building of the triplanes, Roe embarked on another single-seater powered by the 35-hp Green water-cooled engine, the Roe IV Triplane. The upper and middle wings were of equal length, but the lower wing was shortened by 12 feet. The control of the aircraft was by a control wheel mounted on top of a column and it reverted back to using wing warping, despite the success of the elevator method. The tail section consisted of a triangular shaped rudder and, for the first time, movable elevators. The undercarriage reverted back to the four wheels mounted either side of extended skids.

Only one of the aircraft was built, and that was retained for use at the newly opened Avro Flying School. Unlike Roe's previous aircraft, the Roe IV Triplane was very sensitive to control and not really the ideal training aircraft as the number of accidents suffered by the aircraft proved. A number of pilots, however, did manage to master the aircraft and completed the course successfully. Even Roe's mechanic, Howard Pixton, passed his aviator certificate exam on the aircraft. One year later, the aircraft was replaced with the Avro Type D, a much superior aircraft in every way.

The abandonment of the triplane design opened up a new venture for the Avro Company. Although the triplane disappeared and a biplane was put in its place, the triangular girder fuselage was retained, as was the two-wheeled undercarriage and skids and triangular shaped tail section. Powered by a 35-hp Green water-cooled engine, with its radiator mounted vertically behind and in front of the pilot, the first of this new breed of aircraft appeared in March 1911. The first flight took place with Howard Pixton at the controls; he said that it was almost without fault, a feeling later endorsed by another pilot, Gordon Bell.

On 6 May 1911, the Avro Type D was entered in the Brooklands to Shoreham race and was to be flown by Howard Pixton, the first time an Avro aircraft had been flown in an event other than by the designer. Pixton, who had also entered the endurance competition for pilot and passenger, had been flying for over 20 minutes in the competition before he realised the race had started and he was well behind the other competitors. With no map and no cross-country flying experience, and an aircraft that had never been farther that the boundaries of Brooklands, he chased after the other aircraft. Inevitably he got lost, and after getting directions from someone on the ground he managed to reach Shoreham – taking three hours to complete the journey. On his way back, he stopped to give a flying demonstration in Haywards Heath.

A. V. Roe was approached by the War Office to give a demonstration of the Avro Type D to the Parliamentary Aerial Defence Committee at Hendon on 12 May. Howard Pixton once again flew the aircraft and gave the demonstration, in which he flew Commander Sampson, RN, a man already establishing a reputation as a first-class pilot.

In June 1911, Commander Oliver Schwann, RN (later to become Air Vice Marshal Sir Oliver Schwann, RAF), who was in charge of the airship tender *Hermione*, had a flight in the Avro Type D. He was so taken with the aircraft that he purchased it for the sum of £700. It was crated and sent by rail to Barrow-in-Furness, where the wheels were removed and replaced with floats that had been designed by Schwann and constructed by members of his crew. A number of other modifications were made including the repositioning of the radiator, covering the rear section of the fuselage with fabric, fitting a small tail float and replacing the triangular tail section with a more conventional one.

The initial taxiing trials were carried out in the Cavendish Dock in Barrow-in-Furness. It soon became apparent that the narrow, flat-bottomed floats caused the tail of the aircraft to adopt a tail-down attitude, while the tail float caused a large wash. The float and the fin it was attached to were removed, and the rudder moved to keep it clear of the water. After a number of experiments with a variety of rudders, Commander Schwann took the aircraft on to the 'step' during taxiing trials. Suddenly, the aircraft became unintentionally airborne to a height of 20 feet; unfortunately Schwann was not a qualified pilot, and the aircraft dropped back into the water and capsized. Rescued unharmed but with a damaged aircraft, Schwann rebuilt the aircraft and left the testing to another naval officer, Lieutenant S. V. Sippe, who was a qualified pilot. Sippe had passed his flying test on 8 January 1912 on a Roe Type D Sesquiplane.

On 9 April 1912, Lieutenant Sippe lifted the aircraft off the water, making it the first seaplane to take off from British waters. In reality it was Commander Schwann who was the first, but the fact that he wasn't a qualified pilot at the time disqualified him from being the first. After a couple of circuits of the dock area, Sippe brought the aircraft back down on to the water and handed it back to Commander Schwann, who had just qualified as a pilot from the Bristol School on Salisbury Plain, Wiltshire.

While the trials of the converted Avro Type D were taking place, A. V. Roe was desperately constructing another Type D for the forthcoming £10,000 *Daily Mail* Circuit of Britain Race. The sale of the aircraft to Commander Schwann had reduced the number of aircraft at the Avro School to one aircraft – the Roe IV Triplane. The modified Type D was built in Manchester under the guidance of its pilot, R. C. Kemp. Powered by a 60-hp E.N.V. eight cylinder water-cooled engine, it retained its triangular girder fuselage, which was lengthened from 26 feet to 28 feet. It was a sesquiplane, the upper wing being 33 feet and the lower wing 23 feet; the tailplane section consisted of the large triangular type fitted on the earlier models.

When completed, the aircraft was sent by rail to Brooklands for the princely sum of £1 16s 6d, a remarkably cheap method of transporting goods even in these early days. A. V. Roe himself carried out the taxiing trials, but R. C. Kemp carried out the first flights. These flights, although initially satisfactory, showed the engine had a tendency to overheat and the rate of climb was very poor with a full fuel load aboard. In an effort to improve the performance, Kemp unofficially authorised work to be done on extending the lower wing to be equal with the upper wing.

The initial test started out all right, but then suddenly the extension to the lower wing section failed and the aircraft spun into the ground. Miraculously, Kemp stepped away from the wreckage unhurt, but A. V. Roe was furious.

A third Type D was constructed, almost identical to the second. The only differences were the repositioning of the radiator to behind the engine, a covered rear section of the fuselage and straight skids on the undercarriage. The first flight took place on 11 September 1911, and so successful was it that instead of using the aircraft for the school, as was originally intended, it was entered in the Michelin Speed Prize. The pilot, F. P. Raynham, took off from Brooklands on 21 September, but because of fog ran into trouble and had to land to ask directions. There were problems with the propeller and the fabric covering the wings, causing him to abort the attempt. He finally returned to Brooklands on 24 September, and the aircraft was placed in the charge of the Avro School.

One week later, the fourth Avro Type D was delivered to Brooklands for testing. It was identical to the previous models in construction but had a specially tuned 45-hp Green engine installed. The results of the flight tests were satisfactory, and it was intended to enter the aircraft for the Michelin long distance prize. Loaded with enough fuel for a proposed eight-hour flight, the aircraft took off only to be forced down some two hours later with an iced up carburettor. The damage was quite extensive so a fifth model was ordered, its specifications were identical to the second Avro Type D model and powered by a 35-hp Green engine. Very little is known about this model, only that it was part of the aircraft fleet at the Avro School.

The arrival of a sixth model, Avro Type D, on 30 September 1911 heralded the arrival of a new engine, the 35-hp five-cylinder, air-cooled Viale radial engine. The aircraft, with its new engine, proved to be a hit with instructors and pupils alike. It was also used by a number of pilots in which to take their Aviator's Certificate test. Then, on 13 January 1912, one of the pupils found himself in trouble during poor visibility and had to carry out a forced landing in Abingdon. Some damage was caused, and the aircraft later returned to the school where it continued to be used for flying instruction. The Viale engine was later removed and replaced with a 50-hp Isaacson for experimental purposes.

In the early days of aviation, it was not unusual for someone to have an aircraft built to their own specifications and it was invariably named after the person who picked up the bill. The Duigan Biplane was no exception. A very wealthy Australian by the name of John R. Duigan designed and built his own aircraft in Australia, and after teaching himself to fly, flew it at Bendigo Racecourse just outside Melbourne. His inexperience and lack of knowledge caused him to have a series of mishaps, so he decided to go to England and learn to fly properly. On arrival in England in October 1911, he went immediately to the Avro Flying School at Brooklands and enrolled. The following month he ordered an aircraft from Avro and went to Manchester to oversee the building of it.

The two-bay biplane had a square, box-girder framed fuselage, consisting of two halves bolted together behind the rear cockpit, with celluloid windows in the floor.

The seating arrangement was in tandem and the aircraft had dual control. The wings were of equal length, and lateral control was achieved by warping the wings. The undercarriage was based on the Nieuport model that incorporated a leaf-spring axle with a centre skid instead of the normal two fitted and single wheels. This design of undercarriage was incorporated into future Avro models as it proved to be most successful.

The Duigan Biplane was powered by a 40-hp horizontally opposed Alvaston engine that had large spiral tube radiators mounted either side of the cockpit for cooling. The first 'hop' tests were carried out by Duigan himself, but when he tried to take off he discovered that the engine power was insufficient to lift the aircraft off the ground. Dejected, he took the aircraft back to Brooklands where a 35-hp E.N.V. engine was fitted. This gave the aircraft the power to take off and a number of successful short flights were made, but when he attempted a long flight he once again discovered that the engine was insufficient for the job. Duigan, undeterred, tuned the engine himself and then made and fitted a propeller to his own design. The result was remarkable, and after a series of flights he completed the tests required for his Aviator's Certificate.

Having obtained the certificate, Duigan headed back to Australia. Once home he designed and constructed another aircraft based on the design of his biplane, but crashed it on its first flight. The Duigan Biplane, still at Brooklands, was sold to the Lakes Flying Company, who modified the airframe to take a Gnome rotary engine, fitted floats in place of the undercarriage and used it as a floatplane, renamed *Sea Bird*, on Lake Windermere.

With the unrest in Europe beginning to have an unsettling effect on Britain, the War Office looked to strengthen the military machine, and one of the areas they looked closely at was aviation. In 1911, they invited designs to a specification that called for a two-seat aircraft capable of carrying a 350-lb payload in addition to the normal equipment it required, at a speed of 55 mph, and at a height of 4,500 feet for 4 to 5 hours. There was one major stipulation: the aircraft had to be designed, built and tested within nine months!

A. V. Roe saw his opportunity and immediately took up the challenge, and using the technology obtained from building Duigan's biplane he created the Avro 500 Type E. The two-seat aircraft had a box-girder fuselage that tapered toward the tail section. The front engine section was covered in a metal plate, while the rear section was fabric covered. Like the Duigan model, celluloid panels were set into the floor to give the pilot and the observer downward vision. The two-bay mainplanes were of equal length, and were constructed in three sections for ease of transport. The undercarriage, with its centre skid, was taken from the Duigan model and a rubber-sprung skid supported the tail section.

The Type E, as it was known, was powered by a 60-hp E.N.V. water-cooled engine, which was mounted on top of the longerons, and was cooled by two-spiral tube radiators mounted on each side of the front section of the fuselage. Two gravity fuel tanks were mounted on the centre section struts, while the main fuel tank was fitted in front of the observer's position.

The first test flight, flown by Wilfred Parke, took place on 3 March 1912 from Brooklands, and it became obvious right from the start that this aircraft was something special. It had a tremendous climb capability and climbed to 1,000 feet in six minutes, which for its time was quite spectacular. A number of successful test flights were carried out over the following weeks, but on taking off for Hendon to take part in a competition for the Mortimer Singer Prize, the aircraft suffered engine failure. Wilfred Parke managed to carry out an emergency landing which demolished the undercarriage and wings. The fuselage rolled onto its side, trapping W. H. Sayers, the engineer travelling with the aircraft, inside. He had to be freed by cutting a large hole in the side of the fuselage and removing auxiliary radiators. When the aircraft was rebuilt, the auxiliary radiators were moved to a lower position.

The re-built Avro 500 Type E was put through its paces at the Farnborough trial in June, and then returned to Brooklands to be used as a test bed for the new 60-hp A.B.C. A number of trials were carried out using the engine, causing a number of modifications to be made to the airframe. At the beginning of 1913 the E.N.V. engine was re-installed, and the aircraft was assigned to the Avro School (now transferred to Shoreham), to be used for instructional purposes. The aircraft was later destroyed in the first fatal accident involving an Avro aircraft.

A. V. Roe had started building a second model late in 1912; this time, he fitted a 50-hp Gnome seven-cylinder rotary engine that was half the weight of the previous engines. The performance of the aircraft was more than A. V. Roe could have wished for. Flown by Wilfred Parke, the second version of the Avro 500 Type E reached a height of 2,000 feet in five minutes and flew a distance of 17 miles in 20 minutes to take part in a series of trials completed during the same afternoon.

The War Office officials who were monitoring the trials at the time were really impressed and after some haggling about the price, ordered two to be built, both to be fitted with dual controls. An order for twelve more, and then an order for six of the aircraft followed this from the Admiralty. The company was now regarded as viable, and so moved to larger premises in Clifton Street, Manchester. Production of the orders went into full swing, and by June 1913 all the War Office orders were completed and the aircraft delivered. All without exception were accepted after just one flight test and assigned to training squadrons. Three civil versions were sold later but no more military versions were ordered. The reason behind this, of course, was that with the First World War imminent, aviation was progressing in leaps and bounds and today's inventions suddenly became yesterday's relics.

While he was building the Avro 500 Type E, A. V. Roe was well aware of the exposure to the elements suffered by both pilots and observers. With this in mind he designed and built an enclosed aeroplane, possibly the first of its type anywhere in the world. Based on the design and construction of the Avro 500 and using the same undercarriage, tail section and small rudder, the Avro Type F monoplane, as it was known, was constructed in May 1912. Although there were a number of celluloid windows in the cockpit, forward view was very restricted, so holes were cut in the fuselage, either side of the pilot, enabling him to put his head through if flying through poor visibility. Access to the cockpit was through an aluminium panel situated in the roof, and the fuel and oil tanks were situated in the fuselage behind the pilot.

Powered by a 35-hp Viale five-cylinder radial engine, the Avro Type F, flown by Wilfred Parke, took off from Brooklands on 1 May 1912. This was the first flight in the world of an aircraft with a completely enclosed cockpit. Over the next few days a number of successful test flights were carried out, but then on 25 May, when the aircraft was due to appear at Hendon for flight tests, the engine failed on takeoff, and the aircraft hit a fence on crash landing. It was dismantled and repaired but stayed in the hangar until September, when R. H. Barnwell took it out for a test flight. Once again the aircraft performed well, but on landing the front skid broke and the aircraft flipped over on to its back, causing considerable damage. The damage was extensive and beyond economical repair, so the Avro Type F was scrapped.

With the loss of the Avro Type F monoplane, A. V. Roe decided to build a second model; this time, it was a two-seat biplane with a fully enclosed cabin. Loosely based on the structure of the Type F, the Avro Type G, as it was known, had a very narrow cabin with a maximum beam of just 2 ft 3 in, tapering to 1 ft 3 in at the end. Powered by a 60-hp Green engine which had spiral tube radiators mounted either side of the cabin, the engine was enclosed in louvered cowlings with the exhaust extending over the roof of the cabin. Access to the cabin was through a hinged door in the fuselage.

Two models were built: the first, No. 6, was to be powered with the 60-hp Green engine; the second, No. 7, was to be fitted with a 60-hp A.B.C. engine. The latter engine was not ready in time and because it was a real rush job, the Green engine was fitted. It was intended to enter the aircraft in the Military Aeroplane Competition at Larkhill, Salisbury Plain. The aircraft was completed, crated and shipped off by rail from Manchester. On arrival, the aircraft was assembled and Wilfred Parke, the pilot, took off on a 3-hour endurance trial. The weather closed in and the air became so turbulent that Parke was forced to return to Larkhill. Landing downwind, the aircraft overturned, causing extensive damage. The Avro Type G No.7 was returned to the factory in Manchester for extensive repairs

In the meantime, aircraft No. 6 had been completed and sent to Larkhill to compete in the competition. All the tests went well, including Parke flying into a heavy rainstorm for almost 45 minutes. The watching military observers were impressed, but not so impressed as to give Avro any orders for the aircraft. The aircraft returned to Shoreham, where it joined the fleet of Avro aircraft at the Avro Flying School. Nothing more was heard of it.

One of the reasons that the Avro Flying School and airfield were moved from Brooklands to Shoreham in the autumn of 1912 was because tests could be carried out on both landplanes and floatplanes. The latter had come about after Commander Schwann's experiments with the Avro Type D that he converted to a seaplane. A. V. Roe had been watching Schwann's experiments with interest, and could see the possibilities in developing a seaplane. The result was the Avro 501, which was an enlarged Avro 500 with a strengthened top wing and floats in place of the undercarriage. It had a wide central float 15 feet long and 7 feet wide, in which were fitted three wheels: one at the front and two at the rear. Because of the large wingspan of 47 ft 6 in, small floats were fitted to the wingtips to stabilise the aircraft when taxiing.

Powered by a 100-hp Gnome engine, the Avro 501 was one of the first amphibians built, and first flew in November 1912. There were stability problems right from the start, and despite a number of modifications the central float was eventually replaced with two separate floats. Tests were carried out, and the fitting of the two floats worked sufficiently well enough for the Admiralty to ask for the aircraft to be delivered to their testing ground on the Isle of Grain.

Encouraged by the interest shown in the floatplane by the Admiralty, Roe produced a larger version of the Avro 501, the Avro 503 Type H. One of the main features of the design was the method of quick dismantling and assembling. The upper wing was 3 feet longer than the lower and fitted with inversely tapered ailerons. The first test flight was a huge success, with company test pilot F. P. Raynham at the controls. Interestingly, he had a passenger, John Alcock, who was later to find fame as being one of the two men to first fly the Atlantic non-stop. A number of other flight tests were carried out in front of Admiralty officials and, surprisingly, a German naval officer, Kapitän Schultz, who flew the aircraft himself. Within a week, he had purchased the aircraft on behalf of the German government and made arrangements to have it dismantled, packed into crates and shipped to Wilhelmshaven. Once in Wilhelmshaven, it was re-assembled and flown by Leutnant W. Langfeld to Heligoland, and from there to Cuxhaven.

The success of the Avro 503 Type H caused the Avro 501 to be cancelled. The single centreline float was removed and replaced with a wheeled undercarriage after the Navy agreed to accept it as landplane. Three more Avro 503 Type H models were purchased by the Navy to be used by the Royal Naval Air Service (RNAS).

One of Avro's most successful aircraft of the First World War was being designed at the end of 1912: the Avro 504. Unlike previous Avro aircraft, which had been designed by A. V. Roe, the Avro 504's fuselage and undercarriage were designed by Roy Chadwick (later to design the world-famous Lancaster bomber) and a man called Taylor, while the wings were designed by H. E. Broadsmith. The fuselage was of a braced, box-girder construction consisting of four spruce longerons and spruce cross struts. The cockpits were in tandem, the pilot occupying the rear of the two seats. The two-bay wings were staggered but of equal length, braced by hollow spruce strut. The undercarriage was similar to that of the Avro 500, but made much simpler and strengthened by means of anchoring the skid to the fuselage by means of steel 'V' struts, to which a steel tube axle was fixed, supported by two main undercarriage legs with built-in rubber shock absorbers. The tailskid was attached to the trademark comma-shaped rudder.

It was decided to enter the aircraft in the 1913 Aerial Derby that was being held at Hendon. Shrouded in secrecy, the unveiling of the aircraft on the day caused a sensation, as it was obvious from the onset that this was an aircraft that was something special. Flown by F. P. Raynham, the Avro 504 finished fourth, but few people realised that the aircraft had only flown once before the race itself and was virtually an untried and untested machine. Another contest, this time with the new Blackburn Monoplane, flown by Harold Blackburn himself, showed the potential of the aircraft.

The trials and competition threw up some anomalies that caused the aircraft to be returned to Manchester for modifications to be carried out. A different engine was proposed, which meant that the engine mountings had to be changed to accommodate it and the streamlined cowlings. The wing warping arrangement was replaced with constant chord-hinged ailerons, and wires replaced the original rods, meaning the wing itself was strengthened.

During the next few months the aircraft was tested extensively, and, despite having to carry out an emergency landing when a carburettor control broke, exceeded a number of flying records, including the height record when it attained a height of 14,420 feet while over Brooklands. At the end of 1913, the aircraft was purchased by the *Daily Mail*, and was flown on publicity flights around the country, giving passenger flights to prominent citizens. A. V. Roe constructed a set of interchangeable floats, so that when the aircraft was in coastal areas it could be used as a seaplane. The original 80-hp Gnome engine was replaced with the more powerful 80-hp Gnome Monosoupape engine.

The first publicity flights took place in April 1914, at Paignton in Devon. There followed flights to Falmouth, Southport and Northern Ireland. On its return to Shoreham on 4 August for servicing, it was immediately taken over by the military as war had been declared. The aircraft was assigned to the RNAS and F. P. Raynham, who had been demonstrating the aircraft for the *Daily Mail*, took off to deliver it. Shortly after take-off the engine failed, and with no water to land on, Raynham had no choice but to put it down on land. The damage was extensive, so much so that it was beyond economical repair.

The information gathered during these flights had been passed on to the company, and during April 1914 production of the Avro 504 commenced, with a contract for twelve of the aircraft from the War Office. The first of the aircraft off the production line was sent to Farnborough, where it was tested to destruction. The next three were assigned to No. 5 Squadron RFC, who took them to France. One of the aircraft was shot down by ground fire while being flown by Lieutenants V. Waterfall and C. G. Bayly. This was one of the first aerial casualties of the war.

Additional orders for the aircraft were announced as the war progressed, but never in large numbers. A batch of fifty was ordered, forty-four of which were two-seaters, the remaining six single-seat fighters given the designation 504D. Deliveries of the first of the two-seaters began in February 1915, and they were assigned to the RFC squadrons in France. The Admiralty then placed an order for seven of the aircraft, and the first was delivered to RNAS Eastchurch on 27 November 1914. The RNAS had established its first forward base at Antwerp, Belgium, in November 1914, quickly followed by a second at Belfort, France. The same month, two aircraft from the base at Antwerp attacked the Zeppelin sheds at Düsseldorf and Cologne. The two pilots, Squadron Commander Spenser-Grey and Flight Lieutenant R. G. L. Marix, each selected the targets; Spenser-Grey attacked Cologne, and Marix Düsseldorf. Spenser-Grey's target was shrouded in clouds, so he attacked a nearby railway station with limited success, but Marix found his sheds easily and from a height of 600 feet dropped his two 20-lb bombs. Seconds later, the Zeppelin hangar erupted in an enormous fireball that reached a height of over 500 feet. The two bombs had scored a direct hit not only on the hangar, but also on the brand-new Zeppelin Z9 inside, which had only just been completed. After coming under heavy machine gun fire, from which his aircraft sustained considerable damage, Marix managed to coax the aircraft back to the Allied lines. Both pilots were awarded the DSO (Distinguished Service Order) for their bravery.

Within days, the aircraft were in action again; piloted by Flt Sub-Lt R. H. Collet, one took off armed with four 16-lb bombs in an attempt to bomb the German submarine depot at Bruges. Unfortunately, the weather closed in over the area so he attacked the Ostend-Bruges main railway line instead. In October, four Avro 504s had been formed at Manchester into a special flight and transported to Southampton under great secrecy. From there, they were shipped to Le Havre, and from there taken to Belfort by train. They were kept overnight in a barn for fear of being seen by German agents known to be operating in the area.

The four Avro 504 biplanes, Nos 179, 873, 874 and 875, were equipped to carry four 20-lb bombs and on 20 November 1914, they took off from Belfort. By the time all but one of the four aircraft had returned, they had flown 250 miles over enemy-held territory, over mountain ranges through extremely difficult weather conditions and had bombed the Zeppelin factory at Friedrichshafen. The raid caused a great deal of damage to enemy material and morale, and had almost destroyed the Zeppelin Z7, which was in for repairs. The one aircraft that did not return was that of Squadron Commander Featherstone-Briggs, whose aircraft was riddled by heavy machine gun fire from the ground. Although wounded, he managed to land his aircraft and was taken prisoner. The Germans treated him with great respect, as they admired the audacity and skill in the preparation and execution of the raid. Briggs managed to escape some weeks later and returned safely to England.

A number of other missions were successfully carried out over the next few months, but then, at the beginning of 1915, the Avro 504 was relegated to training duties. A. V. Roe developed the 504, and produced a purpose-built trainer for the RFC – the Avro 504A. Literally hundreds of these aircraft were built over the next few years, as it proved to be one of the finest training aircraft available. The Admiralty also ordered a number for training purposes and these were designated the Avro 504B. From this was developed the 504C, which was a long-range, armed single-seater that was used for anti-airship patrols in the North Sea and English Channel. The RFC counterpart to this model was the 504D, of which only six were built, and they ended up on advanced training duties.

Such was the demand for the Avro 504As that a number of other aircraft manufacturers were brought in to keep up with the demand. The 100-hp Gnome Monosoupape engine was installed in the later models, giving increased power. The RNAS modified an Avro 504B by having the rear cockpit moved further back, and having the space in between used to contain the main fuel tank. The stagger in the wings was reduced by 15 inches and a 100-hp Gnome Monosoupape engine powered the aircraft. Ten of the aircraft were modified and given the designation Avro 504E.

One of the 504Cs was fitted with a 75-hp Rolls-Royce Hawk six-cylinder, in-line engine and given the designation Avro 504F. The intention was that if the marriage of the engine with the aircraft were successful, then an order for thirty of them would be placed. It proved to be a failure however, as it was found that the aircraft was desperately underpowered.

The RFC ordered another variant to be used as a gunnery trainer. Powered by a 130-hp Clerget engine and fitted with forward-firing synchronised Vickers machine guns and a Lewis gun attached to a Scarff ring in the rear cockpit, ten of the Avro 504G, as it was designated, were built and assigned to various training establishments.

The last of the variants was a strengthened Avro 504C, which had a special padded seat. The aircraft, flown by Flight Commander R. E. Penny, was to be used in catapult trials from warships, one of the first aircraft ever to be launched from a ship.

The Avro 504 was one of the most successful aircraft built by A. V. Roe during the First World War.

In Manchester, while other models of Avro aircraft were being built, the company was also creating other types of aircraft and one of these was the Avro 508. Designed as two-seater reconnaissance two-bay biplane, the aircraft had its aileron cables running inside the leading edge of the lower wing using buried pulleys. The aircraft was powered by an 80-hp Gnome rotary pusher engine, which was mounted behind the pilot and observer. The design of the aircraft and the engine's location gave it the appearance of a back-to-front Avro 504. Only the one model was built and it was never flown. The RFC showed little or no interest in the aircraft.

Interest in the development of the seaplane was always prominent in the mind of A. V. Roe and when the 1914 Circuit of Britain Race was proposed, Roe designed and built the Avro 510. The aircraft was built in Manchester in July 1914, and the first test flight took place there. The aircraft was then dismantled and shipped in crates by rail to Calshot, Southampton, where the race was to start. It was a one-off and bore no resemblance to any machine that A. V. Roe had built before. The only trademark, if you could call it that, was the comma-shaped rudder.

The two-seat fuselage was of the box-girder configuration, consisting of four spruce longerons braced by steel tubing. The undercarriage was of a completely new design, consisting of a rectangular tube-steel frame to which the floats were attached. This in turn was fixed to the fuselage by four steel struts. The two-bay wing consisted of an extended upper wing that was 24 feet longer than the lower and incorporated the ailerons that were fitted onto the extending sections. The aircraft was powered by a 150-hp Sunbeam engine, giving it a top speed of 70 mph.

A. V. Roe arrived at Calshot to assemble the aircraft, only to hear that war had been declared and the race cancelled. Despite this, he assembled the aircraft and carried out flight tests with members of the Admiralty watching. The results were particularly successful, the newly-designed floats making landing on the sea much easier and smoother. With the trials completed, much to A. V. Roe's astonishment, Captain A. Longmore, RN, (later Air Vice Marshal Sir Arthur Longmore) from the Admiralty asked the cost of the aircraft, and immediately handed over a cheque for the full amount. He also ordered, on behalf of the Admiralty, five more Avro 510s, stipulating a number of modifications to be made to them. All six aircraft were to be eventually stationed at Calshot, some fitted with the 160-hp Gnome engine.

The Admiralty also looked at another single-seat, two-bay biplane that had been built for them early in 1916: this was the Avro 519. It was almost identical to the Avro 510 seaplane, but with an enlarged central wheeled skid replacing the floats, and the fitting of the large fin and rudder that was on the Avro 504B. One of the noticeable differences was the pilot's streamlined headrest, which gave rise to the assumption that it was to have been used for long-distance reconnaissance missions.

Four prototypes were built, two for the RNAS and two for the RFC, the latter being designated the Avro 519A and constructed as a two-seater. Powered by a 150-hp Sunbeam Nubian engine, the aircraft were sent to Farnborough for testing and evaluation, but were not accepted, being considered underpowered with a poor rate of climb.

Another variant of the Avro 504 appeared at the end of 1915, a two-seat fighter/ trainer, the Avro 521. The 521 was in reality a hybrid: the short span ailerons and the tail assembly were from a 504A, the positioning of the cockpit and the centre section struts from a 504E, the undercarriage assembly from a 504G, the streamlined headrest from the 519 and the top longerons from the 504 prototype. The aircraft was powered by a 110-hp Clerget engine, giving it a top speed of 80 mph

(128 km/h). The initial test flight was carried out at Trafford Park, Manchester, flown by F. P. Raynham with H. E. Broadsmith standing up in the rear cockpit holding a dummy machine gun to test the drag quotient. It was not a successful flight, and problems with the handling at low speeds caused some concern. The War Office delivered the aircraft to Farnborough for flight test and evaluation and much to everyone's surprise, twenty-five were ordered.

A number of proposals were made and modifications suggested, but none came to fruition and only the one prototype was ever built. An accident at the Advanced Flying Training School at Gosport in 1917, in which Captain Garnett, RN, was killed, happened in the Avro 521 prototype.

The increasing interest by the Admiralty in some of A. V. Roe's aircraft prompted him to set up an experimental establishment with an airfield on the Hamble, near Southampton. The site had a mile of foreshore and Roe had a Manchester architect design the new establishment, together with homes for 350 of his employees. Roe intended to move his entire workforce down to the South Coast and close the Manchester factory. Unfortunately, the war restricted the availability of building supplies and so only twenty-four of the houses were built, which meant only some of the key employees were moved and the Manchester factory remained open.

The first aircraft to be delivered to the new site was the first twin-engined aircraft built by the Avro Company. The Avro 523 had been designed by Roy Chadwick as a long-distance photo-reconnaissance/short range bomber, and was powered by two 160-hp Sunbeam pusher engines. The pilot's cockpit and the front machine gunner's position were just in front of the three-bay wings, while the rear gunner/observer's position was just behind. Both gunners had Lewis guns mounted on rotatable ring mountings, enabling their field of fire to cover a considerable area. The large, wide undercarriage was sprung with enlarged versions of the rubber shock absorbers that were fitted to almost all Avro's previous aircraft.

Flight tests were excellent, and the handling qualities gave no rise for concern. But the Pike, as the aircraft had been named, was too late to be considered, as contracts for a similar aircraft had been given to the Short Brothers Aircraft Company and production was well under way.

A. V. Roe persevered with the aircraft and a second aircraft was built with two 150-hp Green tractor engines, the Avro 523A, in an effort to improve performance. But the Admiralty were not interested in the aircraft; however, they were impressed enough to order an improved version, known as the Avro 529.

The Avro 527 and 528 appeared at the same time as the Avro 523, but were in fact modified versions of the Avro 504G. The 527 was fitted with a 150-hp Sunbeam engine with twin exhaust stacks that projected upwards in front of the pilot, severely restricting his view. The 527 retained the central skid undercarriage and was fitted with the fixed fin, which up to then had only been fitted on aircraft of the RNAS. A second version had an increased 6 feet wingspan, and that was designated a 527A. The type 528 was almost identical to the 527, the exception being the fitting of a 225-hp Sunbeam engine. None of the three aircraft lived up to expectations, and only the prototypes were built.

Although the Admiralty had selected Short Brothers to provide their short-range bomber, and had turned down the Avro 523, they were sufficiently impressed with the 523A to order two enlarged versions of the aircraft. The Avro 529, as it was designated, had three-bay folding wings, distinguished from the 523 by the curve of the top wing and its semi-circular balance area. The first prototype was built in Manchester but assembled in Hamble, and was powered by two uncowled 190-hp Rolls-Royce Falcon engines mounted midway between the wings.

The second prototype was built and assembled at Hamble because of the increased production of the Avro 504K. Known as the 529A, the second model was powered by two 230-hp B.H.P. engines which were housed in nacelles and mounted on top of the lower wing. The specifications varied hardly at all, and they were almost identical in appearance. The rear cockpits were fitted with Scarff rings, on which Lewis machine guns were mounted.

The Admiralty regarded the flight tests of both aircraft as good, but for some unknown reason no production contracts were issued and only the prototypes were built.

One of the most successful aircraft designed and built by Avro was the Avro 530, which unfortunately came along at the same time as the Bristol Fighter. The 530 was a two-seat fighter that was powered by a 200-hp Hispano-Suiza water-cooled engine. The engine earmarked for the aircraft was the 300-hp Hispano-Suiza, but for a variety of reasons it was not available. The 200-hp version was available, but almost all had been acquired for the S.E.5a. The first flight in July 1917 showed a great deal of promise but lacked the right engine.

The construction of the Avro 530 consisted of a deep box-girder fuselage, which was wire-braced and covered with fabric. This was stretched over formers that gave the aircraft a very streamlined look. The tail section resembled that of the prototype 503 Pike, to which a sprung steel skid was attached. The undercarriage went totally away from the normal Avro design and consisted of two 'V' struts covered in faired metal sheeting attached to an axle, to which the wheel were fixed. The two-bay equal length wings were mounted so that the upper wing was level with the pilot's eyes, thus ensuring good forward and upward views. In the rear cockpit, the observer/gunner had a single Lewis machine gun mounted on a Scarff ring, which gave him an excellent rearward and downward field of fire.

The Avro 530 was powered by a 200-hp Hispano-Suiza engine, which was cooled by a large frontal radiator, covered by a hollow, open-fronted spinner. In an effort to resolve the problem of the engine, the 200-hp Hispano-Suiza was replaced with a 200-hp Sunbeam Arab and the open spinner removed. The fairing on the undercarriage struts was removed and a larger tail fin installed. But it was to no avail; the RFC and Admiralty showed no interest, and the project was scrapped.

Still convinced that the Avro 503 would have provided the Air Ministry and the Admiralty with a good medium-range reconnaissance fighter/bomber, A. V. Roe produced the Avro 533 Manchester. This was a three-seat, twin-engined photo-reconnaissance fighter/bomber powered by two 320-hp A.B.C. Dragonfly 7-cylinder radial engines. Retaining the box-girder fuselage construction, it also improved the crew accommodation necessary for long flights. The construction of the aircraft took place at Hamble and adhered rigidly to the design requirements laid down by the Air Ministry.

In October 1918, the aircraft was completed, but without the A.B.C engines, which still had not arrived from the manufacturers due to problems. So as not to delay the testing of the aircraft, two 300-hp Siddeley Puma high-compression water-cooled engines were installed. The aircraft was designated the Avro 533A Manchester Mk II, the first flight-tests taking place at the beginning of December 1918. On completion of the tests, the aircraft was sent to No. 186 Development Squadron at Gosport. A second model, the Avro 533 Manchester Mk I, was fitted with the A.B.C. Dragonfly engines and was almost identical, save for the tail surfaces on the Mk I, which were larger than those of the Mk II.

This marked the end of A. V. Roe's involvement with military aviation, but this was rekindled twenty years later when the skills of his designers and engineers were once again put to the test.

SPECIFICATIONS

Roe I

Wing Span:	30 ft 0 in (9.1 m)
Length:	23 ft 0 in (7.0 m)
Height:	7 ft 2 in (2.1 m)
Weight Empty:	350 lb (158 kg)
Weight Loaded:	650 lb (294 kg)
Max. Speed:	Not known
Engine:	One 9-hp J.A.P.
	One 24-hp Antoinette

Roe I Triplane

Wing Span:	20 ft 0 in (6.0 m)
Length:	23 ft 0 in (7.0 m)
Height:	7 ft 2 in (2.1 m)
Weight Empty:	300 lb (136 kg)
Weight Loaded:	450 lb (204 kg)
Max. Speed:	25 mph (40 km/h)
Engine:	One 9-hp J.A.P.
	One 20-hp J.A.P.

Roe II Triplane

Wing Span:	26 ft 0 in (7.9 m)
Length:	23 ft 0 in (7.0 m)
Height:	11 ft 1 in (3.3 m)
Weight Empty:	150 lb (68 kg)
Weight Loaded:	550 lb (249 kg)
Max. Speed:	40 mph (64 km/h)
Engine:	One 35-hp Green

Roe III Triplane

Wing Span Upper:	31 ft 0 in (9.4 m)
Wing Span Lower:	20 ft 0 in (6.0 m)
Length:	23 ft 0 in (7.0 m)
Height:	11 ft 1 in (3.3 m)
Weight Empty:	350 lb (158 kg)
Weight Loaded:	750 lb (340 kg)
Max. Speed:	40 mph (64 km/h)
Engine:	One 35-hp Green
	One 35-hp J.A.P.

Roe IV Triplane

Wing Span Upper:	32 ft 0 in (9.7 m)
Wing Span Middle:	32 ft 0 in (9.7 m)
Wing Span Lower:	20 ft 0 in (6.0 m)
Length:	34 ft 0 in (10.3 m)
Height:	11 ft 2 in (3.3 m)
Weight Empty:	350 lb (158 kg)

Weight Loaded: 650 lb (294 kg)
Max. Speed: 40 mph (64 km/h)
Engine: One 35-hp Green

Avro Type D

Wing Span Upper:	31 ft 0 in (9.4 m) – Standard and seaplane
	33 ft 0 in (10.0 m) – Sesquiplane
Wing Span Lower:	31 ft 0 in (9.4 m) – Standard and seaplane
	23 ft 0 in (7.0 m) – Sesquiplane
Length:	28 ft 0 in (8.5 m)
Height:	9 ft 2 in (2.8 m)
Weight Empty:	350 lb (158 kg)
Weight Loaded:	500 lb (226 kg)
	1,000 lb (452 kg) – Seaplane
Max. Speed:	50 mph (80 km/h)
Engine:	One 35-hp Green
	One 45-hp Green
	One 35-hp Viale
	One 50-hp Issacson
Range:	100 miles (160 km)

Avro Type D (Duigan's Biplane)

Wing Span:	34 ft 0 in (10.3 m) – Duigan Biplane
	39 ft 4 in (11.9 m) – Sea Bird
Length:	29 ft 4 in (8.9 m)
Height:	10 ft 6 in (3.2 m)
Weight Empty:	350 lb (158 kg)
Weight Loaded:	500 lb (226 kg)
Max. Speed:	40 mph (64 km/h) – Duigan Biplane
	62 mph (99 km/h) – Sea Bird
Engine:	One 35-hp E.N.V Type D – Duigan Biplane
	One 40-hp Alvaston – Duigan Biplane
	One 50-hp Gnome – Sea Bird
Range:	100 miles (160 km)

Avro 500 / Type E

Wing Span:	36 ft 0 in (10.9 m)
Length:	30 ft 6 in (9.2 m) – Type E prototype
	29 ft 0 in (8.8 m) – Avro 500
Height:	9 ft 9 in (2.9 m)
Weight Empty:	1,100 lb (498 kg) – Type E prototype
	900 lb (408 kg) – Avro 500
Weight Loaded:	1,650 lb (748 kg) – Type E prototype
	1,300 lb (589 kg) – Avro 500
Max. Speed:	50 mph (80 km/h) – Type E prototype
	61 mph (98 km/h) – Avro 500
Engine:	One 60-hp E.N.V.Type F – Type E prototype
	One 60-hp A.B.C. – Type E prototype
	One 50-hp Gnome – Avro 500
	One 100-hp Gnome – Avro 5
Endurance:	6 hours

Avro Type F

Wing Span:	28 ft 0 in (8.5 m)
Length:	23 ft 0 in (7.0 m)
Height:	11 ft 2 in (3.3 m)
Weight Empty:	500 lb (226 kg)
Weight Loaded:	800 lb (362 kg)
Max. Speed:	65 mph (104 km/h)
Engine:	One 35-hp Vaile rotary

Avro Type G

Wing Span Upper:	35 ft 3 in (10.7 m)
Wing Span Lower:	35 ft 3 in (10.7 m)
Length:	28 ft 6 in (8.6 m)
Height:	9 ft 9 in (2.9 m)
Weight Empty:	1,191 lb (540 kg)
Weight Loaded:	1,792 lb (812 kg)
Max. Speed:	62 mph (99 km/h)
Engine:	One 60-hp Green

Avro 501

Wing Span Upper:	47 ft 6 in (14.4 m)
Wing Span Lower:	39 ft 6 in (12.0 m)
Length:	33 ft 0 in (10.0 m)
Height:	12 ft 6 in (3.8 m)
Weight Empty:	1,740 lb (789 kg)
Weight Loaded:	2,700 lb (1,224 kg)
Max. Speed:	55 mph (88 km/h)
Engine:	One 100-hp Gnome

Avro 503 Type H

Wing Span Upper:	50 ft 0 in (15.2 m)
Wing Span Lower:	47 ft 0 in (14.3 m)
Length:	33 ft 6 in (10.2 m)
Height:	12 ft 9 in (4.0 m)
Weight Empty:	1,740 lb (789 kg)
Weight Loaded:	2,200 lb (997 kg)
Max. Speed:	50 mph (80 km/h)
Engine:	One 100-hp Gnome

Avro 504 A/B/C/D/E/F/G/H

Wing Span:	36 ft 0 in (10.9 m)
Length:	29 ft 5 in (8.8 m)
Height:	10 ft 5 in (3.1 m)
Weight Empty:	924 lb (419 kg) – landplane
	1,070 lb (485 kg) – seaplane
	1,050 lb (476 kg) – 504A
Weight Loaded:	1,574 lb (713 kg) – landplane
	1,719 lb (779 kg) – seaplane

	1,700 lb (771 kg) – 504A
Max. Speed:	82 mph (131 km/h) – landplane
	75 mph (120 km/h) – seaplane
	86 mph (138 km/h) – 504A
Engines:	One 80-hp Gnome. – 504/A/B/C/D/G/H
	One 80-hp Gnome Monosoupape – 504/E
	One 80-hp Le Rhône – 504/A/B
	One 100-hp A.B.C. – 504/A
	One 75-hp Rolls-Royce Hawk – 504F

Avro 508

Wing Span:	44 ft 0 in (13.4 m)
Length:	26 ft 9 in (8.1 m)
Height:	10 ft 1 in (3.0 m)
Weight Empty:	1,000 lb (453 kg)
Weight Loaded:	1,680 lb (762 kg)
Max. Speed:	65 mph (104 km/h)
Engine:	One 80-hp Gnome
Endurance:	4½ hours

Avro 510

Wing Span Upper:	63 ft 0 in (19.2 m)
Wing Span Lower:	38 ft 0 in (11.5 m)
Length:	38 ft 0 in (11.5 m)
Height:	11 ft 1 in (3.3 m)
Weight Empty:	2,080 lb (943 kg)
Weight Loaded:	2,800 lb (1,270 kg)
Max. Speed:	70 mph (112 km/h).
Engine:	One 150-hp Sunbeam Nubian
	One 160-hp Gnome
	One 35-hp J.A.P.

Avro 501

Wing Span Upper:	47 ft 6 in (14.4 m)
Wing Span Lower:	39 ft 6 in (12.0 m)
Length:	33 ft 0 in (10.0 m)
Height:	12 ft 6 in (3.8 m)
Weight Empty:	1,740 lb (789 kg)
Weight Loaded:	2,700 lb (1,224 kg)
Max. Speed:	55 mph (88 km/h)
Engine:	One 150-hp Sunbeam Nubian

Avro 523

Wing Span:	60 ft 0 in (18.2 m)
Length:	39 ft 1 in (11.8 m)
Height:	11 ft 8 in (3.5 m)
Weight Empty:	4,000 lb (1,814 kg)
Weight Loaded:	6,064 lb (2,750 kg)
Max. Speed:	97 mph (156 km/h)

Engine: Two 160-hp Sunbeam – Avro 523
                           Two 150-hp Green – Avro 523A
Endurance: 7 hours

Avro 530

Wing Span Upper: 36 ft 0 in (10.9 m)
Wing Span Lower: 36 ft 0 in (10.9 m)
Length: 28 ft 6 in (8.6 m)
Height: 9 ft 7 in (2.8 m)
Weight Empty: 1,695 lb (768 kg)
Weight Loaded: 2,680 lb (1,215 kg)
Max. Speed: 114 mph (183 km/h)
Engine: One 200-hp Hispano-Suiza
                           One 200-hp Sunbeam Arab

Avro 533

Wing Span Upper: 60 ft 0 in (18.2 m)
Length: 37 ft 0 in (11.2 m)
Height: 12 ft 6 in (3.8 m)
Weight Empty: 4,887 lb (2,216 kg) – Mk I
                           4,574 lb (2,074 kg) – Mk II
Weight Loaded: 7,390 lb (3,352 kg) – Mk I
                           7,158 lb (3,246 kg) – Mk II
Max. Speed: 112 mph (181 km/h)
Engine: Two 320-hp A.B.C. Dragonfly
                           Two 300-hp Siddeley Puma

Armstrong Whitworth (AWK)

Armstrong Whitworth had started life as two separate engineering companies in the 1800s. The Armstrong Company had been an engineering company involved in the making of guns which then progressed to making warships and merchant ships. The Whitworth Company was also an engineering company which, among other things, found itself in the gun-making business when it invented a new method of tempering steel to make it stronger. Eventually, in 1897, the two companies merged and became one of the main manufacturers of guns and warships. Then, in 1910, it was asked to repair a Gnome engine and rebuild a Farman aircraft after it had hit a flagpole during a demonstration flight. On completion of the repairs, the aircraft was sold to the Avro Flying School at Brooklands.

Such was the skill shown in the repair that the Avro Company approached Armstrong Whitworth with a suggestion that they manufacture Avro aircraft under licence. This was politely turned down, but little did the company realise that in later years they would be doing just that.

In December 1912, the Armstrong Whitworth Company started to build the All British Engine Company Ltd. (A.B.C.) aircraft engine, designed by Granville Bradshaw. The first of the engines was put into the government engine competition under Armstrong Whitworth's name, but it failed the preliminary tests. It was decided to move the engine section of the factory to Elswick, Newcastle upon Tyne, and an Avro biplane was purchased (at the cost of £500) to test the engines. It was decided after the first engines had failed their preliminary tests that the designer, Granville Bradshaw, would have to be in residence at Elswick to oversee the construction of his design, and if he didn't agree then Armstrong Whitworth would build their own engines. Bradshaw refused to go to Elswick, and that was the end of the association.

The Admiralty approached Armstrong Whitworth in March 1913, and invited them to put forward a tender to build one large rigid airship, one large non-rigid airship and three small non-rigid airships. The War Office also approached the company to build aircraft and engines specifically to their designs, with the result that a new aviation department was set up within the company. Captain I. F. Fairbairn-Crawford, who up to this point had been assistant manager of the Elswick engine plant, headed the department. His assistant was a Dutchman, Frederick Koolhoven, a design engineer who had been chief engineer for the British Deperdussin Syndicate Ltd in London.

In preparation for the opening of the department, Fairbairn-Crawford went to France and visited the aircraft factories there to observe the production methods and the layouts of their production lines. In 1915, he himself was to learn to fly after taking a course at Hendon.

A new factory was built at Scotswood, Newcastle upon Tyne, and it was here that the first aircraft, the B.E. (British Experimental) 2a was built. They were flight-tested at Farnborough in April 1914 and passed with flying colours. The company was complimented on the high level of workmanship in its aircraft construction. An order for eight B.E.2as and twenty-five B.E.2bs quickly followed, and in order to cope with this amount the company rented a disused skating rink at Gosforth to be used as an aircraft factory. Gosforth, which was situated at the western end of Duke's Moor, close to Newcastle's Town Moor, had been selected because there was a field close by that could be used as an airfield where the aircraft could be tested. Initially it appeared to be very satisfactory, but it was soon realised that the airfield was only 600 yards long and 150 yards wide and surrounded by trees. This left very little room for mistakes when testing the aircraft, although fortunately there were no accidents. Nevertheless, a new airfield was found just northeast of the Town Moor.

The first of the Armstrong Whitworth aircraft designed by Koolhoven appeared at the beginning of 1914: the F.K.1 single-seater. Originally designed as a monoplane, the F.K.1 was altered to a biplane in mid-construction. It was a single-bay model with no stagger to the wings, and was powered initially by a 50-hp Gnome engine. The first flight of this aircraft was carried out by Koolhoven himself, and it was discovered to be seriously underpowered. An 80-hp Gnome engine was fitted later, but that was not successful either. This was followed in 1915 by the F.K.2, a two-seater, two-bay, equal span biplane powered by a 70-hp Renault air-cooled engine. The cockpits were in tandem, with the pilot sitting in the rear cockpit. The tail section consisted of a large vertical fin with unusually long elevators. The letters 'AW' with a small Union Flag were painted on the rudder.

At the outbreak of war, seven of the aircraft were ordered and they bore a very strong resemblance to the B.E.2c, the only notable difference being the tail section on the F.K.2. The initial enthusiasm for the F.K.2 waned after reports from pilots, who criticised its aileron control and found it difficult to handle in rough weather. Its 28-gallon fuel supply was also found to be inadequate, and so it was relegated to training duties. Even the fitting of a 90-hp R.A.F.1a engine could do nothing to improve the aircraft's performance.

Production of the B.E.2c was now at full height, and it was while in the development of this aircraft that Koolhoven designed and built the F.K.3. This was a distinct improvement on the B.E.2c and a large number were ordered. However, bureaucracy once again reared its ugly head and the F.K.3 was not allowed to compete with the government's own design of aircraft. This was to be the pattern throughout the First World War with regard to any aircraft designed by Koolhoven, even though his aircraft proved to be superior to any of the government designs. An example of this was the F.K.8, which was built in greatly reduced numbers to that of the R.E. (Reconnaissance Experimental) 8, and although superior in every way, it was relegated to the same duties as the R.E.8, carrying out artillery observation. The development of the later F.K.10 quadruplanes fared no better.

The majority of the F.K.3 production models were fitted with the 90-hp R.A.F.1a engine, but a small number of them were fitted with the 120-hp Beardmore engine. There were conflicting stories around this time regarding the supply of engines, and in the magazine *The Aeroplane* an article appeared stating that there was a serious shortage of 90-hp R.A.F engines, and that the War Office had ordered the 120-hp Beardmore to replace them. Then, an article the following week said that there was no longer a shortage and that manufacture of the 90-hp RAF engine was back in full production! This was all utter nonsense, and it has to be pointed out that the magazine was edited by C. C. Grey, whose hatred of the anything connected with the Royal Aircraft Factory was legendary, so he was not going to let the truth get in the way of a good story.

Nearly all of the F.K.3s were assigned to training duties in Britain, but No. 47 Squadron, RFC were assigned some of the F.K.3s and took them with them when they were moved to Macedonia. The squadron's inventory of aircraft consisted of a number of different makes, and the F.K.3 was assigned to bombing, artillery spotting and reconnaissance duties, in which it gave a good account of itself.

Frederick Koolhoven had not been idle, and at the beginning of June 1916 he produced the F.K.7 two-seater bomber/reconnaissance aircraft. It was an enlarged version of the F.K.3, but with an undercarriage strengthened with oleo shock absorbers, and with a rudder with a pointed horn-balance area. The aircraft was taken to the CFS by Captain E. D. Horsfall, and on arrival was put through the usual range of trials. All the criticisms levelled at the aircraft were ones that were easily remedied, and the aircraft was passed on to the Royal Aircraft Factory for further testing.

The results from both test establishments convinced the War Office to order an equal number of F.K.7s to those already ordered of the R.E.8. The first of the production models was designated the F.K.8 and fitted with a synchronised, forward-firing, Vickers machine gun, which was mounted within the fuselage on the port side and just behind the engine.

The first squadron to be equipped entirely with the F.K.8 was No. 35 Squadron, RFC, which, almost immediately on receiving the aircraft, were sent to France. The synchronisation mechanism fitted to the first production models was the Arsiad type, as the Armstrong Whitworth model had not been properly tested at this point. While operating under combat conditions a number of other faults were found, and a number of modifications had to be made, especially to the undercarriage. Landing on a succession of rough airfields caused a large number of tailskids to break off, and the oleos on the undercarriage were often damaged and had to be replaced. The Armstrong Whitworth gun synchronising system proved to be unsatisfactory and was hurriedly replaced by the Constantinesco system, which in reality was not a great deal better.

The ongoing problem with the undercarriage was resolved when the undercarriage from a standard Bristol Fighter was fitted. This, of course, caused problems with the production of the Bristol Fighter when a number of their undercarriages were given to the squadrons who had the F.K.8.

Because of its dependability, the F.K.8 was used for a variety of roles: reconnaissance, artillery spotting, day and night bombing, contact patrol and ground attack duties were among its tasks. In one incident, an F.K.8 from No. 2 Squadron RFC, flown by 2nd Lt A. A. McLeod, was attacked by eight Fokker Dr.Is. McLeod was hit five times, while his observer, Lt A. W. Hammond, was hit six times. Despite their injuries, they managed to shoot down three of the enemy aircraft before crashing themselves. Although badly wounded and bleeding profusely from his injuries, McLeod extricated himself from the wreckage and pulled his observer clear from the now fiercely burning wreckage. For this dramatic incident, McLeod was awarded the Victoria Cross. Their F.K.8 had sustained serious damage, but still was able to fly – a fitting testament to the men who designed and built her.

Inspired by the appearance of the Sopwith Triplane, Frederick Koolhoven designed the first of his quadruplanes, the F.K.9. The Sopwith Triplane may have inspired it, but it had none of the sleek, feisty-looking attributes of the Sopwith. In fact, it was quite an ugly-looking aircraft: the mainplanes had no dihedral, and had the small ailerons inserted into the wingtips. The undercarriage, consisting of a single main leg on either side, cross-braced to the fuselage and fixed to a thin steel bar, looked flimsy. The tail section was small and looked incapable of giving any support to the aircraft's controls.

The first flight took place on 24 September 1916, powered by a Clerget engine lent by the War Office. Despite its appearance, the results were encouraging and four days later the aircraft took to the air once again, this time with a representative of the Admiralty, Wing Commander Alec Ogilvie, observing. At the end of the flight the aircraft touched down, and as it reached the end of the runway it ran into Ogilvie, who suffered slight injuries. Despite being run down by the aircraft, Wing Commander

Ogilvie showed a real enthusiasm for the F.K.9 and discussed with Koolhoven the need for a number of modifications to be made, and the re-design of the aircraft to take the 200-hp Hispano-Suiza engine.

Unfortunately, the company was exclusively attached to the War Office and Ogilvie represented the Admiralty. The directors of Armstrong Whitworth were reluctant to upset what was their main beneficiary in terms of aircraft orders. Fortunately for them, there were no Hispano-Suiza engines available at the time; after all, Britain was in the middle of a war and everything was in short supply. In order to supply the Admiralty, Armstrong Whitworth gave another manufacturer, Hewlett & Blondeau, an order for three of the aircraft. The order was later transferred to another company, the Phoenix Dynamo Manufacturing Company of Bradford, but only for two of the quadruplanes. The third one was to be built by Armstrong Whitworth themselves.

The modifications that Wing Commander Ogilvie discussed were carried out and a second F.K.9 was produced. On the positive side, the tests showed the aircraft to be extremely light on the controls and very manoeuvrable; on the other hand, the cockpit itself was so small that it allowed the pilot very limited room to use the controls, and the structure of the fuselage was so weak that it had to be trued up after every landing. This was obviously totally unacceptable, and so it was refused. For some unknown reason the War Office decided to order two more if further modifications were made, and so the F.K.10 was designed and constructed. The F.K.10 had a deeper fuselage, the tail section had been re-designed and the undercarriage had been retained. A 130-hp Clerget 9B engine powered the aircraft, and the first test was carried out at Martlesham Heath at the beginning of March 1917. Like the F.K.9, it too was extremely light on the controls and very manoeuvrable, but its performance figures were even worse than those of the F.K.9. Even so, five of the aircraft were built, but all ended up at Orfordness to serve as static damage-assessment targets for various types of gunfire.

Armstrong Whitworth may not have made huge impression in the military field of aviation, but in later years they produced a number of excellent aircraft for the commercial market.

SPECIFICATIONS

Armstrong Whitworth F.K.1

Wing Span:	40 ft 0 in (12.1 m)
Length:	29 ft 0 in (8.8 m)
Height:	11 ft 10½ in (3.5 m)
Weight Empty:	1,386 lb (628 kg)
Weight Loaded:	2,447 lb (1,109 kg)
Max. Speed:	68 mph (109 km/h)
Engine:	One 70-hp Renault air-cooled V-8

Armstrong Whitworth F.K.2

Wing Span:	40 ft 0 in (12.1 m)
Length:	29 ft 0 in (8.8 m)
Height:	11 ft 10½ in (3.5 m)
Weight Empty:	1,386 lb (628 kg)
Weight Loaded:	2,447 lb (1,109 kg)
Max. Speed:	78 mph (125 km/h)
Engine:	One 90-hp R.A.F.1a

Armstrong Whitworth F.K.3

Wing Span:	40 ft 1 in (12.2 m)
Length:	29 ft 0 in (8.8 m)
Height:	11 ft 10½ in (3.5 m)
Weight Empty:	1,682 lb (762 kg)
Weight Loaded:	2,056 lb (932 kg)
Max. Speed:	92 mph (148 km/h)
Engine:	One 90-hp R.A.F.1a
	One 120-hp Beardmore

Armstrong Whitworth F.K.7 & 8

Wing Span:	43 ft 6 in (13.2 m)
Length:	31 ft 0 in (9.4 m)
Height:	11 ft 0 in (3.3 m)
Weight Empty:	1,916 lb (869 kg)
Weight Loaded:	2,811 lb (1,275 kg)
Max. Speed:	98 mph (157 km/h)
Engine:	One 160-hp Beardmore
Armament:	One forward firing fixed .303 Vickers machine gun
	One Scarff-mounted .303 Vickers machine gun in rear cockpit
	Eight 25 lb Cooper bombs

Armstrong Whitworth F.K.9 & 10

Wing Span:	27 ft 10 in (8.4 m)
Length:	22 ft 3 in (6.7 m)
Height:	11 ft 6 in (3.5 m)
Weight Empty:	1,226 lb (556 kg)
Weight Loaded:	2,038 lb (924 kg)
Max. Speed:	98 mph (157 km/h)
Engine:	One 110-hp Clerget 9Z – F.K.9
	One 110-hp Le Rhône 9J – F.K.10
	One 130-hp Clerget 9B – F.K.10
Armament:	One forward firing fixed .303 Vickers machine gun
	One Scarff-mounted .303 Vickers machine gun in rear cockpit

Blackburn Aircraft Company Ltd

The beginnings of the Blackburn Aircraft Company Ltd lie in 1906, when Robert Blackburn left university with an engineering degree and went to work for Thomas Green & Sons Ltd, steamroller and lawn mower manufacturers, in the design and drawing office. Within a couple of months, Robert Blackburn realised that the current engineering practices and his own forward thinking were not compatible, and so he left to continue his studies by working for various engineering companies in Germany, France and Belgium. It was while working for an engineering company in Rouen, France, that he saw Wilbur Wright flying his aircraft at Le Mans. Intrigued by the engineering concept in aviation, he continued to watch a number of other aviation pioneers at the time, like Farman, Blériot and Latham, testing their aircraft at Issy, near Paris.

Fired by enthusiasm, Robert Blackburn decided to design and build his own aircraft, and went to live in Paris to concentrate on his design. Satisfied with the results of his design, he returned to Leeds and, after persuading his father to back him, opened his first workshop and produced his first aircraft, the First Blackburn Monoplane. Powered by a 35-hp Green water-cooled engine, the aircraft began trials on the stretch of sands between Marske-by-the Sea and Saltburn. The trials consisted of taxiing trials with short hops, but it soon became obvious that the engine was not powerful enough. During one attempt at a short hop, the port wing dropped and dug into the sand, with the result that the aircraft turned over and was wrecked.

The wreckage was returned to the workshop, and parts of what could be re-used were incorporated into a completely new design. The Second Blackburn Monoplane was almost identical in appearance to the French Levavasseur Antoinette monoplane, but that is where the similarity ended, because there were a number of very detailed improvements in Blackburn's model. The aircraft was powered by an Isaacson 40-hp 7-cylinder, air-cooled, radial engine. The advantage of this engine over the Green model was that the working parts were easily accessible for maintenance and repair purposes. There were some problems with the construction of the aircraft, however. The undercarriage was found to be weak, meaning the wingtips had to be supported when stationary, so urgent modifications were made and the undercarriage strengthened. The first flight on 8 March 1911 resulted in the aircraft sideslipping into the ground, but after repairs the second flight was extremely successful and Robert Blackburn was in the aviation business.

The third aircraft to appear was the Blackburn Mercury (Mercury I), which was in fact a larger two-seat version of the Second Blackburn Monoplane. The aircraft was exhibited at the Olympia Aero Show in March 1911, after which it was flown to Filey to join the newly-created Blackburn Flying School, which was part of the Blackburn Aeroplane Company. Over the next three years, the company produced the Mercury II, followed by the Blackburn Monoplane Type B, and the Mercury III. The company's first expedition into the field of military aviation was with the Blackburn Type E. This was a two-seat, all-metal monoplane based on the successful design of the Mercury series of aircraft. The aircraft was in response to a War Office specification that called for:

1. A two-seater reconnaissance aircraft
2. Able to carry a useful load of 250 lb over and above the normal requirements
3. Maintain a height of 4,500 ft for one hour
4. A climb rate of 200 ft per minute
5. An endurance of 4½ hours
6. A maximum speed of 55 mph
7. Transportable by crate from one area to another

The time allowed to produce such an aircraft was just nine months, which would be just in time for the Military Trials on Salisbury Plain in August 1912.

The Blackburn Type E was powered by a 60-hp 4-cylinder, inline, water-cooled Green engine. When completed, it was painted grey overall and the inscription 'Indian Aviation Co. Ltd' painted on the lower rudder, and the name *L'Oiseau* on the engine cowling. It was taken to Brooklands for trials, and such was the company's confidence that it was entered for the Round-London Aerial Derby on 8 June. It was pulled out at the last moment because of trouble with the engine, which was replaced by the 70-hp air-cooled Renault engine. It is interesting to note that up to this point the aircraft hadn't actually flown, and when it was taken by road to Knavesmire, Yorkshire, to be test-flown by Norman Blackburn, Robert's brother, it proved to be far too heavy to leave the ground. The ultimate fate of the aircraft is not known.

Two more monoplanes followed, both for the civilian market, the Blackburn Single-seat Monoplane and the Blackburn Type I. The monoplane, powered by a 50-hp Gnome, had been ordered by Mr Cyril E. Foggin, and had been designed as a sporting aircraft. The first flight was carried out in November 1912 by Harold Blackburn, and was very successful. A number of other test flights were flown during the following months, and it wasn't until March 1913 that the owner actually managed to get his hands on the controls. The aircraft was sold the following month to a fellow aviator, Montague Glew, who crashed the aircraft on his father's farm some weeks later.

The Type I was a two-seat version of the monoplane, both occupants sitting in tandem in a large cockpit. Like its predecessor, the aircraft flew well and was exhibited around Yorkshire on a number of occasions by Harold Blackburn. It is interesting to note that the owner, Mr M. G. Christie, had taken a course of instruction as a pilot, but had not qualified. He employed Harold Blackburn as his personal pilot and accompanied him on the demonstration flights. On 21 September 1913, the aircraft was entered in the *Yorkshire Evening News* Challenge Cup Race. The race from Leeds to York, Doncaster, Sheffield, Barnsley, and back to Leeds was between a Manchester-built Avro 504 prototype, flown by F. P. Raynham with A. V. Roe as passenger, and the Type I. Billed as the 'War of the Roses', the two aircraft battled their way through poor visibility and rain, with the Type I coming through as the eventual winner.

Another Type I two-seater was built for the Aero Show in Olympia, which opened on 16 March 1914. In the meantime, the original model was carrying out a number of exhibition flights all over Yorkshire, and was attracting the attention of the military. When war was declared, both Type I aircraft were commandeered by the War Office and placed under guard at their field. Two days later, their canvas hangar was doused in petrol and set on fire by saboteurs, thought to be two local German waiters, although it was never proved. The aircraft were rescued by one of the aviation students, who was badly burned in the process.

In October 1915 one of the Type Is was fitted with floats, and trials were carried out on Lake Windermere. Almost no modifications were required to complete the transition from landplane to floatplane, and all the trials were very successful. A large number of RNAS pilots carried out their initial training on the aircraft. It was written off after a crash on 1 April 1916.

The Type I was not the Blackburn Company's first purpose-built floatplane; that was the Blackburn Type L. This was the first biplane built by the Blackburn Company, and was a two-seat model with a square-shaped fuselage, unlike all the previous models, which had a triangular-shaped fuselage. It was powered by a 130-hp Canton-Unné water-cooled radial engine that was being produced under licence by the Dudbridge Iron Works at Stroud, Gloucestershire. The aircraft was produced just in time for the proposed Circuit of Britain seaplane race, which attracted nine entries from Avro, Beardmore, Eastbourne, Graham-White, White & Thompson and Sopwith. Scheduled to start at 0600 hours on 10 August 1914 from Calshot, some of the aircraft were actually on their way to the starting point when war was declared and the Admiralty immediately commandeered all the seaplanes. The Blackburn Type L was flown to Scarborough, where it was used for reconnaissance missions around the North Sea.

The company was also involved in the manufacture of aircraft from other companies: the B.E.2c, the Sopwith torpedo bomber, and the Sopwith Cuckoo, all of which they built in large quantities. While they completed these contracts, they were working on their own design for a long-range Zeppelin interceptor night bomber. The result was the Blackburn T.B. (Twin Blackburn), a large biplane powered initially by two 150-hp Smith engines, then later by two 100-hp Gnome Monosoupapes, and then by two 110-hp Clerget 9b engines. The Admiralty ordered nine of the aircraft, but there were problems from day one. Like so many of the aircraft designed and built during the First World War, the Blackburn T.B. was underpowered. Problems were also discovered in the wire-braced sections, and the means of communication between the crewmembers was by hand signals, which during a night-time mission were useless. They were taken off charge, and seven of the aircraft were sent to RNAS Killingholme, where they were stored and eventually broken up. The other two were taken to the RNAS depot at Crystal Palace, where they remained until they, too, were broken up.

While the construction of the unsuccessful Blackburn T.B. had been taking place in one part of the factory, another aircraft was taking shape – the Blackburn Triplane. Designed late in 1915, the Blackburn Triplane (N502) fighter aircraft had equal, unstaggered single-bay wings and was powered by a 100-hp Gnome Monosoupape radial engine. The cockpit nacelle was mounted on top and in front of the centre wing, with a single forward-firing machine gun mounted in the nose. The tail section was connected to booms, and consisted of two large rudders with a tailplane mounted on top. Strut-connected ailerons on each of the six wingtips achieved lateral control. After tests, a 110-hp Clerget engine was fitted to try and improve the aircraft's performance, but the results were minimal and the aircraft faded into obscurity.

Despite the setback of the Blackburn T.B., the company pressed ahead with the design and construction of a three-seat, long-range, anti-submarine seaplane bomber called the Blackburn G.P. (General Purpose). The three-bay biplane prototype (1415), which had unequal wings, had two 150-hp Sunbeam Nubian engines that powered four-bladed propellers, which gave the aircraft a maximum speed of 97 mph. The wings were constructed with a wing-folding mechanism that enabled the wings to be folded back against the fuselage, so that the aircraft could be kept in a conventional hangar. The three-man crew consisted of a bomb-aimer/gunner in the nose, pilot and rear gunner, whose cockpit was aft of the wings. The bomber carried two Lewis machine guns mounted on Scarff rings, and four 250-lb bombs in racks beneath the wings. The prototype was taken to the Isle of Grain for trials, where it underwent extensive taxiing trials in rough weather. There is no evidence however that it took to the air at anytime.

A second prototype (1416) was built, powered by two 190-hp Rolls-Royce engines. The main differences between the two models were limited to the use of stronger metals, the repositioning of the engine exhaust pipes and the repositioning of the oil tanks. Like No. 1415, the trials were not successful, and no contracts were secured for production of the aircraft. Both aircraft were later broken up.

The demise of the two seaplane versions of the Blackburn G.P. did not bring an end to the design. A landplane version was produced powered by two 250-hp Rolls-Royce Falcon II engines with four-bladed propellers – the Blackburn R.T.I Kangaroo. Like its predecessor, the Kangaroo retained the unequal three-bay wings, the wing-folding mechanism and the wooden airframe covered in fabric. The engines, however, were raised into the mid-gap position of the first bay, and the radiators were moved from the side of the engines to the front. The undercarriage consisted of four wheels in two separate units, one under each engine position. There were no shock absorbers fitted to the undercarriage, the only form of springing was that absorbed by the pneumatic tyres. The armament was the same as that of the G.P., but the split undercarriage made it the ideal vehicle for carrying a torpedo, which for some unknown reason was never done.

On 3 January 1918, the prototype was delivered to Martlesham Heath for trials to begin. The pilot was Clifford B. Prodger, an American test pilot who was at the time testing the Handley Page HP O/400 bombers. The tests took three weeks, and although the results were quite favourable, there were some defects, including excessive loads on the control column. In an engine-off glide mode, the rear section of the fuselage tended to twist when coming out of a steep turn and the gunners' positions prevented them from operating satisfactorily. Nineteen of the aircraft were under construction at the time, and a number of modifications were requested by the Admiralty, who had placed the order, after reading the extensive report from the tests. A statement from the Blackburn Company read:

> The 20 Kangaroos, which are already well in hand at Blackburns, will be similar to the machine in the attached report. It is understood that no more are to be ordered and no steps have been taken to modify the machine.

Modifications must have taken place despite this statement being put out, because there were no problems experienced in any of the production models that eventually entered service with the RAF.

The initial use for the Blackburn Kangaroo was to have been as a night bomber, but they were never used in that role; instead, they flew convoy protection and reconnaissance missions for the remainder of the war. No. 246 Squadron, RAF had been supplied with ten of the aircraft and had some success with them. They had sighted twelve U-boats, sank one and damaged four between 1 May 1918 and 11 November 1918. The remaining ten Kangaroos were assigned to training establishments and despite the original test reports, no complaints about the aircraft were received from crews who flew it.

After the war, the Blackburn Kangaroos that remained airworthy were sold to private buyers and experienced some success as commercial aircraft.

The first landplane produced by the Blackburn Aircraft Company in the First World War was the Blackburn N113, which was the prototype for the Blackburn Blackburd (*sic*). The aircraft came out of a requirement by the Admiralty in 1917 for a single-seat torpedo carrying aircraft, powered by a 350-hp Rolls-Royce Eagle VIII engine, and capable of delivering a 1,400-lb Mk VIII torpedo. Blackburn produced a two-bay biplane with equal unstaggered wings with the torpedo slung beneath the fuselage between split undercarriage units.

Three prototypes were built, and the first of these was fitted with skids as well as wheels. Just after takeoff the wheels would be jettisoned, and after launching its torpedo the aircraft would then return to land on the skids. If a situation arose whereby the aircraft had to put down on the water, the N113 had internal floatation gear fitted inside the fuselage. It was distinctive in its overall design with its constant deep and box-shaped fuselage. The second prototype, the N114, had small floats fitted beneath the lower wings, but still retained the box-shaped fuselage.

Blackburn and another company, Short's, were involved in the development of this type of aircraft, but after exhaustive tests both aircraft were found to be greatly inferior to the Sopwith Cuckoo. No orders were placed with either Blackburn or Short's for their aircraft.

SPECIFICATIONS

Blackburn Mercury

Wing Span (Mercury I):	38 ft 4 in (11.5 m)
Wing Span (Mercury II):	32 ft 0 in (9.7 m)
Wing Span (Mercury III):	32 ft 0 in (9.7 m)
Length (Mercury I):	33 ft 0 in (10.1 m)
Length (Mercury II):	31 ft 0 in (9.4 m)
Length (Mercury III):	31 ft 0 in (9.4 m)
Height (Mercury I):	6 ft 9 in (2.1 m)
Height (Mercury II):	8 ft 6 in (2.5 m)
Weight Empty:	Not known
Weight Loaded (Mercury I):	1,000 lb (453 kg)
Weight Loaded (Mercury II):	700 lb (317 kg)
Weight Loaded (Mercury III):	800 lb (362 kg)
Max. Speed (Mercury I):	60 mph (96 km/h)
Max. Speed (Mercury II):	70 mph (112 km/h)
Max Speed (Mercury III):	75 mph (120 km/h)
Engines (Mercury I):	One 50-hp Isaacson
Engines (Mercury II):	One 50-hp Gnome
Engines (Mercury III):	One 60-hp Renault
	One 50-hp Isaacson
	One 50-hp Gnome
	One 50-hp Anzani

Blackburn Type E

Wing Span:	38 ft 4 in (11.5 m)
Length:	31 ft 2 in (9.4 m)
Height:	6 ft 9 in (2.1 m)
Weight Empty:	Not known
Weight Loaded:	950 lb (430 kg)
Max. Speed:	80 mph (128 km/h)
Engines:	One 60-hp Green
	One 70-hp Renault

Blackburn Type I

Wing Span:	38 ft 0 in (11.5 m)
Length:	28 ft 6 in (8.6 m)
Height:	6 ft 9 in (2.1 m)
Weight Empty:	950 lb (430 kg)
Weight Loaded:	1,500 lb (680 kg)
Max. Speed:	70 mph (112 km/h)
Engines:	One 80-hp Gnome

Blackburn Type L

Wing Span Upper:	49 ft 6 in (15.0 m)
Wing Span Lower:	35 ft. 0 in (10.6 m)
Length:	35 ft 0 in (10.6 m)
Height:	12 ft 6 in (3.8 m)
Weight Empty:	1,717 lb (778 kg)
Weight Loaded:	2,475 lb (1,122 kg)
Max. Speed:	80 mph (128 km/h)
Engines:	One 130-hp Canton-Unné

Blackburn T.B.

Wing Span Upper:	60 ft 6 in (18.4 m)
Wing Span Lower:	45 ft 0 in (13.7 m)
Length:	36 ft 6 in (11.1 m)
Height:	13 ft 6 in (4.1 m)
Weight Empty:	2,310 lb (1,047 kg)
Weight Loaded:	3,500 lb (1,587 kg)
Max. Speed:	86 mph (138 km/h)
Engines:	Two 150-hp Smith
	Two 100-hp Gnome Monosoupapes
	Two 110-hp Clerget 9bs

Blackburn Triplane

Wing Span:	24 ft 0 in (7.3 m)
Length:	21 ft 5½ in (6.5 m)
Height:	8 ft 6 in (2.6 m)
Weight Empty:	1,011 lb (458 kg)
Weight Loaded:	1,500 lb (680 kg)
Max. Speed:	86 mph (138 km/h)
Engines:	One 100-hp Gnome Monosoupape
	One 110-hp Clerget 9b

Blackburn G.P.

Wing Span Upper:	74 ft 10¼ in (22.7 m)
Wing Span Lower:	52 ft 10½ in (16.0 m)
Length:	46 ft 0 in (14.1 m)
Height:	16 ft 10 in (5.1 m)
Weight Empty:	5,840 lb (2,649 kg)
Weight Loaded:	8,600 lb (3,900 kg)
Max. Speed:	97 mph (156 km/h)
Engines:	Two 150-hp Sunbeam Nubian
	Two 190-hp Rolls-Royce

Blackburn Kangaroo

Wing Span Upper:	74 ft 10¼ in (22.7 m)
Wing Span Lower:	53 ft 1 in (16.1 m)
Length:	44 ft 2 in (13.4 m)
Height:	16 ft 10 in (5.1 m)
Weight Empty:	5,284 lb (2,396 kg)

Weight Loaded:	8,017 lb (3,636 kg)
Max. Speed:	98 mph (158 km/h)
Engines:	Two 250-hp Rolls-Royce Falcon II
	Two 190-hp Rolls-Royce Falcon III

Blackburn Blackburd

Wing Span Extended:	52 ft 5 in (15.9 m)
Wing Span Folded:	17 ft 1 in (5.2 m)
Length:	34 ft 10 in (10.6 m)
Height:	12 ft 4½ in (3.7 m)
Weight Empty:	3,228 lb (1,464 kg)
Weight Loaded:	5,700 lb (2,585 kg)
Max. Speed:	95 mph (157 km/h)
Engines:	One 350-hp Rolls-Royce Eagle VIII
Armament:	Two Lewis machine guns – one forward, one aft
	Four 230 lb bombs

The prototype of the D.H.1, seen at Hendon.

A prototype of the D.H.2 fitted with an enlarged rudder.

A D.H.2 of No. 14 Squadron RFC in the Middle East.

Airco D.H.3.

An Airco D.H.4 fitted with floats.

Three D.H.4s being prepared for flight at a training school.

A prototype of the D.H.5.

A D.H.6 just off the production line.

A D.H.9 from No. 49 TDS with an American star marking on the fuselage.

A D.H.9 on patrol.

A D.H.9 overflying an airfield on which can be seen several Bristol F2b fighters.

The R.I., a Russian copy of the D.H.9a.

The first production model of the D.H.10.

The only model of the D.H.11, seen on a rare test flight.

Alliott Verdon Roe.

The Avro II Triplane coming to mishap after ground-looping.

A. V. Roe at the controls of his Avro III Triplane as the engine is about to be started.

The Avro Type G at the Military Trials in 1912.

Another view of the Avro Type G at the Military Trials.

The Avro 508 at the Aero Show, Olympia.

The crew of an Armstrong-Whitworth F.K.3 adjusting their cameras before setting out.

The Armstrong-Whitworth F.K.5, designed by Franz Koolhoven.

Another view of the F.K.5.

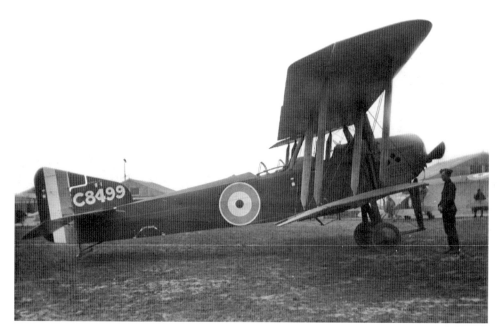

Armstrong-Whitworth F.K.8, No. C8499.

An F.K.8 preparing to take off.

F.K.8 No. C3655.

The instrument panel for an F.K.8.

A rare aerial photograph of an F.K.8 pursuing a German Rumpler.

A rare aerial photograph of a F.K.8 going down, trailing black smoke.

The wreckage of an F.K.8 after a landing accident.

An Armstrong-Whitworth F.K.10 Quadraplane.

A Blackburn Kangaroo of the RNAS being serviced.

A Blackburn Blackburd (*sic*) under construction.

Blériot Aéronautique

Louis Blériot's entry into the world of aviation was not the most spectacular. His first attempt, in 1903, concerned the development and construction of an ornithopter that never even got off the ground. One year later he built a floatplane glider that crashed and sank just after getting airborne. There followed a succession of disasters, but despite all these setbacks, Blériot persevered until he designed and built the Blériot XI in 1909.

After a number of flights and mishaps, including crashing into the pond at Trou-Salé et Buc, near Versailles, Blériot completed the trials of his XI. The aircraft was originally powered by a REP (Robert Esnault-Pelterie) engine; however, in May 1909, Alesandro Anzani produced his Anzani engine, which Blériot then fitted into his XI. This came after a time in 1908 when the *Daily Mail*, owned by Lord Northcliffe (a strong supporter of aviation), offered a prize of £500 for the first aeroplane flight between England and France. Because there had been no response from aviation circles, it had been decided to double the prize money to £1,000. It had also been decided that any attempt would have to be under the control of the Aero Club in London and the International Aeronautical Federation.

Louis Blériot was among a number of pilots to register with the ruling bodies, including the favourite to complete the flight, Hubert Latham. On 25 July 1909, Louis Blériot's Blériot XI lifted off from Calais and, 37 minutes later, landed at Dover Castle, winning him a worldwide reputation. He and his aircraft had been the first to fly the English Channel.

The Blériot XI was a two-seat monoplane with shoulder-wings and a box-shaped fuselage with rectangular cross-sections and a small balanced rudder as the tail section. It was constructed of wood, with only the forward section of the fuselage covered in plywood and fabric. The undercarriage was raised and made of wood, reinforced with steel cables, giving it a spindly, fragile appearance. All-round visibility was excellent, but downward visibility was very poor indeed, especially as the observer was seated in front of the pilot and over the centre of the wings.

In 1912, a second model of the Blériot XI was entered in the Military Trials at Larkhill and impressed the military hierarchy to the extent that they ordered one and assigned it to the RFC. Interestingly enough, there was another Blériot entered in the trials, the Blériot Type 21. This was said to have been owned by a Lieutenant R. A. Cammell, who flew it from his camp at Larkhill. It was later taken over by the Air Battalion and re-designated B2. It was later transferred to No. 3 Squadron, where it was in effect abandoned after trials with various engines.

Thirteen Blériot XIs were ordered: four with 50-hp Gnome engines, and the remaining nine with 80-hp Gnome engines. They were assigned to Nos 3 and 6 Squadrons, RFC. The Blériot Company opened up a subsidiary in England called Blériot Aeronautics and started to produce the aircraft at their new factory. Further contracts were issued for the Blériot XI, three of which were built in Britain, the remaining nine in France. Then, just before the war, a further twenty-eight were ordered and were assigned to Nos 3, 6, 9 and 16 Squadrons, all of which were serving on the Western Front.

The RNAS ordered thirty-five Blériot XIs, all to be fitted with the 80-hp Gnome engines, which were assigned as trainers and reconnaissance aircraft to No. 1 Wing RNAS and Eastchurch. A further fifteen were ordered and assigned to Nos 1 and 3 Wings, RNAS.

As the war progressed so the aircraft became faster and more deadlier, leaving aircraft like the Blériot XI behind, so those that were left were transferred to training squadrons where they continued train more pilots and observers.

In August 1913, Blériot produced another version of the XI, the Blériot Parasol. The main difference between the two aircraft was that the shoulder-mounted wings of the XI were slightly shorter, and now mounted above the fuselage in one piece and supported by a double inverted V-like structure mounted on top. The tail section was the same as that fitted to the 50-hp Blériot XI, and the fuselage and undercarriage as that of the 70-hp Blériot XI.

A total of fifteen of the aircraft were ordered by the RFC, five built in France and the remaining ten built by Blériot Aéronautique in England. Five of them saw service in France with Nos 3, 5 and 9 Squadrons, RFC; the remainder were assigned to training squadrons in England. Among the mechanics that looked after the Blériot Parasol in No. 3 Squadron was Air Mechanic J. T. B. McCudden, who later became one of the outstanding British fighter pilots of the war. In later years, McCudden remembered one incident with the Parasol; Lieutenant Conran's Blériot Parasol was loaded with sixteen hand grenades, two shrapnel bombs and a Mélinite bomb, all to be manhandled over the side of the aircraft, and took off to bomb Laon railway station. It is not recorded whether or not the raid was a success.

The majority of pilots who flew the Blériot Parasol liked the aircraft, and when better and faster aircraft superseded it, those that were left were dispatched to training squadrons like their predecessors.

The Blériot factory was also involved in constructing aircraft for a number of other companies during the war, including the SPAD.

SPECIFICATIONS

Blériot XI

Wing Span:	29 ft 3 in (8.9 m)
Length:	24 ft 11 in (7.6 m)
Height:	8 ft 4 in (2.5 m)
Weight Empty:	738 lb (335 kg)
Weight Loaded:	1,289 lb (585 kg)
Max. Speed:	62 mph (100 km/h)
Engines:	One 70-hp Gnome
Armament:	Rifles, Flechettes and bombs

Blériot Parasol

Wing Span:	29 ft 3 in (8.9 m)
Length:	25 ft 2 in (7.9 m)
Height:	8 ft 4 in (2.5 m)
Weight Empty:	617 lb (280 kg)
Weight Loaded:	926 lb (420 kg)
Max. Speed:	68 mph (110 km/h)
Engines:	One 80-hp Gnome
Armament:	Rifles, Flechettes and bombs

Société des Avions Louis Breguet

The first fixed-wing aircraft designed and built by the Breguet Company was a two-bay biplane that had a biplane tail and used wing warping for lateral control. They had experimented with various types of other aircraft, but none had met with any success. With the success of the first flight of the Breguet I, the company Société des Avions Louis Breguet was formed in 1911. The first military aircraft, the Breguet L.1, was built in June 1910. It had been designed and built in response to a request by Colonel Hirschauer for an artillery spotter and reconnaissance aircraft.

The Breguet L.1 was a two-bay biplane fitted with a 50-hp Renault tractor engine and a four-wheeled undercarriage. The aircraft attracted the attention of the RFC, who purchased one of the aircraft and subjected it to stringent trials with a view to purchasing more if acceptable. The tests showed that the aircraft was extremely difficult to fly and required tremendous strength to control. It was destroyed in a crash landing after a trial.

In 1913, the Breguet Company opened up a subsidiary company in England called the British Breguet Plane Limited Company, and developed their latest aircraft at the plant, the Breguet U2. The U2 was of an unusual design and construction. It was a two-bay biplane with flexible wings, and was powered by a 110-hp Canton-Unné tractor engine. The fuselage, which had a circular cross-section, was constructed of wood and covered with aluminium, tapering to almost a point at the tail section where a cruciform all-flying tail was fitted. It was this unusually shaped fuselage that gave rise to the aircraft's nickname, 'Tin Whistle'.

The RFC obtained two Breguet U2s from France and evaluated them during the Military Trials at Larkhill on Salisbury Plain in 1912. Neither of the aircraft was accepted, as they never measured up to the requirements set by the RFC. One was later purchased from the British Breguet Company and was assigned to No. 4 Squadron, RFC, but served only as a training aircraft.

The development of the Breguet-Michelin bombers was one of the company's more unsatisfactory projects. The first of these was the BU.3, and this was initially designed as a fighter with a crew of two. The design consisted of a twin-boom fuselage, extending from behind the top and bottom wings and converging at the tail section, which consisted of a single large rudder with two elevators, one either side, that had vertical fins fitted.

The Breguet BUM.3 was powered by a 200-hp Canton-Unné 2M7 pusher water-cooled radial engine. The armour-plated tandem two-seat cockpit nacelle was mounted on the lower wing of the three-bay biplane. The observer/gunner sat behind the pilot; to use the machine gun, he had to stand and fire over the pilot's head. On later variants the observer/gunner's position was moved to the nose of the aircraft, giving him a greater field of fire, and a number of different weapons were trialled, including the 37 mm Hotchkiss cannon.

Fifty of the aircraft were built, thirteen of which were ordered by the RNAS at the beginning of 1916. The Breguets de Chasse, as the British called them, were all fitted with the 225-hp Sunbeam engine and assigned to Nos 1 and 3 Wing, RNAS. By June 1916, it was realised that the aircraft were obsolete: they were too slow, too cumbersome and useless against the fighters of the German Imperial Air Service. All were withdrawn from service.

A further development of the BUM.3 was the SN.3. This came about after a competition to find an aircraft capable of carrying 200 kg bombs over a radius of 600 km with the intention of bombing the town of Essen (hence the designation SN). The 600 km was the distance from Nancy to Essen and back. The aircraft was required to have a speed of 120 km/h, and have a ceiling of 2,000 meters. Powered by a 250-hp Renault engine, the SN.3 had unequal wingspan, which resulted in a decrease of wing area from 70.5 sq m to 54 sq m. The SN.3 was placed first in the competition, but was not put into production because it was thought that its defence was inadequate and it lacked sufficient range for long distance bombing raids. The Breguet Company immediately began work on an improved version, and developed the BM (Breguet Michelin) 4. This was a very similar design to that of the SN.3, but was powered by a Renault 8Gd engine. The prototype was tested by the Aviation Militaire and, despite discovering that the range and bomb load was reduced, they placed an order for 200 of the aircraft.

The BM.4 was soon in action, heavily involved in attacks on railway stations and troop trains. Many of the BM.4s were fitted with searchlights and used in night bombing missions. But difficulties with maintenance of the aircraft were causing serious problems, and slowly they were replaced.

Two other countries acquired the BM.4; Romania and Russia. The Romanian aircraft, although belonging to Romania, were part of the French Escadrille BM.8 and crewed by French airmen. They were involved in numerous missions, including the daring attack on German warships in Braila Harbour on 31 March 1917, in which one ship was sunk and several others were damaged. The Russians purchased one of the aircraft, but they found it woefully inadequate for their needs.

The relative success of the use of the cannon in the Breguet BU.3 led the Breguet Company to install it in their latest aircraft, the Breguet 5. This was a three-bay, unequal span biplane powered by a 225-hp Renault 12Fb engine. The tail section was the same as that of the Breguet BU.3, with four tail booms extending from the upper and lower wings. The RNAS purchased fifty-nine Breguet 5s from the Breguet factory and ordered an additional thirty from the Graham-White Aviation Company, but only ten were ever built in Britain. Twenty-five of the Breguet 5s built in France had the 250-hp Rolls-Royce engine installed; the remaining models were powered by the 225-hp Renault engine.

The next design was a radical one: the Breguet 11 Corsair. This was a three-engined aircraft with two pushers and one tractor. The two pusher engines were mounted on the lower wing, either side of the main fuselage, in nacelles that resembled it, each with its own tricycle undercarriage. The three-bay, unequal span wings had ailerons mounted in the upper wings, but despite a favourable test report, the aircraft was declined in favour of smaller models. The 90-ft (27.6 m) wingspan was one of the reasons it was declined, because it was felt that the relatively slow speed of the aircraft, 91 mph (149 km/h), coupled with its enormous size made it an easy target for anti-aircraft guns.

What was to follow was some of the best French aircraft produced during the First World War: the Breguet 13 and 14. Over 8,000 Breguet 14s were built and sold to twenty-two countries. There were fourteen variations that included using a number of different engines and a large number of modifications.

The designs of these aircraft looked nothing like the previous designs. The Breguet 13, or AV 1, as it was known at the time, had a more conventional look. The prototype took to the air on 21 November 1916 with Louis Breguet at the controls. After extensive trials by company test pilots, the aircraft was delivered to Aviation Militaire in January 1917 for their assessment. It immediately became apparent that the aircraft was far in advance of anything the British or the Germans had. The STAé (Section Technical Aeronautique) had stipulated earlier in November that they wanted four types of aircraft, a three-seat, long-range reconnaissance plane, a three-seat bomber, a two-seat army co-operation plane and a two-seat fighter. Breguet submitted the aircraft stating that variants of the aircraft could cover all the requirements.

On 6 March 1917, impressed by the aircraft, the Aviation Militaire ordered 150 Breguet AV 1s (Breguet 13) to be used for reconnaissance. At the same time, the Michelin Company received an order for 150 Breguet AV 2s (Breguet 14), the bomber version. Because the aircraft were almost identical, it was decided to use the same designation for both – Breguet 14. In the months up until September 1917, orders totalling another 475 aircraft were placed.

Because demand was now outstripping supply, other companies were brought in to build the Breguet 14 under licence: Ballanger (300), Darracq (330), Farman (220), Sidam (300) and Paul Schmitt (275). The Paul Schmitt Company was already in the process of building a bomber, but the Breguet 14 had to take precedence, although they still managed to complete their own orders.

One of the exciting things about the Breguet 14, as far as the military were concerned, was its adaptability. It underwent numerous modifications, none of which affected its performance. On some of the aircraft, the wingspan and flap size was reduced. Different engines were tried, and various types of armament were installed and tested. Among these was one of the first air ambulances – the Breguet 14S (Sanitaire). The fuselage was modified to enable two stretchers to be carried inside.

Almost every escadrille was supplied with the Breguet 14, including the overseas units. During the short period of the war in which the USAS was involved, they purchased almost 400 of the aircraft. The first of their bombardment units, the 96th Aero Squadron carried out their first mission in June 1918 using Breguet 14 bombers. After the war, the Breguet 14 was used by a number of countries as a small passenger aircraft.

An enlarged version of the Breguet 14 appeared at the beginning of 1918, the Breguet 16 Bn2. This was designed for use as night-bomber, and the increased wingspan of 17 metres enabled it to carry sufficient fuel for long missions, as well as armament for major attacks.

At the same time as the Breguet 16 was being developed, a two-seat fighter, a version of the Breguet 14, was being built. It had originally been on the drawing board back in 1916, and had been submitted to the STAé for consideration. Rejected by them, the design had stayed on the drawing board, but the requirement for a long-range escort fighter at the beginning of 1918 caused it to be resurrected.

Powered by a 450-hp Renault 12 engine, the Breguet 17, as it was called, looked very similar to the Breguet 14. However, it had a larger tail fin and rudder, a shorter wingspan, a deeper under-camber and increased armament. The first test flight took place in June 1918 but again, like the Breguet 16, there were problems and the aircraft wasn't available until after the Armistice. Only ten of the aircraft were built.

The Breguet Company, despite a slow start, had contributed greatly to the Allies' war in the air and, like many other aircraft manufacturers, left their mark in the world of aviation.

SPECIFICATIONS

Breguet U2

Wing Span:	44 ft 4 in (13.5 m)
Length:	27 ft 10 in (8.5 m)
Height:	8 ft 4 in (2.5 m)
Weight Empty:	1,234 lb (560 kg)
Weight Loaded:	2,116 lb (960 kg)
Max. Speed:	68 mph (110 km/h)
Engines:	One 110-hp Canton-Unné
Armament:	None

Breguet 5

Wing Span:	57 ft 5 in (17.5 m)
Length:	32 ft 5 in (9.9 m)
Height:	12 ft 8 in (3.9 m)
Weight Empty:	2,976 lb (1,350 kg)
Weight Loaded:	4,167 lb (1,890 kg)
Max. Speed:	81 mph (131 km/h)
Engines:	One 220-hp Renault 12Fb
	One 250-hp Rolls-Royce
Armament:	One 37 mm Hotchkiss cannon
	One Lewis machine gun

Breguet 13

Wing Span:	49 ft 7 in (15.3 m)
Length:	27 ft 10 in (8.5 m)
Height:	10 ft 9 in (3.3 m)
Weight Empty:	2,094 lb (950 kg)
Weight Loaded:	2,976 lb (1,350 kg)
Max. Speed:	62 mph (100 km/h)
Engines:	One 160-hp Gnome
Armament:	One Hotchkiss machine gun and Flechettes

Breguet 14

Wing Span:	46 ft 9 in (14.3 m)
Length:	29 ft 5 in (8.9 m)
Height:	10 ft 8 in (3.3 m)
Weight Empty:	2,271 lb (1,030 kg)
Weight Loaded:	3,450 lb (1,565 kg)
Max. Speed:	114 mph (184 km/h)
Engines:	One 300-hp Renault 12Fc
Armament:	One synchronised 7.7 mm Vickers machine gun
	Two Lewis machine guns in observer's cockpit
	Four 120 mm bombs

British & Colonial Aeroplane Company (Bristol Aeroplane Company)

One of the most famous aircraft companies in the world started life not as one company, but as four. They consisted of:

The Bristol Aeroplane Company Limited
The Bristol Aviation Company Limited
The British & Colonial Aeroplane Company Limited
The British & Colonial Aviation Company Limited

Formed by Sir George White in 1910, the Bristol Aeroplane Company was inspired by the first powered flight by the Wright brothers at Kittyhawk, North Carolina. An entrepreneur and highly-regarded businessman, George White approached the board of the Bristol Tramways Company, of which he was president, and announced that they were going into the aircraft building business. The company was started with £25,000, and all the money came from the White family. This was due to the fact that Sir George White knew it would be useless trying to raise the money from other sources, because when he announced the project everyone in the business world thought that he was mad.

Sir George White's nephew, Herbert J. Thomas, was sent to Paris to meet with representatives from the Société Zodiac, and after examining the designs and manufacturing methods an agreement was reached for the Bristol Company to build the Zodiac biplane under licence. One of the Zodiac biplanes was sent to the Olympia Aero Show, and afterwards was taken to Brooklands, where the Bristol Company had leased a hangar. A French pilot who had been hired to test fly the aircraft could not even get the Zodiac off the ground, no matter how hard he tried, and told the company that the best thing they could with the aircraft was to scrap it. His suggestion was to purchase the Henri Farman biplane, which was already making a name for itself. The Bristol Company had already started making five of the Zodiac aircraft at Filton, and on hearing of the problems, they immediately stopped work on them. The aircraft were scrapped and the Bristol Company claimed 15,000 francs in compensation from Zodiac for misleading them about the aircraft's airworthiness.

George Challenger, whose father was the general manager of the Bristol Tramways Company, was appointed engineer and works manager of the Bristol Aircraft Company and immediately became interested in the design of the Henri Farman biplane. He was involved in the design of a Farman-type biplane, and fitted the new 50-hp Gnome engine that had just arrived from France. There were some half-hearted complaints from the Farman Company regarding the infringement of their patent, but the two companies remained friends.

The first Bristol aircraft was the Bristol biplane, also known as the Boxkite, which was almost identical to the Henry Farman biplane; the only difference was that the steel clips and aluminium sockets were of a much better quality. It was the addition of these items that made the biplane a far better and more reliable aircraft than its French counterpart. The French company started legal proceedings against the Bristol Company with regard to infringements of patent, but when the Bristol Company produced a defence that they had carried out substantial improvements to the design and construction, the case was dropped. A total of sixteen Bristol Boxkites were built: the first nine remained in Britain and were involved in various military trials and competitions; Nos 10 and 12 were sent to Australia and India respectively for trials; No. 11 was later shipped to Australia as spares for No. 10; No. 9 was used as spares for No. 12; the remaining four aircraft (Nos 13, 14, 15 and 16) remained in Britain.

The aircraft was a complete success, and the various trials proved that it was a reliable and sturdy aircraft capable of being flown anywhere in the world. Convinced, the War Office placed an order for four of the aircraft on 14 March 1911, all to be powered with the 50-hp Gnome rotary engine. Over the next couple of years, a number of Bristol Boxkites were built and sold to a number of countries: Spain, Russia, Bulgaria, Rumania, Sweden and South Africa. A variety of engines were tried and tested, using the Boxkite as a flying test-bed. When the First World War broke out, the Bristol Company had already produced over six different models of aircraft, and was among the leaders in aviation manufacture.

Just prior to the war, a Romanian engineer by the name of Henri Coanda joined the company. Coanda was the son of the Romanian War Minister and had trained as an engineer in France under the guidance of Gustav Eiffel, who had built the world's first wind tunnel. Henri Coanda's first design was of a two-seat tandem monoplane based on the design of the Prier-Dickson model. The wings consisted of two steel spars, onto which ribs were fitted and fixed with clips that allowed them to rotate around the spars for warping purposes. In previous designs based on this idea, the front spars were always longer than those of the rear, which restricted the range of warping. Coanda's design went the opposite way: the rear spars were longer than the front ones and braced with steel tubes above and below to steel pylons. The slab-sided fuselage tapered toward the tail to a conventional, semi-circular, fixed style tailplane, with a balanced rudder and a one-piece elevator. The aircraft was powered by a 50-hp Gnome engine, which was covered with a circular metal cowl to prevent oil being thrown back over the cockpits. A military version of the Bristol Coanda Monoplane was entered into the Military Aeroplane Competition. The rules surrounding the entrants were surprisingly rigid, considering the relatively short time the manufacturers had to prepare for the event. The aircraft had to be taken to Larkhill in a railway carriage and be no longer than 32 feet, and be capable of being towed on its own wheels or on a purpose-built trolley behind an army column.

The trials went well, but then an accident in one of the monoplanes that killed two army officers caused the War Office to ban all military pilots of the Royal Flying Corps from flying monoplanes. This in effect ruined all chances of selling the aircraft to the RFC, but fortunately the ban did not apply to the Admiralty, who ordered a few of the aircraft. Overseas sales to Italy and Romania of the military version of the Coanda Monoplane continued, but in only small numbers.

As if to compensate for their loss of orders, the War Office awarded Bristol a contract to build the B.E. (British Experimental) 2 biplane. This aircraft had been ineligible for the Military Aeroplane Competition, but tests had shown it to be far superior to the winners of the competition. This prompted Henri Coanda to look toward designing a two-seater biplane, encouraged by the fact that the company had received a number of enquiries from overseas customers for a long-range two-seater aircraft.

Given the designation Bristol B.R.70 (later shortened to B.R.7), the first of the models was built at the same time as the B.E.2. Seven of the aircraft were built in total, and during the next year the company embarked on a number of trials concerning floatplanes, including the Bristol-Burney Flying Boats. One of these, the X-3, was trialled for use aboard a submarine, but the results came to nothing and the design was dropped.

At the end of 1913, the Bristol Company, through their many contacts in Europe, were aware of the rumours of unrest that were spreading across the continent. They were also aware of the need for military aircraft in the event of Britain becoming involved in a conflict. With this in mind, Henri Coanda set to work re-designing the S.B.5 Prier monoplane powered by an Anzani engine; he turned it into a single-seat, high-speed, reconnaissance biplane. Previously destined for the Italian Government, it was now known as the 'Baby-biplane' or 'Scout', a very simple aircraft with a 22-ft single-bay wingspan which was powered by an 80-hp Gnome engine. A number of modifications were carried out on the Scout, including the fitting of longer wings that reduced the landing speed without affecting the performance.

Two more of the aircraft were built and given the designation Scout B. Both were then subjected to intensive trials and took part in a number of competitions. On 4 August 1914, the First World War broke out, and immediately the War Office requisitioned both the aircraft. After further testing at Farnborough, they were assigned to Nos 3 and 5 Squadrons RFC in France. There they were flown by Lieutenant Cholmondeley and Major J. A. Higgins, who were so impressed with the aircraft that they nicknamed them the 'Bristol Bullets'.

Word soon filtered back to the War Office, and the company received a contract for twelve improved versions to be given the designation Scout C. Another order from the Admiralty for twenty-four of the aircraft quickly pushed the factory into full production. Problems arose when the Admiralty demanded that they be given priority as they had placed the largest order and they were the Senior Service. In an effort to appease, the first Scout C off the production line was sent to the Admiralty while the next eleven went to the War Office. On 16 March 1915, the War Office placed a second contract for seventy-five Scout Cs, all to be fitted with the 70-hp Gnome engine.

The aircraft were distributed among the various squadrons as reconnaissance scout aircraft, but never in fact made up a squadron in their own right. Although not officially armed, the individual pilots fitted carbines for protection, and in one incident on 25 July 1915, Captain Lanoe Hawker from No. 6 Squadron RFC, who was on patrol at the time, encountered three German two-seaters, all armed with machine guns. His aircraft was armed with a Martini carbine mounted on the starboard side of the fuselage, and with a mixture of brilliant flying and considerable luck he managed to force the three enemy aircraft down. For this feat he was awarded the Victoria Cross.

The success of the Scout C was followed by the Scout D, a modified version of the C which was powered by a 100-hp Mono-Gnome engine. On 3 August 1915, the War Office issued a contract for a further fifty Scouts, subject to a number of design changes including an alternative wing design with smaller but longer ailerons and a larger rudder. Three months later, a further contract for fifty more Scout Ds was issued, and these were to be equipped with standard gun mountings. The Admiralty also ordered an additional thirty Scout Ds, with the promise of another contract later in the year. The last contract had to be declined, as the company was at full stretch producing the B.E.2 two-seat fighter in addition to its own aircraft.

In July 1915, the War Office put out a requirement to the various aircraft manufacturers for a twin-engined, two-seater defence aircraft. The following month Captain Frank Barnwell, the company's former chief designer, who had gone to Australia to work, returned to his old job. He immediately set to work on a preliminary design for the twin-engined aircraft. Two aircraft were required, and four 150-hp R.A.F.4a engines were set aside for the aircraft. The Bristol T.T. (Twin Tractor) A model had a two-bay wing section with the engines mounted in nacelles between the wings. At the rear of the nacelles were the oil and gravity-fed fuel tanks. The undercarriage consisted of twin wheels beneath each nacelle and a fixed skid under the nose. The tail section consisted of a single balanced rudder with a flat tailplane. Both cockpits were fitted with controls, although the observer's controls consisted of pedals, as there was no room for the normal rudder bar and they were there for emergency use only.

Tests on the aircraft showed it to have a top speed of 87 mph and a climb rate of 400 feet per minute. This was barely acceptable to the War Office, and when further criticisms about the design of the aircraft were made, it was sufficient for them to refuse it for squadron service.

As the war entered its second year, the Royal Flying Corps was becoming increasingly concerned that the number of their scout/fighter aircraft was dwindling rapidly. The Fokker fighters of the German Army Air Service were far superior to anything the Allies had at that time, so a new type of fighter that could match the Fokker was needed. The Bristol Company had been working on such an aircraft based on a design by Captain Barnwell. This was a monoplane with a conventional fuselage with wire-braced longerons. The wings, which were raked at the tips, were attached to the top longerons with wire braces fitted to the bottom longerons, and to a hooped structure above the pilot's head. This structure also served as protection for the pilot in the event of the aircraft turning over while taking off or landing. The undercarriage consisted of two wheels fitted to a V-shaped steel tube frame connected by a sprung-rubber axle. The aircraft was powered by a 110-hp Clerget engine fitted with a domed spinner that reduced the drag coefficient.

The Bristol M.1A, as it was called, had its first test flight on 14 July 1916 at Filton, and was flown by test pilot Fred Raynham. The little aircraft even astounded Fred Raynham when he reached the speed of 132 mph, and he was delighted with the handling qualities as he flew it under the Clifton Suspension Bridge. The War Office, who ordered a further four to be built with slight modifications, then evaluated the aircraft. The Bristol M.1B was the first of the modified models, with a Vickers machine gun mounted on the port wing root and the overhead structure arranged in a pyramid shape. The last of the four models was fitted with the 130-hp Clerget rotary engine, and later a Bentley A.R.1 rotary engine.

Although the aircraft met all the requirements for the RFC, there were some serious criticisms from combat pilots regarding the high landing speed. A production order for 125 of the aircraft, designated the Bristol M.1C, was awarded, but with a centrally-fitted synchronised Vickers machine gun, fitted with either the Sopwith-Kauper or the Constantine Constantinesco interruptor mechanism, and the 110-hp Le Rhône engine. Five squadrons were equipped with the aircraft: Nos 17, 47, 150, which flew mostly against the Turks and Bulgarians out of Salonika; No. 72 Squadron, which flew from Basra; and No. 111 squadron in Palestine.

Once again they were not the success hoped for, and the majority of those not assigned to squadron were distributed among flying schools, and some ended up as personal taxis for some senior officers.

Also at this time, one of the problems that were starting to appear was the shortage of timber, like the silver spruce, suitable for the building of airframes. In 1914, a number of designers had looked at the feasibility of building an all-metal version of the B.E.2c, to be known as the B.E.10. Because production of aircraft at Filton was expanding rapidly, the project had to be abandoned in favour of mass-produced fighter aircraft, and there were a number of shortcomings with the aircraft that needed to be resolved.

Then, in July 1916, Captain Barnwell was looking at a similar project with the intention of altering the layout of the R.2A reconnaissance biplane to accommodate the 190-hp Rolls-Royce engine. Using his knowledge of the development of the B.E.10, and remembering the shortcomings that were discovered, he developed the Bristol M.R.1.

The fuselage was of the standard monocoque design, but built in four sections bolted together. The front section carried the engine bulkhead and bearers, the second section the pilot's cockpit and all that went with it, the third section contained the observer's cockpit and the fourth section contained the tail and rudder assembly. The wing assembly was a direct swap from wood to duraluminium, and the building of the wing was put out to The Steel Wing Company of Gloucester, which had developed a rolled high-tensile steel strip suitable for construction.

Because of the length of time taken to construct the steel wing, it was decided to build conventional wooden wings so that flight tests could take place. All the tests were successful, and the aircraft was taken over by the Air Board for further evaluation. The second of the two models ordered, complete with metal wings, wasn't delivered until the end of 1918, and was fitted with a 180-hp Wolseley Viper engine. It is not known what happened to the first model (no doubt it was just scrapped), but the second model crashed on the runway at Farnborough while in the process of being delivered to the Royal Aircraft Establishment by its designer, Captain Barnwell. He was unhurt, but the aircraft was damaged beyond repair and no more were built.

At the beginning of 1916, the Bristol Company had contracts to build more than 600 B.E. two-seater fighters, with contracts to build a further 550 B.E.2d and B.E.2e models by the end of 1917. While these aircraft were being built, their designated successor, the R.E.8, was about to be produced. Captain Barnwell had had sight of the designs and specifications, and was not impressed. With this in mind, he set to work designing a two-seat fighter that would perform better than anything else comparable at the time. In March 1916, he produced the R.2A, which was powered by a 120-hp Beardmore engine. The two-bay aircraft was fitted with two cockpits, the front one for the pilot and the rear for the observer/gunner. The observer's gun was mounted on a rotating ring that allowed him a much larger field of fire, and also enabled him to fire over the top of the pilot's head. The pilot's gun was a synchronised Lewis machine gun mounted on the starboard upper longeron.

It soon became apparent that the aircraft was underpowered, and so a second model, the R.2B, was designed and built, powered by a 150-hp Hispano-Suiza engine. Then Barnwell was offered the latest 190-hp Rolls-Royce engine, and set about redesigning a new aircraft around the engine instead of modifying the existing designs. The result was the Bristol F.2A, which was to become one of the company's most successful aircraft designs of the First World War.

Based on the R.2A, the new design incorporated a new tail unit with an adjustable tail plane attached to a cambered horizontal knife-edge fuselage, which greatly reduced the observer's 'blind spot'. Two prototypes of the Bristol Fighter, as the aircraft became colloquially known, were built. The first was completed in July 1916, the second in the October, and the first flight took place on 9 September 1916 with Captain Hooper at the controls. Everything was perfect, except for the fact that Hooper said the aircraft could not climb above 6,000 feet according to the altimeter. Everything was checked and double-checked, but again there was the same report. Captain Barnwell sent for his brother, Harold Barnwell, who was chief test pilot for Vickers at the time. He experienced a similar result, but insisted that he had thought, like Hooper, that he had flown much higher than that. The altimeter was changed, and it was discovered that the original instrument had been faulty and the aircraft had in fact flown to 10,000 feet in just 15 minutes.

The aircraft was then taken to Upavon for military trials, and exceeded all expectations. The only thing that was altered was the radiator. Originally, the Rolls-Royce engine had two radiators mounted vertically either side of the fuselage, just ahead of the wings, but this restricted the pilot's downward view on landing. Barnwell designed a new circular radiator with shutters in the front, to be mounted in the nose of the aircraft.

Contracts for the aircraft were issued, and the Bristol Company began production of the F.2A Bristol Fighter at the end of 1916. Fifty of the aircraft were built at the Filton Works, and an additional contract for a further 200 was issued for the improved version, the F.2B Bristol Fighter. This had come about after the second prototype had been modified with various alterations and improvements.

The first squadron to receive the new F.2A fighter was No. 48 Squadron RFC, under the command of Major A. Vere Bettington, based at Bellevue, near Arras. The squadron had some of the most experienced fighter pilots within its ranks, and couldn't wait to pit this new fighter against the German Albatros D.IIIs. Their chance came on 5 April 1917 when six F.2A Bristol Fighters, led by Captain Leefe Robinson, VC, were on patrol over Arras. They were attacked by six Albatros D.IIIs, led by the legendary Manfred von Richthofen. In the ensuing battle, four of the F.2As were shot down, including Leefe Robinson's. Six days later, four more F.2As were shot down with the loss of just two Albatros D.IIIs. Then, on 16 April, there was a further disaster when a patrol of five aircraft ran out of fuel over enemy lines and had to put their aircraft down. They managed to set fire to the aircraft before the enemy could get to them, but this was a loss of thirteen F.2As in less than a month; not the auspicious start envisaged.

The Bristol F.2B came off the production line at the beginning of 1917, and was immediately dispatched to Nos 48 and 11 Squadrons in France. Within days, the F.2B was in action and proved to be superior to the F.2A in every way. Demand for the aircraft, however, far outstripped the numbers coming off the production line, so it was decided to issue contracts to build the aircraft to other firms; these included Armstrong Whitworth and Angus Sanderson of Newcastle-on-Tyne, the Standard Motor Co. of Coventry, the National Aircraft Factory No. 3 at Aintree, Marshall & Sons of Gainsborough, the Gloucestershire Aircraft Co. at Cheltenham and Austin Motors and Harris & Sheldon of Birmingham.

Although the first choice of engine for the F.2B was the Rolls-Royce Falcon, for obvious reasons, demand far exceeded the output, so various other engines were fitted with varying results; these included the Hispano-Suiza, Siddeley Puma and Sunbeam Arab. To accommodate these different engines, a number of modifications had to be made to the airframe that changed the shape of the aircraft to a certain extent.

Throughout the war, the F.2B fought in almost every theatre, from the arid wastes of Palestine to the seas of mud in France. In Britain, it was only the Bristol F2B of the Home Defence squadrons that could get within range of the Zeppelins. When America entered the war in April 1917, the Bristol F.2B was one of the first British aircraft to be proposed for large-scale production in the United States. When engineers from Filton went over to America to the Curtiss Aeroplane & Motor Corporation, the principal manufacturer of the aircraft, they discovered to their horror that the engine proposed for the Curtiss-built F.2B was the 400-hp Liberty 12. It was immediately noticed that the engine was far too heavy, and was incorrectly installed. Captain Barnwell, who headed up the British team, immediately raised an objection to the choice of engine but was overruled by the Curtiss board. The first flight of the Liberty engine-powered F.2B was disastrous, as Barnwell had predicted, and the aircraft crashed soon after take-off. The US Army blamed the design of the aircraft, not the engine. The fact that the weight of the engine was a contributory factor to the crash, and that the Bristol Fighter F.2B had been fighting in almost every theatre of the war in Europe without any similar problems, seems to have eluded the American military hierarchy. Nevertheless, the proposed 2,000 aircraft to be built was drastically reduced to just twenty-seven, and the remainder were cancelled.

The success of the Bristol Scouts A, B, C and D prompted the company to consider improving the model. At the end of 1916, the Bristol Fighter had not been delivered to the RFC squadrons and the air force were desperate for new single-seat fighters that were better than Germany's latest Fokker fighters. It was with this in mind, and after hearing of a new 200-hp ten-cylinder, two-row water-cooled radial engine named the 'Cruciform' being developed, that Captain Barnwell decided to build an aircraft around it. Designed by W. T. Reid, the new model, the Bristol Scout E, was an equal two-bay biplane with a conventional fuselage and a standard V-type undercarriage connected to a rubber-sprung axle. The 'Cruciform' engine was to be installed with an annular radiator positioned forward, which was covered by a spinning annular which surrounded a central cone. With the Bristol Scout E prototype ready, it soon became obvious that the 'Cruciform' engine was nowhere near ready, and there were some doubts if it ever would be.

Urgent modifications had to be made to the aircraft's design so as to accommodate a 200-hp Hispano-Suiza engine instead, so the wing arrangement was changed to one of unequal span with the ailerons on the top wing only. The single Lewis gun, which had been mounted on the upper wing, was removed and two synchronised Vickers machine guns were mounted on top of the fuselage, ahead of the pilot. There were also a number of minor modifications made, and because of these alterations to the aircraft it was re-designated the Bristol Scout F. Then another blow came when it was discovered that because of the demand for the Hispano-Suiza engine, the Bristol Scout F was to be powered with the unreliable 200-hp Sunbeam Arab engine.

The aircraft performed well throughout all its trials, but because of the engine and its unreliability it was not accepted. Then a lifeline was thrown to the aircraft in the shape of a new engine, a 315-hp Cosmos Mercury radial. The company had a contract to build 200 of these engines and was looking for a suitable aircraft in which to install it, and the Bristol Scout F fitted the bill perfectly. The aircraft, with its new engine, was put through its paces by the company's new test pilot, Cyril F. Unwins, very successfully, and was delivered to Farnborough for further trials. The Armistice intervened, and the contract for the building of the Cosmos Mercury engine was cancelled, which in effect put paid to any further development of the Bristol F.1.

There were some later experimental designs regarding bombers, and although they were built for use during wartime they did manage to serve a purpose after the war in helping develop civilian passenger-carrying aircraft.

SPECIFICATIONS

Bristol Boxkite

Wing Span Standard:	34 ft 6 in (10.5 m)
Wing Span Military:	47 ft 8 in (14.5 m)
Length:	38 ft 6 in (11.7 m)
Height:	11 ft 10 in (3.5 m)
Weight Empty Standard:	800 lb (362 kg)
Weight Empty Military:	900 lb (408 kg)
Weight Loaded Standard:	1,050 lb (476 kg)
Weight Loaded Military:	1,150 lb (521 kg)
Max. Speed Standard:	40 mph (64 km/h)
Max. Speed Military:	40 mph (64 km/h)
Engines:	One 50-hp Gnome
	One 50-hp Grégoire
	One 50/60-hp E.N.V.
	One 60-hp Renault
	One 70-hp Gnome
Armament:	None

Bristol Coanda Monoplane

Wing Span Standard:	41 ft 3 in (12.5 m)
Wing Span Military:	42 ft 9 in (13.0 m)

Length Standard:	27 ft 0 in (8.2 m)
Length Military:	29 ft 2 in (8.8 m)
Height:	7 ft 0 in (2.1 m)
Weight Empty Standard:	770 lb (349 kg)
Weight Empty Military:	1,050 lb (476 kg)
Weight Loaded Standard:	1,100 lb (498 kg)
Weight Loaded Military:	1,775 lb (805 kg)
Max. Speed Standard:	65 mph (104 km/h)
Max. Speed Military:	71 mph (114 km/h)
Engines:	One 50-hp Gnome
	One 80-hp Gnome
Armament:	None

Bristol Scout A – D

Wing Span A/B/C/D:	24 ft 7 in (7.4 m)
Length A:	19 ft 9 in (6.0 m)
Length B/C/D:	20 ft 8 in (6.3 m)
Height A/B/C/D:	8 ft 6 in (2.5 m)
Weight Empty A/B/C/D:	750 lb (340 kg)
Weight Loaded A/B:	1,100 lb (498 kg)
Weight Loaded C/D:	1,440 lb (653 kg)
Max. Speed Standard:	100 mph (104 km/h)
Engine A/B/C/D:	One 80-hp Gnome
	One 80-hp Le Rhône
	One 80-hp Clerget
Engine D:	One 100-hp Mono-Gnome
	110-hp Clerget
	110-hp Le Rhône
Armament:	None (Officially)

Bristol Scout F

Wing Span:	29 ft 7 in (9.0 m)
Length:	20 ft 10 in (6.3 m) Arab engine
	20 ft 0 in (6.0 m) Cosmos Mercury engine
Height:	8 ft. 4 in (2.5 m)
Weight Empty:	1,440 lb (653 kg)
Weight Loaded:	2,200 lb (997 kg) Arab engine
	2,260 lb (1,025 kg) Cosmos Mercury engine
Max. Speed:	138 mph (222 km/h) Arab engine
	145 mph (233 km/h) Cosmos Mercury engine
Engines:	One 200-hp Sunbeam Arab
	One 315-hp Cosmos Mercury Radial
Armament:	None fitted
	Two synchronised Vickers machine guns mounted side-by-side on top of the engine

Bristol T.T.A.

Wing Span:	53 ft 6 in (16.3 m)
Length:	39 ft 2 in (11.9 m)
Height:	12 ft 6 in (3.8 m)
Weight Empty:	3,820 lb (1,732 kg)

Weight Loaded: 5,100 lb (2,313 kg)
Max. Speed: 87 mph (139 km/h)
Engines: Two 120-hp Beardmore
Armament: Two Lewis machine guns mounted on telescopic
                          pillars in the observer's nose cockpit, one forward
                          and one rearward firing.

Bristol M.R.1

Wing Span: 42 ft 2 in (12.8 m)
Length: 27 ft 0 in (8.2 m)
Height: 10 ft 3 in (3.1 m)
Weight Empty: 1,700 lb (771 kg)
Weight Loaded: 2,810 lb (1,274 kg)
Max. Speed: 110 mph (176 km/h)
Engines: One 140-hp Hispano-Suiza
                          One 180-hp Wolseley Viper
Armament: None fitted

Bristol M.1A/B/C

Wing Span: 30 ft 9 in (9.4 m)
Length: 20 ft 4 in (6.3 m)
Height: 7 ft 10 in (2.3 m)
Weight Empty: 900 lb (408 kg)
Weight Loaded: 1,350 lb (612 kg)
Max. Speed: 132 mph (212 km/h) M.1A
                          125 mph (201 km/h) M.1B
                          130 mph (209 km/h) M.1C
Engines: One 110-hp Clerget – M.1A/B
                          One 110-hp Le Rhône – M.1C
                          One 130-hp Clerget – M.1B
                          One 150-hp Bentley A.R.1 – M.1B
Armament: One Vickers machine gun

Bristol F.2A/2B

Wing Span: 39 ft 3 in (11.9 m)
Length: 25 ft 10 in (7.9 m)
Height: 9 ft 6 in (2.8 m)
Weight Empty: 1,700 lb (771 kg)
Weight Loaded: 2,700 lb (1,224 kg)
Max. Speed: 110 mph (176 km/h)
Engines F2A: One 190-hp Rolls-Royce Falcon I
                          One 150-hp Hispano-Suiza
Engines F2B: One 190-hp Rolls-Royce Falcon I
                          One 220-hp Rolls-Royce Falcon II
                          One 275-hp Rolls-Royce Falcon III
                          One 200-hp Hispano-Suiza
                          One 200-hp Sunbeam Arab
                          One 200-hp R.A.F.4d
                          One 180-hp Wolseley Viper
                          One 230-hp Siddeley Puma
                          One 300-hp Hispano-Suiza

Armament (F2A):	One synchronised Lewis machine gun mounted on the starboard upper longeron
	One Lewis machine gun mounted on a rotating ring in cockpit behind the pilot
Armament (F2B):	Two Lewis machine guns mounted in the nose cockpit
	One Lewis gun in the observer's cockpit firing aft

Caudron Aircraft Company

Inspired by the exploits of the Wright Brothers after seeing them demonstrate their aircraft in France, René and Gaston Caudron decided to enter the world of aviation. Their first aircraft was the Caudron Type A, an ambitious project, which initially was to have been powered by two engines but ended up as a glider because of the unavailability of the engines. Over the next five years the brothers developed their skills, producing better and better aircraft.

The first of their aircraft to come to the attention of the military was a twin-seat, twin-float tractor biplane of unequal wingspan powered by a 100-hp Gnome engine, presented at the Expositions Internationales de Aéronautiques in 1913. The twin floats of the J Type, as it was called, also contained a pair of wheels that enabled it to be manoeuvred more easily when brought ashore. It had been intended to use the aircraft as a trainer, but it drew interest from China, Russia and the United Kingdom as a reconnaissance aircraft, and each country purchased a small number.

Then, in 1914, the Caudron Company produced their first combat military aircraft, the Caudron G.2, a total of ten of which were built. Four were purchased by the Australian Flying Corps (AFC) and one by the RNAS; the remaining five were assigned to Escadrille CM (Caudron Monoplace) 39.

The Caudron G.2 had flexible wings of unequal span, which the pilot warped to get lateral control. The wings of the Caudron had scalloped trailing edges that were to become a trademark of the aircraft. The two-seat cockpit nacelle was situated between the wings, and had four booms made of wood, two ash (upper) and two fir (lower), to which twin rudders were connected. The undercarriage consisted of two pairs of wheels attached to the lower part of the nacelle fuselage.

In 1915, further development of the G.2 resulted in the G.3, which attracted the attention of the RFC. In March 1915, the RFC obtained one of the Caudron G.3s and subjected it to a series of flight tests before accepting it. The aircraft was assigned to No. 1 Squadron on 27 March 1915, followed by two more the following month.

The Caudron G.3 was a two-bay, unequal span, tractor biplane. The wings were supported at the tips by oblique angle struts, and were made of ash and spruce. The short fuselage section had the pilot sitting behind the observer, with a 100-litre fuel tank and 5-litre oil tank situated between them. The tail section was fixed to four ash and fir booms, and consisted of twin triangular fins and rudders. The landing gear consisted of two pairs of wheels connected to the forward section of the lower fuselage booms, with rubber bungees acting as shock absorbers. The engine was mounted in front of the observer, and was covered with an aluminium cowling that prevented the two occupants from being sprayed with hot oil and smoke from the exhaust.

With orders coming in from the RFC and the RNAS, the Caudron brothers opened another company called British Caudron. A total of 250 Caudron G.3s were built for the RFC and the RNAS, the majority of them only seeing service as trainers.

The two Caudron brothers reverted back to their original idea of a twin-engined aircraft when they designed the Caudron G.4. Basically, the aircraft was an enlarged twin-engined version of the Caudron G.3 and it appeared in March 1915. It was powered by either two 80-hp Le Rhône engines or two rotary 100-hp Anzani engines, which gave the aircraft an increased range and the ability to carry a heavy machine gun in the nose. Like the G.3, the tail section, consisting of four rudders and twin elevators, was fixed at the convergence point by four booms. The double-wheeled undercarriage was fixed to the two lower booms underneath the engines.

The first of the Caudron G.4s to be obtained by the RFC arrived at No. 1 Aircraft Depot in Saint-Omer on 14 January 1916, but after tests it was not accepted. The RNAS, on the other hand, already had twelve in service with No. 1 Wing, RNAS in France and at the end of 1915 had placed an additional order for twelve more. The ones supplied to the RNAS had been built by the British Caudron Company under an Admiralty contract, and were used by No. 4 and No. 5 Wings for long-range bombing operations on German airfields. A number of missions were carried out, and the majority were very successful. One in particular, on 2 August 1916, was on the St Denis Westerem airfield, and the raid helped divert German aircraft away from the Somme front. Attacks on the airship sheds at Brussels, the docks at Ostend and the ammunition dump at Lichtervelde proved the aircraft to be a great asset to the Allies.

By the end of 1916, however, the role of the Caudron G.4 had been superseded by the arrival of the Sopwith 1½-Strutter and the Short Bomber. Also by this time, the RNAS had taken delivery of the Handley Page O/100 and the D.H.4, so the G.4's role was reduced to that of a trainer.

This did not deter the Caudron Brothers, and they re-designed the G.4, coming up with the G.5. This was in response to the Avation Militaire's request for a three-seat light bomber and reconnaissance aircraft. The fuselage of the G.5 became more conventional than the previous models. Two 80-hp Le Rhône engines, mounted mid-wing, were supposed to give the aircraft sufficient power, but after tests it was found to be seriously underpowered. Only a small number were built, and were quickly superseded by the superior G.6 that arrived shortly afterwards.

The G.6 proved to be the most reliable of all the aircraft produced by Caudron. The aircraft was powered by two 130-hp Le Rhône engines, which were mounted in nacelles suspended between the equal-span wings. The prototype was fitted with a very short nose that protruded just in front of the engines, but because this restricted the field of fire to a certain degree, a longer nose was fitted. The spars for the upper and lower wings were made from spruce and ash with plywood ribs. The fuselage was constructed from four spruce longerons held together with piano wire and covered with fabric. The tail section consisted of a single horizontal stabiliser and a rudder, to which was attached a fixed forward fin. The undercarriage was made up of an oval cross section with two 'N' struts, to which two pairs of wheels were attached.

The first flight took place in June 1916, and almost immediately the Aviation Militaire placed orders for the aircraft. By the end of the year, fifty Caudron G.6s had been built and delivered to front-line Escadrilles. In total, 512 of the aircraft were produced and delivered to Aviation Militaire by August 1917.

With the relative success of the G.6, the Caudron Company was approached by Aviation Militaire to design a reconnaissance bomber based on the A3 requirements. The result was a three-bay, unequal span biplane powered by two 130-hp Renault 12Db engines. The R.4, as it was called, carried a crew of three with a gunner in the nose and a second gunner/observer situated behind the pilot. The engines were mounted between the wings, under which a paired wheel undercarriage was fitted. A single nose wheel was fitted to the nose of the aircraft, and had been installed purely to prevent the aircraft from ground looping when landing on rough terrain. The prototype was passed to the Aviation Militaire for testing as a long-range bomber and reconnaissance aircraft. The initial tests showed the aircraft to be underpowered, which affected the handling qualities of the aircraft.

Modifications were carried out, and the next test flight was carried out by Gaston Caudron himself; it was nearly his last, as the aircraft crashed on landing. At first it was thought that the engines had failed but subsequent examination revealed that the wing spars, close to the centre portion of the wing, had failed. Further modifications were carried out, and the next test flight was carried out by Gaston's brother, René. The tests were satisfactory, so the aircraft went into full production and a total of 249 R.4s were built.

Two were purchased by the Royal Flying Corps for use as long-range bombers, but ended up being used as test beds for armament and wireless communications systems. The United States Army Air Service also purchased two in October 1918, and they were assigned as escorts for bombers of the 88th and 96th Aero Squadrons.

A number of other variations and models were built, but none ever saw active service.

SPECIFICATIONS

Caudron G.3

Wing Span:	43 ft 4 in (13.2 m)
Length:	22 ft 7 in (6.9 m)
Height:	8 ft 6 in (2.6 m)
Weight Empty:	959 lb (435 kg)
Weight Loaded:	1,565 lb (710 kg)
Max. Speed:	65 mph (105 km/h)
Engines:	One 80-hp Le Rhône
	One 70-hp Renault
	One 100-hp Anzani
Armament:	Rifles or pistols

Caudron G.4

Wing Span:	55 ft 24 in (16.8 m)
Length:	23 ft 7 in (7.2 m)
Height:	8 ft 6 in (2.6 m)
Weight Empty:	1,863 lb (845 kg)
Weight Loaded:	2,976 lb (1,350 kg)
Max. Speed:	80 mph (130 km/h)
Engines:	One 80-hp Le Rhône
Armament:	One nose-mounted Lewis machine gun

Curtiss Aeroplane & Motor Corporation

Glenn Hammond Curtiss was born in the small wine-producing area of Hammondsport, New York, on 21 May 1878. Even at an early age, speed and the technology associated with it fascinated him. After leaving school, he worked as a telegraph messenger and studied electricity before finding serious employment with the Eastman Kodak Company. In 1901, he went into business for himself building bicycles, which progressed to motorcycles, then motorcars and, inevitably, aviation.

In 1907, Curtiss was invited to join Alexander Graham Bell's newly created organization, the Aerial Experiment Association (AEA). Together with other members of the AEA, they created a series of aircraft, starting with the AEA Aerodrome (name given for the aeroplane at the time) No. 1, *Red Wing*. The following year, the group built and flew four different types of AEA aircraft, all flown by Glenn Curtiss himself. For a number of reasons the group decided to split and go their own separate ways in March 1909. Curtiss himself was now heavily committed to the designing and building of aircraft, and started his own company. Over the next five years the Curtiss Company produced a number of aircraft, predominantly flying boats.

The RNAS had already purchased some of the aircraft built by Curtiss; this was the Curtiss JN-3. This was the forerunner of the Curtiss JN-4A, also known as the Curtiss Jenny. The JN-3 was a two-seat, two-bay, unequal span, single-engine tractor biplane. Six were initially purchased at the end of 1914 and allocated to No. 1 Squadron RNAS. This was followed in May 1915 by seventy-nine from Curtiss in the United States and a further twelve from the Curtiss factory in Toronto, Canada. One hundred were transferred to the RFC, and the first of these was sent to Farnborough, where Lt-Col. D. B. Fulton, Chief Inspector of the Aircraft Inspection Department (AID), examined it. He was not impressed, and in a letter to the Secretary of the War Office he said:

> I think it necessary to place on record that constructionally this machine leaves a great deal to be desired. The workmanship and material throughout are of a cheap and typically American kind. It is impossible to effect any improvement in the machine without practically scrapping all the existing fittings and making new ones. The use of these machines is only justified by war necessity.

These comments were supported by Captain E. N. Fuller, commanding officer of No. 17 Squadron, when he wrote to the OC Fifth Wing, RFC saying,

> I have carefully examined the construction of the Curtiss No.5404 (JN-3) and I recommend that an effort be made to prevent any more of these machines from being allotted to the Fifth Wing.

The aircraft was powered by a 90-hp Curtiss OX-5 engine, which was ideal for training purposes, but not powerful enough for active service. In 1915, four Canadian-built Curtiss JN-3s (which were known as Cannucks) were sent to Egypt and assigned to No. 22 Reserve Squadron at Abu Qir. These had been heavily modified with an additional diagonal strut on either side and a modified centre-section bracing. The four aircraft were used for reconnaissance and patrol missions, and were operational throughout the war.

The arrival of the Curtiss JN-4 (Jenny) brought a new type of trainer to both the RFC and the RNAS. It was to turn out to be more widely used for training purposes than any aircraft built during the First World War. Very similar in appearance to the JN-3, the JN-4 differed inasmuch as it had completely revised tail surfaces, an enlarged rudder, an enlarged tailplane with straight leading edges and a simplified tailskid. The same 90-hp Curtiss OX-5 engine powered the aircraft, but the exhaust pipes were of the stack type that thrust upwards in front of the wings. The Admiralty ordered 250 aircraft, 100 of which were almost immediately transferred to the RFC and the AFC to help boost their training programme. Seventy of the aircraft were never delivered because of cancellations by the Admiralty, as better and faster aircraft became available.

The arrival of the Curtiss H.4 in January 1912 heralded the start of what was to be a long association between Britain and America with regard to aircraft. When the First World War started, the White & Thompson Company of Bognor, Sussex, had acquired a licence, and was already producing Curtiss aircraft in England. Among the staff of Curtiss in America was an Englishman by the name of John Porte, who was one of their chief designers. He had served in the Royal Navy for some years, and at the onset of war returned to England and rejoined the RNAS as a Squadron Commander. He persuaded the Admiralty to purchase two Curtiss flying boats, given the designation of Curtiss H.4.

The Curtiss H.4 had a boat-shaped wooden hull covered in fabric, two-bay, unequal span wings, carried a crew of four and was powered by two 150-hp Sunbeam, or 100-hp Anzani engines. Twelve of the aircraft were ordered by the RNAS initially, followed by a further thirty-eight two months later. A variety of engines were tried in the aircraft when it was discovered that the two 90-hp Curtiss engines supplied with the aircraft had insufficient power. Called 'Small America' by the RNAS, the Curtiss H.4 was used for training and patrol work, but suffered from poor seaworthiness.

John Porte worked tirelessly to improve the design of the Curtiss flying boats, and the arrival of probably the most famous of them all, the Curtiss H.12, highlighted his input into the design of the hull. It was, in reality, an enlarged version of the H.4, but with a number of modifications that improved the design and construction. Again, the Curtiss engines supplied with the aircraft were found to be seriously underpowered and it wasn't until two 275-hp Rolls-Royce Eagle I engines were fitted that the true potential of the aircraft came to the fore. The H.12 was employed on anti-submarine reconnaissance patrols, and as an anti-Zeppelin fighter.

Despite its size, the H.12 proved to be a worthy fighter against the Zeppelin menace and claimed its first Zeppelin on 14 May 1917. Flown by Flt Sub-Lt Robert Leckie and F/Lt John Galpin, a Curtiss H.12, No. 8666, left Great Yarmouth on that date and intercepted the Zeppelin L.22 commanded by Kapitänleutnant Ulrich Lehmann and shot it down.

There were successes against the U-boats, too. On 20 May 1917, the UC-36, commanded by Oberleutnant Buch, was bombed while on the surface just off the Needles, Isle of Wight. A second U-boat, the UB-20 commanded by Oberleutnant Glimpf, was bombed on 28 July off Zeebrugge by two H.12s, adding to the aircraft's reputation as a submarine 'killer'. On 20 August, another H.12, together with a Q-ship, took part in an attack on the German submarine UC-72, commanded by Kapitänleutnant Voigt, and sank it with all hands.

Towards the end of the war, the Curtiss Company produced and enlarged a version of the Curtiss H.12, the H.16. Also known as the 'Large America', the flying-boat had a hull designed by John Porte and was significantly stronger and more seaworthy that any of the previous Curtiss flying boats. This brought the aircraft on a par with the British Felixstowe flying boats, giving Britain the strongest flying-boat squadrons in the world. The aircraft were fitted with twin 250-hp Rolls-Royce Eagle VIII engines, and an initial order for fifteen of the aircraft was quickly followed by a further order for 110. Meanwhile, the US Navy had set up bases in England and southern Ireland and was also operating the Curtiss H.16, but twin 330-hp Liberty engines powered these.

The H.16 carried out numerous patrols, and played a significant part in keeping the U-boats at bay in the Western Approaches. The end of the war caused the Admiralty to cancel fifty of the 110 H.16s ordered. The Curtiss Aircraft Company had provided some of the finest flying boats of the war, and had made a significant effect on the protection of convoys against the U-boat threat.

SPECIFICATIONS

Curtiss JN-3

Wing Span:	43 ft 10 in (13.3 m)
Length:	27 ft 3 in (8.2 m)
Height:	9 ft 11 in (3.0 m)
Weight Empty:	1,300 lb (589 kg)
Weight Loaded:	1,918 lb (870 kg)
Max. Speed:	70 mph (112 km/h)
Engines:	One 90-hp Curtiss OX-5
Armament:	None

Curtiss H.4

Wing Span:	72 ft 0 in (21.9 m)
Length:	36 ft 0 in (10.9 m)
Height:	16 ft 0 in (4.8 m)
Weight Empty:	2,992 lb (1,357 kg)
Weight Loaded:	4,983 lb (2,260 kg)
Max. Speed:	80 mph (130 km/h)
Engines:	Two 90-hp Curtiss OX-5s
	Two 100-hp Anzanis
	Two 110-hp Clergets
	Two 150-hp Sunbeams
Armament:	One nose-mounted Lewis machine gun
	100-lb bombs beneath lower wing

Curtiss H.12

Wing Span:	92 ft 8½ in (28.2 m)
Length:	46 ft 6 in (14.1 m)
Height:	16 ft 6 in (5.0 m)
Weight Empty:	7,293 lb (3,308 kg)
Weight Loaded:	10,650 lb (4,830 kg)
Max. Speed:	85 mph (139 km/h)

Engines: Two 275-hp Rolls-Royce Eagle I
                            Two 345-hp Rolls-Royce Eagle VII
                            Two 375-hp Rolls-Royce Eagle VIII
Armament: Four Lewis machine guns
                            Four 100-lb bombs beneath lower wing

Curtiss H.16

Wing Span: 95 ft 0 in (29.0 m)
Length: 46 ft 6 in (14.1 m)
Height: 17 ft 8 in (5.4 m)
Weight Empty: 7,363 lb (3,339 kg)
Weight Loaded: 10,670 lb (4,839 kg)
Max. Speed: 85 mph (139 km/h)
Engines: Two 320-hp Rolls-Royce Eagle VIII
                            Two 345-hp Rolls-Royce Eagle VIII
Armament: Four Lewis machine guns
                            Four 100-lb bombs beneath lower wing

Louis Blériot and Alexandre Anzani.

A Blériot XI-2 powered by a 70-hp Gnome engine.

A Blériot Monoplane.

Blériot parasol flown by Capitane de Marancourt.

A Breguet BM.4 known as *Queen Mary*.

A Breguet 5 in the workshop.

The second prototype of the Breguet Av.2, also known as the Breguet 14.

Breguet 14 production model.

A Breguet 14B about to land.

Breguet 17 long-range escort fighter.

Breguet 18 Bn2.

Bristol Coanda BR.7.

Bristol Baby Tractor Biplane, or Scout A.

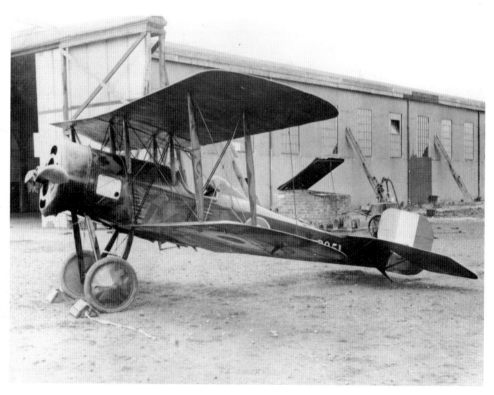

Bristol Scout D (8951) with added head-rest and no wing-tip skids.

A Bristol Scout D of the RNAS carrying our aerobatics.

Bristol Twin-Tractor (TTA) biplane.

Bristol M.1C aircraft of No. 72 Squadron RFC starting their engines prior to going on a mission.

Bristol F2b Fighter A3304 at Filton.

Bristol F2b Fighter A7231 in German markings after being forced down.

Cockpit of a Bristol F2b.

Capt. Ross Smith and Lt Mustard of No. 1 Squadron AFC in their Bristol F2b Fighter in Palestine.

Bristol F2bs of No. 139 Squadron in Italy.

A captured Bristol F2b in German markings. The words on the wings read '*Nicht Schiessen! Gute Leute*', or 'Do not shoot! Good people'.

Caudron G.5, seen outside the factory.

Caudron G.6 of Escadrille C.30.

Caudron G.6 of Escadrille C.56.

Caudron R.4 bomber.

Curtiss J.3 of the RNAS.

Curtiss H-16, powered by twin Liberty engines.

Fairey Hamble Baby.

Fairey IIIC in Russia with the North Russian Expeditionary Force.

Fairey Aviation Company

The creation of the Fairey Aviation Company began in 1915, when Charles Richard Fairey, who was the chief engineer with the Short Brothers Company, started his own aircraft manufacturing company. It is said that Richard Fairey, at the beginning of the First World War, applied to join the Royal Naval Air Service (RNAS) but was rejected. Then, after receiving his call-up papers in error, he applied to join the Royal Flying Corps (RFC) but Commodore Murray F. Sueter (later Rear Admiral), Director of the Air Department of the Admiralty, intercepted his application. Commodore Sueter pointed out in no uncertain manner that Richard Fairey could give no greater contribution to the war effort than to design and build bigger and better aeroplanes. Fairey is said to have responded by saying that if he had a contract and a company with which to build the aircraft, he would be more than willing to do so.

Commodore Sueter, realising that there was a desperate need for more aircraft, arranged for Fairey to be given a contract to build twelve Short 827 seaplanes as a sub-contractor. Three wealthy friends of Fairey, realising that this was possibly a good investment, backed him to the sum of around £50,000. With the financial backing in place, Fairey set about finding a suitable place where he could build the aircraft and test them. The place decided upon was a half-share in a factory in Hayes, Middlesex, used by the Army Motor Lorries Co. There were also a number of skilled workers available, mostly refugees from Belgium. In a nearby field, which was close to a railway line belonging to the Great Western Railway (GWR), Fairey constructed a hangar that could be used for the final assembly of the aircraft before they were transported by rail to Hamble Spit, near Southampton. The Admiralty offered the site, which was at the mouth of the Hamble River on Southampton Water, to Fairey who built a wooden slipway and repair shops close by.

By the middle of 1916 the last of the twelve Short 827 floatplanes had been built, tested by test pilot Sydney Pickles and delivered. In the meantime, negotiations had taken place with the Admiralty and another contract was obtained, this time for 100 Sopwith 1½-Strutters for the RNAS. All the time production was going on for other companies, Richard Fairey had been working on a design of his own, a twin-engine, three-seat, long-range fighter – the Fairey F.2. This was to be the first aircraft to be designed and built by the Fairey Aviation Company.

Looking more like a bomber than a fighter, the Fairey F.2 was more of a general-purpose aircraft. There were a number of variations of this aircraft on the drawing boards, but only one was ever built, and that was powered by two 190-hp Rolls-Royce Falcon 12-cylinder, liquid-cooled tractor engines. The opposite-rotating propellers almost eliminated the torque from the engines and greatly reduced the swing of the aircraft on landing and take-off. The F.2 was a three-bay biplane with the upper wing extensions braced to the interplane struts on the lower wing. The wings folded back from a point just outboard of the engine nacelle. The undercarriage consisted of four wheels fitted to a 'bedstead' arrangement (one in each corner), which reduced the chances of ground looping on touchdown.

The pilot's cockpit was situated just in front of the wings, together with a gunner's cockpit in the nose fitted with a Lewis machine gun mounted on a Scarff ring. The observer's cockpit, situated aft of the wings and almost mid-fuselage, was also fitted with a Lewis machine gun mounted on a Scarff ring.

The Fairey F.2 was developed no further than the one prototype and a number of designs for variations.

The first aircraft to be designed and built exclusively by Fairey in any quantity was the two-seat patrol seaplane, the Fairey Campania. It was the result of an Admiralty demand for an aircraft that would match their specifications. Because the intended use for the aircraft was in the North Sea area and seaplanes at the time were invariably flimsy, it was decided that the seaplane could be launched from the deck of an aircraft carrier. The ship chosen for the trials was HMS *Campania*, which was a converted Cunard liner, built in 1893 for service on the North Atlantic. The early use of aircraft carriers was fraught with danger during the First World War, as they had to stop to pick up their aircraft by hoisting them aboard using cranes. This, of course, left them vulnerable to attack by submarines, and after the initial trials it was decided to catapult-launch the aircraft from the decks of battleships and cruisers as well.

Launching a seaplane from the deck of an aircraft carrier in the early years was carried out using a wheeled trolley which was attached to the aircraft's floats and dropped as the seaplane lifted off the deck. The Fairey Campania was designed as a two-bay biplane of unequal span, made of wood and covered in fabric. Two small pontoons were fitted to the underside of the lower wing. Ailerons were fitted to the upper wings only, and the wings folded back against the conventional box-shaped fuselage. The undercarriage consisted of two pontoon-shaped main floats, which were attached to the fuselage by crossbars. The tail section consisted of a large tail rudder that was connected to a water rudder beneath the fuselage.

Known by their construction numbers, serial numbers N1001 (F.17) to N1009 (F.22), the only difference between these models was the variety of engines that were fitted. However, there were considerable differences between N1000 (F.16), the prototype, and N1001 (F.17), the production model. The prototype (F.16) had slab radiators fitted either side of the 250-hp Rolls-Royce Mk.IV engine, while the exhaust pipes extended upwards through the centre section in front of the main spar of the wings. The production model, which was to be officially known as the Campania (F.17), was powered by a 275-hp Rolls-Royce Eagle V engine, which was mounted slightly more forward so the exhaust pipes extended upwards ahead of the wing. The wing-folding procedure was simplified by reducing the centre-section chord, the wingtip float struts were shortened and the tail section had a longer fin.

The third model was the F.22, which was very similar in appearance to the F.17, the main difference being that it had a 260-hp Sunbeam Maori II engine with a frontal radiator and a single upward-extending exhaust pipe. The Maori and Rolls-Royce Eagle engines were fitted to the majority of Campanias that were built. Later models that were assigned to tropical areas were fitted with larger frontal radiators with adjustable shutters below the propeller shaft. Of the sixty-two Campanias built, fifty were built by Fairey Aviation and the remaining twelve by Barclay, Curle & Co. on Clydeside, Scotland.

Although small in numbers, the Campania seaplane contributed in no small way to the various expeditionary forces it supported throughout almost every theatre of the war.

One of the most revolutionary of all aircraft built by Fairey Aviation in the early years was the Hamble Baby. The aircraft itself was a redesigned version of the Sopwith Baby, but with a number of new innovations. The main one was the introduction of trailing edge flaps that could be adjusted to increase lift when taking off or landing. Known as the 'Fairey Patent Camber-changing gear', it was to be used on a succession of aircraft right up to the Fairey Swordfish that was flown in the Second World War. The advantage of this innovation for seaplanes was the increased lift it generated at low speeds, enabling the aircraft to get on the top of the water more easily, thus creating less drag.

The wings of the Hamble Baby were 2 ft longer than those of the Sopwith Baby, and had rounded wingtips instead of the blunt planform of the original aircraft. The tail section was redesigned, giving the Hamble Baby a square-cut fin and rudder. The floats were given their box-shape and a larger tail-float fitted. The trials were very successful, and production began in 1916 at both the Hayes & Hamble plants and at Parnall & Sons at Bristol. In fact, out of a total of 180 aircraft built, Parnall & Sons built 130.

Because of the initial success of the seaplane, it was decided to make a landplane version known as the Hamble Baby Convert. The conversion consisted of replacing the floats with skids, to which wheels were attached. The end result was a wider than average undercarriage. There was a distinction between the Parnall-built seaplane models and the ones built by Fairey, and that was that Parnall retained the Sopwith floats, tail-fins and rudder.

During the First World War, the Hamble Baby carried out raids and reconnaissance missions similar to those carried out by the Sopwith Baby. The Hamble Baby Convert was used mainly for training and coastal reconnaissance flights.

The success of the seaplanes prompted Fairey to build larger versions, and in the spring of 1917 the first of these was designed and built – the N.9. The design of the aircraft was based on an Admiralty specification, and was a single-bay biplane with an unusually long top wing, which later gave rise to the description 'sesquiplane'. The N.9 was powered by a 200-hp Rolls-Royce Falcon I, V-12, liquid-cooled engine. The revolutionary Camber-changing gear, first used on the Hamble Baby, resulted in flaps being installed along the whole length of the lower wing, and between the centre-sections and ailerons on the upper wing. The fuselage was of the standard box configuration, and the tail section was of the standard Fairey design. Armament consisted of a single Lewis gun mounted on a Scarff ring in the observer/gunner's cockpit situated in the rear.

Initially the N.9 had been designed to operate from seaplane-carriers, but because of the success the Americans had had launching scout seaplanes from warships, it was decided to carry out experiments launching the N.9 by means of a catapult from a warship. The ship selected for the tests was a former dredging support ship with the appropriate name of HMS *Slinger*. The tests were carried out under the control of Lieutenant-Colonel H. R. Busteed, who in fact carried out most of the flight tests himself.

The tests were a complete success, but the war came to an end before the aircraft could be put into production and only the one model was ever built. It was eventually returned to Fairey in 1919, where it was re-engined with a 250-hp Sunbeam Maori II and the lower wings extended so that they were of equal length.

While the tests with the N.9 were going on, a second experimental model, the N.10, was being built. This was a two-bay, equal span biplane with folding wings, an enlarged tail fin and a fuselage that was identical to that of the N.9. Like the N.9, the N.10 was fitted with Camber-changing gear, giving full flaps on the lower wing only, while the upper wing was fitted only with ailerons. Powered by a 260-hp Sunbeam Maori II engine with slab-sided radiators, the N.10 carried out all its initial tests successfully and was later converted to a landplane, the Fairey IIIA, but like the N.9, the war ended before it could be put to any military use.

Fifty of the landplane versions (Fairey IIIA) were built for the RNAS; fitted with either wheels or skids, they were destined for use as a carrier-borne aircraft. They were declared obsolete by the time the war ended, and none saw any active service. The Fairey IIIB, however, was a seaplane designed specifically as a bomber. Twenty-five of these aircraft were built and assigned to coastal stations, but none saw any action before the Armistice.

The Fairey IIIC, a development of the IIIA and IIIB, did see some active service, even though it was delivered to the RNAS at the Great Yarmouth Air Station just weeks before the Armistice. A total of thirty-five of the aircraft were built and distributed to various Naval Air Stations. Seven Fairey IIICs were placed aboard HMS *Pegasus* and took part in the North Russian Expeditionary Force of 1919, based at the Russian port of Archangel. During this time they carried out bombing raids on Bolshevik ships and attacked rail communications.

Although a number of other seaplanes were on the drawing boards and some under were construction, none were ever used under wartime condition, but the information learned from the development of these aircraft was to stand Fairey in good stead for the future.

SPECIFICATIONS

Fairey F.2

Wing Span:	77 ft 0 in (23.5 m)
Length:	40 ft 6 in (12.3 m)
Height:	13 ft 6 in (4.1 m)
Weight Empty:	2,810 lb (1,274 kg)
Weight Loaded:	4,880 lb (2,213 kg)
Max. Speed:	93 mph (150 km/h)
Engines:	One 190-hp Rolls-Royce Falcon
Armament:	One Lewis machine gun in nose cockpit
	One Lewis machine gun in observer's cockpit

Fairey F.16 (Prototype)

Wing Span:	61 ft 7 in (18.77 m)
Length:	43 ft 4 in (13.21 m)
Height:	15 ft 1 in (4.59 m)
Weight Empty:	3,725 lb (1,690 kg)
Weight Loaded:	5,252 lb (2,382 kg)
Max. Speed:	80 mph (129 km/h)
Engine:	One 250-hp Rolls-Royce Mk IV (Eagle IV)
Armament:	None fitted on prototype

Fairey F.17 (Production model) and F.22

Wing Span:	61 ft 7 in (18.77 m)
Length:	43 ft 1 in (13.11 m)
Height:	15 ft 1 in (4.59 m)
Weight Empty:	3,713 lb (1,684 kg)
Weight Loaded:	5,530 lb (2,508 kg)
Max. Speed:	89 mph (143 km/h)
Engine:	One 275-hp Rolls-Royce Mk IV (Eagle V)
	One 260-hp Sunbeam Maori II (F.22)
Armament:	One Lewis machine gun in observer's cockpit mounted on a Scarff ring
	Bombs carried in racks beneath the fuselage

Fairey Hamble Baby

Wing Span:	27 ft 9 in (6.4 m)
Length:	23 ft 4 in (7.10 m)
Height:	9 ft 6 in (2.89 m)

Weight Empty:	1,386 lb (629 kg)
Weight Loaded:	1,946 lb (883 kg)
Max. Speed:	90 mph (145 km/h)
Engine:	One 110-hp Clerget Rotary
	One 130-hp Clerget Rotary
Armament:	Two 65-lb bombs

Fairey N.9

Wing Span:	50 ft 0 in (15.2 m)
Length:	35 ft 6 in (10.8 m)
Height:	13 ft 0 in (3.9 m)
Weight Empty:	2,699 lb (1,224 kg)
Weight Loaded:	3,812 lb (1,729 kg)
Max. Speed:	90 mph (145 km/h)
Engines:	One 200-hp Rolls-Royce Falcon I
Armament:	None fitted – but provision made

Fairey N.10

Wing Span:	46 ft 2 in (14.1 m)
Length:	36 ft 0 in (10.9 m)
Height:	11 ft 10 in (3.6 m)
Weight Empty:	2,970 lb (1,347 kg)
Weight Loaded:	4,159 lb (1,886 kg)
Max. Speed:	104 mph (167 km/h)
Engine:	One 260-hp Sunbeam Maori II
Armament:	None fitted – but provision made

Fairey IIIB

Wing Span:	62 ft 9 in (19.1 m)
Length:	37 ft 1 in (11.3 m)
Height:	12 ft 1½ in (3.8 m)
Weight Empty:	3,392 lb (1,538 kg)
Weight Loaded:	4,892 lb (2,219 kg)
Max. Speed:	95 mph (152 km/h)
Engine:	One 260-hp Sunbeam Maori II
Armament:	One Lewis machine gun mounted on a Scarff ring in observer's cockpit.
	Provision made for bomb racks beneath the fuselage

Fairey IIIC

Wing Span:	46 ft 1¼ in (14.1 m)
Length:	36 ft 0 in (10.9 m)
Height:	12 ft 1½ in (3.8 m)
Weight Empty:	3,392 lb (1,538 kg)
Weight Loaded:	4,800 lb (2,177 kg)
Max. Speed:	110 mph (176 km/h)
Engine:	One 375-hp Rolls-Royce Eagle VIII
Armament:	One forward firing synchronised Vickers machine gun One Lewis machine gun mounted on a Scarff ring in observer's cockpit

Avions Henri et Maurice Farman

Although it is often assumed that the Farman brothers were French, they were in fact British citizens who had chosen to live in France. The three brothers, Henri, Maurice and Richard opened up a car factory in 1902, which they slowly developed. Then, in 1907, Henri purchased a Voisin biplane and, after a number of modifications, entered it in the Archdeacon Cup race. A bitter row sprang up between Henri Farman and Voisin after Henri discovered that they were incorporating the modifications he had made into their own aircraft, without his permission. This annoyed Henri Farman to the extent that he decided to build his own aircraft, and in 1909 he opened up a factory in Mourmelon.

Henri's brother, Maurice also decided to enter the world of aviation and opened his factory at Mallet in the same year. After each had produced their first aircraft, the two brothers decided to amalgamate their two companies, and in the next five years produced a series of aircraft, all based on the same basic pusher design. Their first military version was designed by Henri Farman, the H.F.20.

This was a two-seat reconnaissance aircraft powered by a 70-hp Gnome Lambada. It had a two-bay wing, the lower wing being considerably shorter than the upper. The tail section was supported by two sets of tail booms constructed from pine, and consisted of a single elevator mounted just ahead of the semi-circular rudder that was fitted at the point of convergence. The tandem-seat nacelle was constructed of wood and covered with aluminium. In the centre was fitted the fuel tank, with the engine mounted at the rear. The design of the aircraft allowed the pilot, who sat in the nose and ahead of the wings, an excellent all-round view. The crew's position was reversed when machine guns were fitted, allowing an excellent field of fire for the gunner/observer. The HF.20 was derived from an earlier model, the HF.16, which had been purchased by the Imperial Russian Air Service, and was being used as a reconnaissance aircraft

The RFC obtained one H.F.20 Type III and used it in army co-operation trials; this was followed by an additional two, which were assigned to No. 2 Squadron, RFC. In 1913, Airco obtained the licence to make the H.F.20 at Hendon and several were built there. It was at Hendon that the experiment of fitting machine guns into the aircraft was successfully carried out. The RFC acquired a total of 145 H.F.20s, and the RNAS a further twenty-seven.

A development of the H.F.20, the H.F.22, produced a single-seat fighter/reconnaissance aircraft. Fifteen of the aircraft were purchased by the RNAS, but it was soon realised that the aircraft had severe limitations as it was unable to carry an adequate payload. However, four more of the aircraft were built by Airco under licence in Britain as floatplanes, three of which were purchased by the RNAS.

When the First World War started, the H.F.20 was immediately put into service as a reconnaissance aircraft. Trials were carried out with the intention of using the H.F.20

as a bomber, but it was discovered that it could not carry anything like a satisfactory bomb load. The Henri Farman Company immediately looked towards developing and aircraft that could carry a full bomb load without affecting the performance. What was developed was the H.F.27, a two-seater pusher, three-bay biplane of equal span and with no stagger, designed by Henri Farman. Unlike all previous Farman aircraft, this model had an all-steel structure and was powered by a 140-hp Gnome engine. The two-wheeled undercarriage was replaced by a four-wheeled version similar to the one used by the Voisin bombers. This increased the aircraft's stability in landing, especially on soft ground. The tail section was almost identical to that of the H.F.20.

The first test flight was carried out in February 1915 and was very successful, so successful in fact, that the Dux Company in Russia obtained a licence to build the aircraft for the Russian Imperial Air Service. The RFC in England also took a keen interest in the aircraft and ordered six to be delivered in the spring of 1914. The first five were assigned to No. 5 Squadron, and the other one to No. 3 Squadron. Pleased with the performance of the aircraft, the RFC ordered a further eight in the November, all of which were delivered in June 1915 and assigned to No. 26 Squadron. In the meantime, the RNAS had ordered twenty of the aircraft and a further forty in September 1915. In an effort to booster the RFC's dwindling aircraft numbers, twenty of the RNAS H.F.27s were assigned to the RFC.

A derivative of the H.F.27 appeared at the end of 1915, the H.F.30. The aircraft still retained the basic design of previous models, but the quadracycle undercarriage was replaced with a pair of wheels mounted beneath the lower wing. The cockpit nacelles were mounted suspended between the unequal wings, and were constructed from four ash longerons covered with plywood and aluminium. The fuselage and tail section were almost identical to that of the H.F.27, and were constructed from steel tubing with a sprung tail-skid as support.

Although not adopted by the Aviation Militaire, the aircraft attracted the attention of the Imperial Russian Air Service once again who, through the Dux factory, then obtained a licence to build the aircraft in Russia. Powered by a 160-hp Salmson engine, over 400 of the aircraft were built and were one of the most important reconnaissance aircraft used by them during the First World War. As late as 1929, the aircraft were still being used as a trainer.

While it must have appeared that Henri Farman was the only designer in the company, his brother Maurice Farman was also designing, and it was his M.F.7 Longhorn that was purchased by the RFC in 1913. This was an unequal-span, three-bay, biplane in which the forward elevator was fixed to extensions of the double-wheeled landing skids that protruded in front of the aircraft. The tail section was supported by two sets of tail booms and consisted of two elevators, the upper one being rectangular, while the lower one had a pronounced curve, each of which were mounted above and below two semi-circular rudders. The M.F.7 Longhorn was powered by a 70-hp Renault 8B pusher engine that was mounted behind the tandem two-seater nacelle.

The rights to build the M.F.7 under licence were taken up by Airco, who entered the aircraft in the Military Trials. Both the RFC and the RNAS acquired a number of the aircraft and used them primarily as trainers, although two did see active service in the Middle East as reconnaissance aircraft. It wasn't until October 1914 that the next Maurice Farman-designed military aircraft appeared – the M.F.11 Shorthorn. The names Shorthorn and Longhorn referred to the short and long skids that protruded in front of the aircraft.

The M.F.11 was almost a refinement of the M.F.7, with the forward elevator and the extended landing skids to which it was attached removed. There were slight reductions in the overall specifications; the cockpit nacelle was mounted between the upper and lower wings, unlike that of the M.F.7, which was mounted on top of the lower wing. The tail section was similar to the M.F.7, the only difference being that the large top oblong-shaped elevator was moved to replace the lower elevator, and was fixed behind the twin rudders.

The Eastbourne Aviation Company was given the licences to build twenty of the ninety M.F.11s purchased by the RNAS, most of which were used for bombing and reconnaissance duties in the Aegean with No. 3 Wing, RNAS. The RFC also purchased a large number of the aircraft, some of which were bought directly from France, the remainder being built under licence by Airco and Whitehead Aircraft Ltd. Virtually all the RFC squadrons had the aircraft to use primarily as a trainer, although some were used in a reconnaissance role. No. 30 Squadron, RFC, when posted to Mesopotamia in the Middle East, used the very low speed of the M.F.11 Shorthorn to create a detailed map of the area around the Tigris area. The map became invaluable for the ground troops during the Battle of Ctesiphon, because it showed the approaches and defence positions.

The M.F.11 Shorthorn's contribution to aviation during this period was relatively brief, but nevertheless important.

A number of other pusher variants were developed by the Farman Company over the next year, none of which attracted the attention of the British until the Farman F.40 bomber arrived. It retained the sesquiplane design with the tail booms, and had the combined features of both Henri and Maurice's designs. Because of this, they became known as 'Horaces'. The F.40 had three-bay wings of unequal span with an ovoid nacelle fuselage, which gave a streamlined appearance, mounted between the wings. It was powered by a 160-hp Renault 8Gc engine, which was mounted at the rear of the nacelle with radiators fitted either side of the fuselage. The pilot sat behind the gunner/observer, whose position in the nose gave him a very clear field of fire and excellent visibility. The tail section consisted of four booms, to which a rudder, with a horizontal stabiliser on top, was joined at the point of convergence.

The first trials of the F.40 were carried out under combat conditions, such was the need for aircraft, and were carried out by Escadrille M.F.16. The reports that came back did not contain many compliments; in fact, there were numerous complaints regarding the aircraft's poor manoeuvrability and nose-heaviness. It was also recommended that the undercarriage be strengthened and the rigging made tighter. In order to combat the nose-heaviness, the cockpit nacelles were moved back 6 cm, and the tail section was reinforced. With the modifications made, the output per day rose to ten and this attracted the attention of the RNAS. They ordered fifty F.40s, thirty of which were to be fitted with 160-hp Renault 8Gc engines, and the other twenty to be fitted with the 150-hp Renault engine. None of the F.40s saw action with the RFC.

In August 1916 it was decided to move the RFC's existing Aerial Gunnery School from Hythe to Loch Doon in Scotland. The location and size of the loch was well suited for the purpose, and with this in mind, the RFC ordered eight Maurice Farman S.11 seaplanes to be ready for the move that was to take place in January 1917. The S.11s were in fact modified M.F.11 Shorthorns with the undercarriage replaced by floats. Powered by an 80-hp Renault engine, the aircraft proved to be seriously underpowered, and all were eventually replaced by F.B.A. Type Bs.

A number of variations and models were designed over the following months, but they resulted in only one or two examples being developed. Then, in late 1917 they submitted a design for a heavy bomber capable of carrying 1,100 lb (500 kg) of bombs over a distance of 620 miles (1,000 km).

Designated the F.50, it was a four-bay biplane of unequal wingspan, powered by two 240-hp Lorraine 8Bb engines. The radiators were mounted on top of the engine nacelles, behind which were fitted the 87-gallon (330-litre) fuel tanks. The undercarriage consisted of a pair of wheels, fitted to the wing beneath the engine nacelles and strengthened by cross-wire bracings.

The fuselage consisted of rectangular cross sections, the longerons of which were made of three pieces of pine. The front section of the fuselage, where the crew were situated, was covered in plywood, while the aft section was fabric-covered.

Test flights with the F.50 were carried out at Villacoubly and were satisfactory, climbing to 4,000 feet in 44 minutes at a speed of 125 km/h (77 mph). During one of the tests, one of the two engines shut down, and the pilot experienced great difficulties and considerable fatigue in keeping the aircraft straight, hampered by the poor positioning of the rudder bar. Subsequent tests discovered that it was almost impossible to keep the aircraft on a level light in the event of one engine failing.

Despite this, a bomber was required, so fifty of the aircraft were ordered. Two modified variants were acquired by the Navy and given the designation F.50T, but by the time of the Armistice only seventeen of the aircraft had been built and had entered service. During this relatively short period, they carried out numerous raids against German troop trains and railway yards, cutting off the supply of men and supplies to the retreating enemy.

After the war a number of these aircraft saw service with countries like Mexico and Japan. In Mexico, they were heavily involved in the battle against the revolutionaries and played a major part in the defeat of the rebels.

SPECIFICATIONS

H.F.20

Wing Span:	43 ft 6 in (13.3 m)
Length:	26 ft 5¼ in (8.6 m)
Height:	10 ft 4 in (3.1 m)
Weight Empty:	795 lb (360 kg)
Weight Loaded:	1,455 lb (660 kg)
Max. Speed:	65 mph (105 km/h)
Engine:	One 80-hp Gnome
	One 80-hp Le Rhône
Armament:	One forward-firing Vickers/Lewis machine gun

H.F.27

Wing Span:	52 ft 9 in (16.1 m)
Length:	30 ft 1 in (9.2 m)
Height:	11 ft 9 in (3.6 m)
Weight Empty:	1,697 lb (770 kg)
Weight Loaded:	2,579 lb (1,170 kg)
Max. Speed:	91 mph (147 km/h)
Engine:	One 155-hp Canton-Unné R9
Armament:	One forward-firing Vickers machine gun
	250 kg bombs

M.F.7 Longhorn

Wing Span:	50 ft 9 in (15.5 m)
Length:	37 ft 8 in (11.5 m)
Height:	10 ft 5 in (3.2 m)
Weight Empty:	1,278 lb (580 kg)
Weight Loaded:	1,889 lb (857 kg)
Max. Speed:	56 mph (90 km/h)
Engine:	One 70-hp Renault 8B

M.F.11 Shorthorn

Wing Span Upper:	51 ft 9 in (15.7 m)

Wing Span Lower:	38 ft 7¼ in (11.7 m)
Length:	30 ft 6 in (9.3 m)
Height:	10 ft 4 in (3.1 m)
Weight Empty:	1,441 lb (654 kg)
Weight Loaded:	2,046 lb (928 kg)
Max. Speed:	72 mph (116 km/h)
Engine:	One 80-hp Renault 8B
Armament:	One forward-firing Vickers machine gun

M.F.40

Wing Span:	57 ft 5 in (17.5 m)
Length:	30 ft 6 in (9.3 m)
Height:	12 ft 8 in (3.9 m)
Weight Empty:	1,649 lb (748 kg)
Weight Loaded:	2,469 lb (928 kg)
Max. Speed:	83 mph (135 km/h)
Engine:	One 160-hp Renault 8Gc
Armament:	One forward-firing Vickers machine gun
	240 kg bombs

Felixstowe

The Felixstowe flying boat was one of the most successful of all the Allied flying boats of the First World War. Surprisingly, it was not the brainchild of a specific company but was developed from a design by Lieutenant Commander John Porte, who had worked for the Curtiss Aeroplane & Motor Company in America. A number of different manufacturers built the hulls, including: S. E. Saunders Ltd, Isle of Wight; Aircraft Manufacturing Co. Ltd, Hendon; Norman Thompson Flight Co., Bognor, Sussex; May, Harden & May, Southampton; and Hutchinson, Summers & Payne. Despite the fact there was no manufacturer as such, it is included because of the outstanding contribution the aircraft made in protecting the convoys in the North Sea and the Western Approaches.

At the outbreak of war, John Porte joined the Royal Navy, but because of his poor health he was not assigned to active duty. His experience in the developing world of flying boats, however, prompted the Admiralty to first appoint him to command a training squadron, then to make him commander of RNAS Felixstowe, and it was while here that he persuaded the Admiralty to purchase the Curtiss H.4 flying boat. During tests by RNAS pilots, it was soon discovered that the aircraft was not up to the standard required by the Navy; in fact, the test pilots stated categorically that the aircraft was 'absolutely unfit for active action.' Despite this, a small number of the aircraft were ordered.

Porte set about redesigning the hull, which was the main bone of contention, along with the underpowered Curtiss engines, and produced an improved, stronger design, fitted with Hispano-Suiza engines. Known as the F.I, the aircraft combined the hull designed by Porte with the wings and tail section of the Curtiss H.4. It still did not meet the requirements of the Navy, but this was due in the main to the underpowered engines. A further modification was the replacement of the one-step hull with a two-step hull that also caused it to be enlarged. The engines were replaced with Rolls-Royce Eagle VIII engines and incorporated into the wings of the Curtiss H.12 (Large America). The Felixstowe F.2A, as it was called, carried a crew of four and inherited the name of Felixstowe from the naval air station at which the idea was conceived. The F.2A was fitted with dual controls and, by carrying extra fuel in cans, was able to stay airborne for up to 9 hours. Unlike the Curtiss, the Felixstowe F.2A had no cabin, leaving the pilot and second pilot in an open cockpit. This improved visibility considerably and improved the aircraft's performance.

Only one variation was made, the Felixstowe F.2C, and only the one was built, although it still served during the war. Flown by Lt-Com. John Porte, it participated in the sinking of the U-boat UC-1 commanded by Oberleutnant Mildenstein, accompanied by two F.2As.

One of the first conquests achieved by the Felixstowe F.2A was the shooting down of the Zeppelin L.62 at 8,000 feet over Heligoland. The Zeppelin, commanded by Kapitänleutnant Kuno Manger, was returning from a bombing raid over Britain when a Felixstowe F.2A (flown by Captains T. C. Pattinson and A. H. Munday) intercepted it and shot it down.

Despite its 5½-ton weight, the F.2A was extremely manoeuvrable, a characteristic that was to prove invaluable during one of the fiercest aerial battles between seaplanes of the First World War. On 4 June 1918, a formation of British flying boats, four Felixstowe F.2As and one Curtiss H.12, led by Captain R. Leckie, RN, were on patrol close to the coastline of Zeebrugge when fourteen German seaplanes attacked them. As they approached the coastline, one of the F.2As dropped out because of a blocked fuel line, and during the action another of the F.2As was forced down with a broken fuel line. The remaining two F.2as and the Curtiss H.12 managed to shoot down six of the enemy seaplanes, forcing the remaining eight to withdraw.

After they had triumphantly returned to base, it was decided to paint the aircraft in distinguishing colours after it was realised that once one of their aircraft had put down on the sea, it was extremely difficult to spot it, especially in rough seas. The ones from Felixstowe painted their aircraft in coloured dazzle stripes; others were painted to the liking of their own crews.

The Felixstowe F.2A controlled the skies over the English Channel up to the arrival of the German Hansa-Brandenburg W.29 fighter seaplane, and despite suffering a number of losses the F.2A distinguished itself right to the very end of the war.

The success of the F.2A prompted the Admiralty to look towards the building of a bigger version that could carry a larger bomb load over a greater range. The result was the Felixstowe F.3. Despite being slower and less manoeuvrable, the prototype appeared to match the Admiralty's requirements and 263 of the aircraft were ordered, the maiden flight of the prototype being made in February 1917. The 345-hp Rolls-Royce engines were replaced with 320-hp Sunbeam Cossacks on the prototype, but the production models were fitted with the Rolls-Royce Eagle VIII engines.

Unlike the F.2A, which operated from the home ports, the F.3 operated mainly in the Mediterranean, carrying out anti-submarine patrols. Such was the demand for the aircraft that it was decided to build them in the dockyards in Malta, and eighteen of the aircraft were completed between the end of 1917 and the Armistice. In fact, only 100 of the 263 ordered were completed, as the end of hostilities resulted in numerous contracts with aviation companies being cancelled.

SPECIFICATIONS

Felixstowe F.2A

Wing Span:	95 ft 7 in (29.1 m)
Length:	46 ft 3 in (14.0 m)
Height:	17 ft 6 in (5.3 m)
Weight Empty:	7,549 lb (3,424 kg)
Weight Loaded:	10,978 lb (4,979 kg)
Max. Speed:	95 mph (152 km/h)
Engine:	Two 345-hp Rolls-Royce Eagle VIII
Armament:	Four free-mounted Lewis machine guns
	Two 230 lb bombs

Felixstowe F.3

Wing Span:	102 ft 0 in (31.0 m)
Length:	49 ft 2 in (15.0 m)
Height:	18 ft 8 in (5.6 m)
Weight Empty:	7,958 lb (3,609 kg)
Weight Loaded:	12,235 lb (5,549 kg)
Max. Speed:	91 mph (146 km/h)
Engine:	Two 345-hp Rolls-Royce Eagle VIII
Armament:	Four free-mounted Lewis machine guns
	Two 230 lb bombs

Franco-British Aviation (F.B.A.)

In 1911, Louis Schreck, the South American representative for the Delaunnay-Belleville automobile company, joined up with two other engineers, Hanriot and Gaudard, to build the D'Artois flying boat. Almost at the same time, they purchased the Tellier Company and acquired the patents for the Donnet-Lévéque flying boats.

Using their combined skills, in 1913, the Franco-British Aviation Company, as it was now called after obtaining funding from British investors, produced the first of their single-engine flying boats, the F.B.A. Type A. Based on the design of the Donnet-Lévéque flying boat, the Type A was a very small, two-bay, unequal span biplane powered by a 50-hp Gnome N1 Omega pusher engine that was mounted on struts between the wings. The boat-shaped fuselage was made of wood and had side-by-side seating for the pilot and observer.

In 1914, one of the Type As was fitted with a 100-hp Gnome engine and entered in the Schneider Trophy Contest at Monaco and came second. It was here that the little flying boat attracted the attention of the RNAS. They had been using the Maurice Farman S.11 seaplane as a trainer, but it had proved to be unsatisfactory and the F.B.A. Type A appeared to be just what they were looking for. In April 1915, the RNAS placed an order for forty-two F.B.A. Type A flying boats, the first two being delivered in May and assigned to No. 1 Wing, RNAS. These were quickly followed by a further ten that also went to No. 1 Wing at Dunkerque, and then another twenty in 1916 which were based at various RNAS stations around the coast of Britain. At the end of 1916, ten more were supplied and again assigned to coastal stations around Britain.

In June 1917, the RFC approached the Progress and Allocation Committee, who oversaw aircraft allocations to the RFC, and requested a few seaplanes to replace the Maurice Farman S.11 seaplanes they had been using at School of Aerial Gunnery at Loch Doon in Scotland. Three of the aircraft were transferred from the RNAS to the RFC, and were modified with rounded leading edges on the rudders and rigid trailing edges on the mainplanes. In the meantime, the Gosport Aviation Co. Ltd had acquired the licence to build the F.B.A. Type A and the latest modified version, the Type B. The RFC approached Franco-British Aviation with an order for thirty F.B.A. Type Bs to be built by Gosport. Problems arose when it was discovered that the RNAS were expecting ten of the aircraft to be built and delivered to them every month. To solve the problem, the French parent company agreed to supply some of the aircraft direct from France, while Gosport's production would be shared equally between the RFC and the RNAS.

A total of eighty Type Bs were built, over half of which saw service overseas with the RNAS. The remaining aircraft were used for reconnaissance and training purposes. A development of the Type B, the Type C, was produced, powered by a 130-hp Clerget 9B rotary engine. A large number – seventy-eight in all – of this model were built, and saw extensive service as an anti-submarine aircraft.

The Russian Naval Air Service purchased thirty of the Type C, and a further thirty-four were built by the Lebedev factory under licence. The Italians too were impressed with the aircraft and purchased thirty-eight. The Italian Savoia (SIAI) Company obtained a licence to build the Type C, but only manufactured a small number. They were finally replaced by the Type H.

A Type H appeared in the summer of 1917, four of which were purchased by the RNAS. Two of the aircraft were sent to Malta where, on 20 August 1917, one of the Type H flying boats attacked a German U-boat and, although inflicting some damage, was unable to sink it. Over 1,000 Type H flying boats were produced, 982 of which were built by the Italian Savoia Company under licence. They fitted the more powerful 170-hp Isotta-Fraschini engine and increased the dimension of the aircraft slightly.

A number of other countries also purchased the Type H: Peru (three), Serbia (three), Spain (two), Uruguay (one) and the United States (twelve). Although there were a number of complaints about the construction of the hull, especially by the American Navy based at Porto Corsini, the results the aircraft achieved far outweighed any problems.

The need for a light bomber/patrol flying boat resulted in a number of designs being submitted. The one selected was the F.B.A Type S. Very similar to the Type H, the Type S had a longer fuselage and a larger wingspan, which folded back against the fuselage for ease of storage. It was powered by a 200-hp Hispano-Suiza 8Bb pusher engine mounted centrally behind the pilot. The aircraft carried a crew of two, but provision was made for a third crewmember to be carried if the need arose.

Over thirty of the aircraft were ordered and all saw service in the English Channel, Atlantic Ocean and Mediterranean Sea. A few variations were constructed, but all were just experimental and none went into production.

The F.B.A. flying boats served the Allies well throughout the war and showed that there was a role to be played by the smaller flying boats.

SPECIFICATIONS

F.B.A. Type A

Wing Span:	38 ft 8 in (11.8 m)
Length:	28 ft 9 in (8.8 m)
Height:	7 ft 1 in (2.1 m)
Weight Empty:	681 lb (309 kg)
Weight Loaded:	1,256 lb (570 kg)
Max. Speed:	67 mph (109 km/h)
Engine:	One 80-hp Gnome 7A
Armament:	None

F.B.A. Type B

Wing Span Upper:	45 ft 0 in (13.7 m)
Wing Span Lower:	33 ft 8 in (10.3 m)
Length:	30 ft 0 in (9.1 m)
Height:	9 ft 6 in (2.9 m)
Weight Empty:	1,265 lb (574 kg)
Weight Loaded:	2,000 lb (907 kg)
Max. Speed:	67 mph (109 km/h)
Engine:	One 100-hp Gnome
Armament:	One Lewis machine gun or two 150 kg bombs

F.B.A. Type H

Wing Span Upper:	46 ft 3 in (14.1 m)
Wing Span Lower:	34 ft 8 in (10.5 m)
Length:	32 ft 5 in (9.9 m)
Height:	9 ft 6 in (2.9 m)
Weight Empty:	2,169 lb (984 kg)
Weight Loaded:	3,131 lb (1,420 kg)
Max. Speed:	93 mph (150 km/h)
Engine:	One 150-hp Hispano-Suiza 8A
Armament:	One Lewis machine gun or two 150 kg bombs

Henri Farman beside the tail of his first aircraft.

Henri Farman H.F.20.

Maurice Farman M.F.7 No. B3.

Farman M.F. 11 reconnaissance bomber.

Maurice Farman M.F.11 Shorthorns.

Corporal Frank Ridd, the first NCO pilot in the RFC, in an M.F.7.

Farman F.40 No. 9162 at RNAS Yarmouth.

Felixstowe F.2A flying boat.

Felixstowe F.2A on patrol in the English Channel.

Frederick Handley Page.

Handley Page Type B.

The Handley Page Type E, also known as the 'Yellow Peril'.

Roland Garros in his Morane-Saulnier fitted with the forward-firing machine gun.

Roland Garros being interrogated by German officers after being shot down.

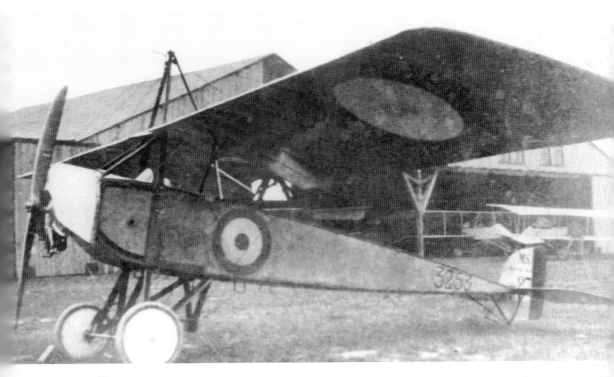

Flt Sub-Lt Warneford's Morane Parasol, in which he shot down the Zeppelin LZ.37.

Morane-Saulnier LA Parasol No. A6607 in RFC markings.

Morane-Saulnier No. A193 of No. 3 Squadron RFC, with General Ashmore climbing in.

Morane-Saulnier Type BB. The large spinner was called 'La Casserole' by the French.

Morane-Saulnier Type AC.

Nieuport 11.

Nieuport 17 of Spa 3, belonging to Georges Guynemer.

Nieuport 17 and 27 Scouts of No. 1 Squadron RFC at Bailleul.

Nieuport 23 with Charles Nungesser's personal insignia on the fuselage.

Charles Nungesser in front
of a Nieuport fighter.

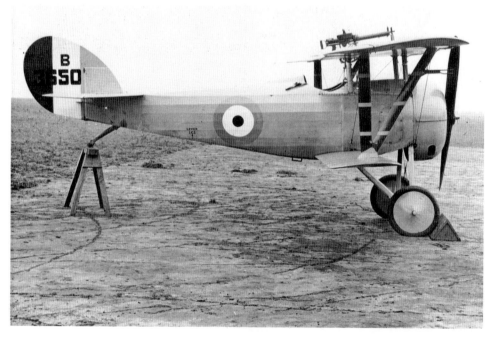

Nieuport 27, No. B3650, of No. 29 Squadron RFC.

Nieuport 27 fighter.

The White & Thompson *Bognor Bloater*.

Norman Thompson NT.4 at anchor in the Solent.

Handley Page Aircraft Company

Frederick Handley Page was born in Cheltenham, Gloucestershire, on 15 November 1885. On leaving school, he entered college to train as an electrical engineer. Within two years of leaving college, he had become the chief designer of an electrical company at the young age of twenty-one. This was the period when the first aeroplanes started to appear, and Handley Page became so fascinated with them that he started his own aviation company in 1908 with a capital of £10,000. This was the first private British company of its kind.

Known primarily for the large heavy bombers it produced during the First and Second World Wars, the company's first aircraft was the H.P.1 (Type A), or *Bluebird* as it was called, built in 1909. This was a single-seat monoplane of the standard wooden construction, fitted with tailskid landing gear and powered by a 20-hp Advance 4-cylinder engine. The first flight was carried out on 24 May 1910, but two days later, on the second flight, the aircraft crashed on landing. Repairs were carried out, and the aircraft was modified and given a new designation, the H.P.3 (Type C). This aircraft never even got off the ground and was scrapped.

Meanwhile, Handley-Page had been working on a new design, the H.P.4 (Type D), also known as the *Antiseptic*. There didn't seem to be any reason given for this strange name. It was a single-seat monoplane with a crescent wing that was wire-braced to a kingpost above the pilot's head, and to the skid landing gear. It was initially powered by a 35-hp Green engine, but a 35-hp Isaacson radial engine was fitted for the first flight on 15 July 1911. The first flight was a disaster, as it crashed on landing. Extensive repairs took place, with the wings and tail section being re-covered in a yellow fabric. When completed, it was given a new designation of H.P.5, but it was also known as the *Yellow Peril* because of the colour of the fabric that covered the aircraft. The results from the tests of this aircraft convinced Handley-Page that if he could produce an aircraft that could carry a passenger, this would create a niche in the market. The result was a larger version of the Type D, a Type E that was a two-seat monoplane with pilot and passenger seated in tandem. The first tests were encouraging, but after a slight accident a new wing was fitted which had ailerons, instead of the usual wing warping for control, and a newly designed tail section. It also gained the nickname *Yellow Peril* because of its brightly-coloured fabric covering, which confused many people because the Type D had the same nickname.

Over the next few years the Type E flew thousands of miles and carried hundreds of passengers without a single problem, but at the onset of war it was considered unsuitable for military service.

The first military aircraft designed and built by Handley Page was the H.P O/100 heavy bomber. This was the world's first heavy bomber, and was the result of a call for such an aircraft from Commodore Murray Sueter of the Admiralty's Air Department.

This had come about after the devastating raids by German Zeppelins on London; Sueter wanted retaliation, calling for a 'bloody paralyser' of an aircraft to do the job. The aircraft that appeared was the H.P. O/100, an enlarged improvement of an earlier design. Powered initially by two 120-hp Beardmore engines, these were found to be underpowered and were replaced by two 250-hp Rolls-Royce Eagle II engines. These incorporated the fuel tanks, and on the prototype the engine nacelles were covered with armour plate, as was the crew cabin. On the production model almost all of this was left off in order to reduce the overall weight of the aircraft, thus increasing the bomb load.

The two-bay bomber had unequal 100-ft wings, making this an enormous aircraft for the day, and in order to be able to store the aircraft in a hangar, the wings were designed to fold back against the fuselage. The upper wings, which were longer than the lower, were constructed in three sections, while the lower wings were constructed in two sections. The whole wing assembly was covered in fabric. The fuselage was of a rectangular box shape configuration with longerons and spacers made of spruce and constructed in four sections. The first section contained the cockpit, the second the bomb bay. The tail section consisted of a single central fin with twin rudders and four elevators.

The undercarriage consisted of four wheels, each pair being supported by a tripod made of steel tubing covered in wood and attached to the fixed section of the lower wing between the engine nacelle and the fuselage. In front of the pilot's cockpit was a gunner's position, in which was mounted either single or twin Lewis machine guns. Behind the pilot, in the observer/gunner's position was mounted either a single or twin Lewis machine guns, and in addition a single Lewis machine gun was mounted in a slot in the floor for downward and rearward defence.

The initial flight tests were carried out on 18 December 1915, using 320-hp Sunbeam Cossack engines. Because of the demand for the Rolls-Royce engine, which far outstripped the supply, two specially boosted 260-hp R.A.F.3a engines replaced them. Over the next few days, a number of test flights were carried out and several problems fixed. It was then sent to Eastchurch on 10 January 1916 for more extensive testing and a number of further problems were discovered, vibration at top speed being just one of them. The Controller of Aeronautical Supplies ordered six H.P. O/100s, and when delivered to the RNAS they were fitted with the 320-hp Sunbeam Cossack engines with frontal radiators.

In September 1916, the H.P. O/100 entered service with the Fifth Naval Wing, RNAS, at Dunkirk; it was initially as a day bomber, but suffered some serious losses, so it was used on night bombing missions. A total of forty-six H.P. O/100 bombers were built, the last six fitted with the 320-hp Sunbeam Cossack engine. By the end of 1917 four squadrons of the RNAS had been equipped with the aircraft, but by this time the enclosed cabin had been removed, as had most of the armour plating. Raids were carried out against U-boat bases, railway yards and aerodromes where the Gotha bombers were based. One H.P. O/100, piloted by Squadron Commander K. S. Savory, was flown in the Aegean and carried out bombing raids on Constantinople and the German battle cruiser SMS *Goeben*. But the H.P. O/100 didn't last long, as it was quickly superseded by the H.P. O/400.

Identical in size to the H.P. O/100, the H.P. O/400 was powered by two 360-hp Rolls-Royce Eagle VIII engines, which gave the aircraft a top speed of 95 mph and an operating height of 8,500 feet. There were some differences, inasmuch as the fuel tanks for the H.P. O/400 were situated inside the fuselage above the bomb bay, as opposed to the H.P. O/100's fuel tanks that were situated in the engine nacelle behind the engine.

Seven bomber squadrons were formed in the Independent Air Force, and the H.P. O/400 became their standard aircraft. A total of 400 H.P. O/400s were built, and an additional 107 were built in the USA for the US Army Air Service by the Standard Aircraft Corporation of New Jersey, but were never flown in combat.

The Handley Page Aircraft Company developed the role of the bomber far better than anyone else, and during the Second World War produced a number of bombers that were to leave their mark on the world of military aviation.

SPECIFICATIONS

H.P.4 *Antiseptic*

Wing Span:	32 ft 0 in (9.7 m)
Length:	22 ft 0 in (6.7 m)
Height:	8 ft 4 in (2.5 m)
Weight Empty:	440 lb (200 kg)
Weight Loaded:	620 lb (281 kg)
Max. Speed:	50 mph (80 km/h)
Engine:	One 50-hp Isaacson radial
Armament:	None

H.P.5 (*Yellow Peril*)

Wing Span:	42 ft 6 in (12.9 m)
Length:	28 ft 2 in (8.6 m)
Height:	9 ft 4 in (2.8 m)
Weight Empty:	800 lb (363 kg)
Weight Loaded:	1,300 lb (590 kg)
Max. Speed:	60 mph (97 km/h)
Engine:	One 50-hp Gnome radial
Armament:	None

H.P. O/100 / O/400

Wing Span:	100 ft 0 in (30.5 m)
Length:	62 ft 10¼ in (19.2 m)
Height:	22 ft 0 in (6.7 m)
Weight Empty:	8,300 lb (3,764 kg)
Weight Loaded:	14,000 lb (6,350 kg)
Max. Speed:	85 mph (136 km/h)
Engine:	Two 250-hp Rolls-Royce Eagle II (O/100)
	Two 360-hp Rolls-Royce Eagle VIII (O/400)
Armament:	Three/Five Lewis machine guns
	2,000 lb bombs

Martinsyde Aircraft Company

The company started business as the Martin & Handasyde Aircraft Company (later changed to Martinsyde), and designed aircraft for the private market. The aircraft drew the attention of the Royal Flying Corps (RFC), who ordered one of their monoplanes and carried out a series of trials with the aircraft. Powered by a 65-hp Antoinette engine, the aircraft was flown by Gordon Bell, and despite the engine firing only on five of its six cylinders, it performed well. Encouraged by the results, Martin and Handasyde decided to enter one of their aircraft at the Military Trials at Larkhill. The trials went well, but because of a ban on monoplanes due to an accident, the aircraft was not accepted.

Then, just before the start of the First World War a small sporting, single-seat, single-bay biplane appeared on the scene and immediately attracted the attention of the military. This was the Martinsyde S.1, which bore a very strong resemblance to the Sopwith Tabloid, the main difference being the ungainly-looking, but solid, four-wheeled undercarriage. It was immediately snapped up by the RFC, and after initial tests was assigned to No. 1 Squadron and used for training purposes. So impressed with the little fighter were the RFC that they ordered a further fifty. Fortunately, H. P. Martin had pre-empted the RFC and gambled that they would want more so they were well into production when the official order came through.

The first production Martinsyde S.1 was sent to join No. 5 Squadron, RFC. A number of modifications made to it, the main one being the fitting of a two-wheeled undercarriage in place of the ungainly looking four-wheeled version on the prototype. As the aircraft came off the production line they were assigned to various squadrons, including No. 6 Squadron, RFC. It was with this squadron that one of the most bizarre incidents occurred concerning a Martinsyde S.1. Lieutenant Louis Strange was on patrol over Menin when he engaged a German Aviatik on a reconnaissance mission. Swooping into attack, he emptied the drum magazine of his Lewis machine gun at the aircraft and then climbed away to change the magazine and attack again. Holding the control stick between his knees, he stood up in the cockpit to change the drum magazine when suddenly the aircraft, which was in a climbing attitude, stalled and went inverted, leaving Lt Strange hanging by his fingertips from the drum magazine. Fortunately, the jammed magazine remained jammed and incredibly, Strange does not recall just how he managed to get back into the cockpit and regain control of the aircraft before it hit the ground.

A number had seen service in Mesopotamia operating from Basra, but the rotary engines suffered badly from the dust kicked up in the dry conditions of the desert. The little aircraft still managed to give a good account of itself, but then they were all withdrawn from service, both in the Middle East and in Europe in the July and August of 1915, to be replaced by the Martinsyde G.100. As with all aircraft at the time, the Martinsyde S.1 was constantly being superseded by improved models.

The Martinsyde G.100 was already on the drawing boards as the S.1 was being built, and by the time the S.1 had been withdrawn from service, the prototype G.100 had been built. It was a two-bay biplane with a slender box-like fuselage with a rounded top. Powered by a 120-hp Beardmore-built Austro-Daimler engine, the single-seat, long-range fighter/reconnaissance aircraft was one of the most powerful of its day. One unusual feature was that the radiator was mounted behind the engine. Because of its ungainly and lumbering appearance, the G.100 earned itself the nickname of 'Elephant'. The one Australian Flying Corps squadron proudly had the emblem of an Elephant painted on the sides of their aircraft.

On 8 September 1915, the G.100 underwent its initial trials at the Central Flying School at Upavon. Two weeks later, it was taken to Farnborough and after further testing was sent to No. 1 Aircraft depot at Saint-Omer, France. It was then assigned to No. 6 Squadron RFC for evaluation, and then on to No. 20 Squadron, RFC for further evaluation. Following the evaluation by No. 6 Squadron, an order for 100 of the aircraft was made and the first arrived in February 1916. A number of minor modifications that had been suggested were taken up, including an improved engine cowling and a simple over-wing mounting for the Lewis machine gun, which had an extended handle for ease of manoeuvrability when lowering and reloading.

The first ten Martinsyde G.100s off the production line were fitted with the 120-hp Beardmore engine, and were assigned to No. 27 Squadron, RFC at Treizennes. There they were used for high-speed scouting and photo-reconnaissance missions. It was quickly realised that an additional rear-facing machine gun was required, so a spigot was fitted just behind the cockpit on the port side that held the second Lewis machine gun. The installation looked impressive, but using the gun with any form of accuracy was almost impossible because of the pilot's ability to move around in the cockpit.

As a fighter, although fast, the G.100 was not ideal for any form of aerial combat and so it was decided to use it as a fighter/bomber, with the emphasis on the bomber. It could carry one 230 lb bomb or two 112 lb bombs which, when combined with the speed of the aircraft, made it a quite formidable adversary.

A further fifty G.100s were ordered in June 1916, and these were fitted with the improved 160-hp Beardmore engine and given the designation G.102. In September 1917, a further seventy G.102s were ordered, followed by an additional fifty at the end of October.

Despite its ungainly appearance, the Martinsyde G.100 and G.102 acquitted itself extremely well, both on the Western Front and in the Middle East. It was during its time in the Middle East that the G.100 was used in a most unusual way. In an effort to stop the grain boats on the Dead Sea, Colonel Williams came up with the bizarre idea of stripping the Martinsyde G.100 of its wings and tail unit, replacing the undercarriage with floats and using the powerful 160-hp Beardmore engine to propel the aircraft/gunboat across the sea. After a great deal of trial and error, which included a number of incidents of capsizing, the problems were solved and the pilot was given a 'free-to-roam' mandate. When the outlandish craft, called *Mimi*, caught up with one of the grain boats, the pilot would stand up in the cockpit and open fire with his top wing-mounted Lewis gun and rake the grain boat from bow to stern. The project was very satisfactory, and caused the sailors on the grain boats to fear the bizarre aircraft/gunboat that appeared from nowhere and shot up their boats.

The disappointment over the G.100 and G.102's lack of manoeuvrability in aerial combat prompted the designers to produce a modified version. The single-bay aircraft that appeared was the Martinsyde R.G. The prototype was powered by the 160-hp Beardmore engine but an improved version of the R.G, the Martinsyde F.3, was powered by the latest 275-hp Rolls-Royce Falcon III engine and fitted with twin synchronised Vickers machine guns.

In September 1917, the aircraft was sent to Martlesham Heath for testing and evaluation and came out with glowing reports from the test pilots. The results prompted the immediate order of 150 of the aircraft and the production lines started to produce the F.3. Then, suddenly and inexplicably, Major General Trenchard, who was commander of the Royal Flying Corps in France at the time, recommended that the project be abandoned and the order cancelled. To this day, no one knows the reason for his sudden and dramatic change of mind. Fortunately his advice was ignored and production continued, this time with an improved engine, the 300-hp Hispano-Suiza.

In January 1918, an improved version of the F.3 appeared, the Martinsyde F.4. The modifications had been made to give the pilot a greatly improved downward view. There were major problems with production of the F.4, none of which were of Martinsyde's making. The problem lay with the delay in delivering the Rolls-Royce Falcon II engine from the manufacturers. The aircraft were completed and in storage, awaiting the delivery of the engine, so it was decided to fit the aircraft with the 300-hp Hispano-Suiza engine.

Because of these problems, it wasn't until June 1918 that the Martinsyde F.4 arrived at Martlesham Heath for testing and evaluation. In the meantime, the production of the F.3 was so slow that only four of the aircraft were ever assigned to operational squadrons before the Armistice. Two F.3s went to No. 39 Squadron, RAF and two to No. 141 Squadron, RAF. The F.4 never went farther than Martlesham Heath, and was abandoned in favour of the Sopwith Snipe.

SPECIFICATIONS

Martinsyde S.1

Wing Span:	27 ft 8 in (8.4 m)
Length:	21 ft 0 in (6.4 m)
Height:	9 ft 4 in (2.8 m)
Weight Empty:	Not known
Weight Loaded:	Not known
Max. Speed:	87 mph (139 km/h)
Engine:	One 80-hp Gnome radial
Armament:	Single Lewis machine gun mounted on top wing
	Six 50 lb bombs, twelve Hales Grenades and
	150 incendiary darts

Martinsyde G.100 / G.102

Wing Span:	38 ft 0 in (11.5 m)
Length:	26 ft 6½ in (8.1 m)
Height:	9 ft 8 in (2.9 m)
Weight Empty:	1,759 lb (798 kg) (G.100)
	1,793 lb (813 kg) (G.102)
Weight Loaded:	2,424 lb (1,099 kg) (G.100)
	2,458 lb (1,114 kg) (G.102)
Max. Speed:	95 mph (152 km/h) (G.100)
	102 mph (164 km/h) (G.102)
Engine:	One 102-hp Beardmore (G.100)
	One 160-hp Beardmore (G.102)
Armament:	Single Lewis machine gun mounted on top wing
	Six 50 lb bombs

Martinsyde F.3 and F.4

Wing Span Upper:	32 ft 10 in (9.9 m)
Wing Span Lower:	31 ft 6 in (9.6 m)
Length:	25 ft 6 in (7.7 m)
Height:	8 ft 8 in (2.7 m)
Weight Empty:	1,859 lb (843 kg)
Weight Loaded:	2,446 lb (1,109 kg)
Max. Speed:	129 mph (207 km/h)
Engine:	One 275-hp Rolls-Royce Falcon II
	One 300-hp Hispano-Suiza 8Fb
Armament:	Twin synchronised Lewis machine guns

Société Anonyme des Aéroplanes Morane-Saulnier

The Morane-Saulnier Company started life in 1910 when Leon Morane, Gabriel Borel and Raymond Saulnier formed a small aircraft company. Leon Morane was already a highly skilled pilot, and had set both a world speed and height record in his Blériot monoplane in the summer of 1910. There was friction between Gabriel Borel and the other two partners almost from the start and so in October 1910 they parted company, leaving just Morane and Saulnier to start a new company, the Société Anonyme des Aéroplanes.

During the next three years, the company produced small training aircraft that were used by the Aviation Militaire and the Russian Air Service. Their test pilot was Roland Garros, who was later to find fame when he demonstrated his Garros-Hue version of the bullet deflector system, which enabled the pilot to fire a machine gun through the arc of the propeller. The aircraft used was the Morane-Saulnier Type G, and it was in this aircraft, fitted with the bullet deflector system, that Garros was shot down and captured by the Germans.

The Type G drew the attention of the Graham-White Company in England, who obtained the rights to manufacture the aircraft under licence. The aircraft proved to be very popular with civilian pilots and ultimately drew the attention of the military. At the beginning of the war, the RFC annexed one of the aircraft and it served first with No. 1 Reserve Aeroplane Squadron, and later with No. 60 Squadron, RFC. The Type H had also appeared on the scene, and the RFC ordered six of both types. The RNAS also obtained two Type Gs; the first was commandeered and assigned to No. 2 (N) Squadron, the second was ordered from the Graham-White Company.

The Type G was a two-seat, parasol fighter/reconnaissance aircraft of simple construction with a fully faired, box-shaped, wooden fuselage, a fixed vertical fin and shoulder-fitted, wire braced wings supported by a central cabane mounted in front of the pilot. It was powered by an 80-hp Le Rhône engine which gave the aircraft a top speed of 85 mph. The Type H was a single-seat parasol fighter almost identical in specification to the Type G, and of the same basic design.

The United Kingdom purchased four Type H aircraft, and then acquired a further twenty-four that were built under licence by the Graham-White Company. Portugal acquired a single version for use as a trainer. What was surprising was that the Pfalz Flugzeugwerk in Germany was granted a licence to build the Type H, from which the company developed the Pfalz Type E fighter. Considering that there were rumblings of war at the time, it is a mystery how they were allowed to do this.

At the end of December 1914, with the war only three months old, the RFC ordered the improved version of the Type L. The design of this aircraft was markedly different from the previous models, inasmuch as the parasol wing was increased in length by one metre, mounted above the fuselage and, like the other models, braced to a tall central cabane. By the end of April, No. 3 Squadron, RFC had fourteen Type Ls, and by the end of 1915 No. 1 Squadron had been re-equipped with the aircraft.

The threat from Zeppelin raids was becoming a cause for concern for the British, and the RNAS endeavoured to intercept these raids as best they could, but they had no aircraft capable of climbing to the heights at which the majority of the Zeppelins operated. On 7 June 1915, however, the RNAS scored its first major success, when Flight Sub-Lieutenant Rex Warneford attacked and destroyed the German Zeppelin LZ37 while it was returning from a patrol. Flying a Morane-Saulnier Type L parasol-winged fighter, Warneford attacked the heavily armed LZ37 as it passed over Ghent. Shutting off his engine, Warneford glided down until he was about 150 feet above the giant Zeppelin, and then released the first of his four bombs. At first he though nothing had happened, so he dropped the second, third and fourth, until the gas inside the Zeppelin suddenly ignited and the LZ37 turned into a flaming inferno. The flaming wreckage plunged to the ground, landing on top of a convent just outside Ghent. Remarkably, one member of the crew, Steurmann (Helmsman) Alfred Mühler, survived the crash with only minor injuries, although a number of civilians were killed and injured when the burning wreckage crashed on top of them, including a nun and a number of orphan children.

Sub-Lieutenant Rex Warneford had given the British the boost that they desperately needed, showing that the Zeppelin menace was vulnerable. He was awarded the Victoria Cross for his bravery.

Another type appeared in 1916, the Morane-Saulnier Type. The aircraft had been developed back in 1913 and given the designation Type I, but had never been offered to the military. The new model was based on the Type N, but had a larger wingspan and elevators. The success the RFC had with the Type N prompted them to order four of the aircraft, but it was soon discovered that it was a very difficult aircraft to handle under combat conditions, and so was relegated to the training squadrons. The Imperial Russian Air Service, however, ordered twenty of the aircraft, all of which were delivered by October 1916.

At the beginning of January 1916, Major General Trenchard gave instructions that fifty Morane-Saulnier Type LAs were to be obtained by May. The problem that faced the procurement department was that there were still thirteen Type LAs still outstanding from a previous order, and the twenty that had been delivered were still awaiting engines. There were also concerns from the manufacturers as stocks of ash wood were fast disappearing, and the only wood available that was suitable was pine.

Slowly but surely the Type L was replaced by the Type LA, and one of the first missions carried out by the aircraft was the attack on the Zeppelin sheds at Brussels, when five B.E.2cs and three Morane-Saulnier Type LAs dropped bombs from 1,000 feet. The fragile and flimsy appearance of the Morane-Saulnier parasol fighter belied the durability and overall strength of the aircraft. The Type L and LA were gradually being phased out by the Type N, which was powered by the 110-hp Le Rhône 9JB engine, giving the aircraft a top speed of 100 mph. The first model prototype arrived for the RFC to test, and the favourable report that it received led the way for an initial order for three aircraft. There was an initial delay with the delivery of the engines, but this was resolved, and a further order for another twenty was placed, and by September 1916 these had been delivered. This prompted a further order for forty-four more Type Ns, but once more the unavailability of the engines caused delays in delivery.

The need for single-seater fighters became increasingly urgent towards the end of 1915, so much so in fact, that because there was a delay in the delivery of the Bristol Fighter, the RFC had to order twenty-seven Morane-Saulnier Type Ns. The Type N design differed from the Type L and LA inasmuch as it reverted back to the original design, where the wings were fitted at the shoulders of the fuselage. Known sometimes as the Morane Bullet or Morane Scout, the RFC flew more Type Ns than the French

Aviation Militaire. A total of twenty-seven of the aircraft was acquired, and were assigned to three squadrons, Nos 1, 3 and 60. During the Battle of the Somme, No. 60 Squadron flew the Type N with great success against the Germans. The aircraft was not the easiest to fly, and some of the British pilots had real problems with its handling at low speed. One other disadvantage was that the Type N bore an uncanny resemblance to the Fokker E.III, which in the early days of aircraft recognition caused many an Allied soldier on the ground to open fire, mistaking it for a German aircraft.

By the time the 110-hp Le Rhône engines became available to fit in the Type N, those fitted with the engine had their designation changed to Type I. Only four were supplied to the RFC and they saw service with No. 60 Squadron, RFC. There appeared yet another version of the Type N at the same time, designated the Type V. This was a redesigned version with an extended wingspan, and an enlarged fuselage that carried a 50-litre fuel tank. Twelve of the aircraft were ordered after a favourable report on a prototype that had been sent to the front for evaluation. Two more were sent to No. 60 Squadron, but after one report from a front-line pilot that stated that the Type V 'was doing its best to kill you', the remainder were returned to England and relegated to training units.

At the beginning of 1915, Morane-Saulnier developed a two-seater biplane, which was a considerable departure from their normal aircraft, all of which up to this point had been monoplanes. The two-bay, equal-span reconnaissance aircraft, known as the Type BB, was powered by an 80-hp Le Rhône engine and used wing warping to obtain lateral control. The prototype was tested by the French Aviation Militaire, who turned it down, but the RFC showed an interest and after evaluating it, placed an order for ninety-two of the aircraft. There was one proviso with the order, and that was that the aircraft had to be powered by the 110-hp Le Rhône engine. Because of the reluctance of the French to release so many of these engines, the RFC reduced the order to eighty.

The aircraft was used widely for reconnaissance, and some were equipped with cameras and radio equipment in place of an observer. Armament consisted of a Lewis machine gun mounted on the top of the upper wing and a movable Lewis machine gun mounted on a ring in the observer's cockpit, when one was carried. Initially the aircraft was assigned to Nos 1 and 3 Squadrons, but as more and more became available, Nos 12 and 60 Squadrons were equipped with the aircraft, although a large number were used for training purposes. A policy statement on 29 January 1916 stated:

> When Morane Parasols are struck off they will be replaced by biplanes as these become available, until there are four biplanes in each of the two Morane Squadrons. These four biplanes will be formed into one flight in each squadron.

It was around this time that Morane-Saulnier produced an improved version of the Type N, the Type P. This coincided with a letter from Major-General Trenchard to Captain Lord Robert Innes-Ker of the British Aviation Supplies Department (BASD), instructing him to reduce the RFC's demand for Morane-Saulnier biplanes because of the crisis in the supply of engines. The Morane-Saulnier Company had intended to phase out the 110-hp Le Rhône engine, but because of increased pressure from the RFC this was shelved.

The order for the Type BB biplane was still being processed when the Type P appeared, and this caused the order to be reduced from thirty-six to twenty-four. Four of the Type Ps were ordered, with a provisional order in place for a further twenty-four if the aircraft passed evaluation. The results of the tests of the Type P were good, so good in fact that Brigadier-General Brooke-Popham increased the order to an additional thirty-six of the aircraft.

The Type P was a newly-designed Parasol with an enlarged fuselage, but incorporating the tail section of the Type LA. The ailerons were operated by the pilot, using a torsion rod that was connected to the vertical-actuating rod on the pilot's controls. There were a number of different modifications to the Type P, including fairings for cameras and wireless sets. In the observer's cockpit a machine gun was fitted with a movable mount, and the synchronised forward-firing machine gun was removed and replaced with a .303 Lewis machine gun mounted on the top of the wing.

The crisis in the delay of spares for the 110-hp Le Rhône engine had reached desperation point and, despite pleadings from the War Office, the French authorities refused to co-operate. The result was that Brigadier-General Brooke-Popham cancelled the order for thirty-six Type Ps and had the French authorities informed that aviation materials such as steel, Lewis and Vickers machine guns, ball bearings and other major parts required by the French would be withheld immediately unless the engines and spares were supplied. The French authorities agreed, and released twenty-four 110-hp Le Rhône 9J engines, all to be delivered before August 1916.

Because of the delay in obtaining the 110-hp Le Rhône 9J engine for the Type P, a number of the engines from the new Type BBs were used. Some of the Type Ps were fitted with the 80-hp Le Rhône, which reduced the operational performance. By the beginning of 1917, all the Type Ps with the 80-hp Le Rhône had been replaced and sent to training units.

After the Type P there were a number of variations produced in prototype form, but none were accepted by the BASD and no more Morane-Saulnier aircraft were ordered or purchased, although another French company was in the process of supplying both the RFC and the RNAS with aircraft – Nieport (Nieuport*)*.

In response to the requirement for a reconnaissance/bomber, the Morane-Saulnier Company put forward a design for a Type S aircraft. This was a three-bay, twin-engine biplane that carried a crew of three – a pilot and two gunners. After tests, the Aviation Militaire placed an order for 300 of the aircraft to be built, at a cost of 60 million francs. The French and British governments decided that this was an excessive amount of money, and ordered that the number of aircraft be reduced to just ninety. Angry at their judgement being questioned and their decision overridden, the Aviation Militaire cancelled the whole order and only the one aircraft was built.

Then, in an effort to placate the company, the Aviation Militaire placed an order for a smaller version of the Type S, known as the Type T. This was a five-bay, twin-engine biplane that carried a crew of three. The undercarriage consisted of the conventional pair of wheels mounted beneath the engines and, unusually, a pair of wheels mounted beneath the fuselage and in line with the other wheels. A large nosewheel was fixed beneath the nose of the aircraft.

The first tests were completed in August 1916 and ninety were ordered. Further testing, however, discovered there were airframe weaknesses that were sufficiently bad to cause a stop on production. Modifications were made and production restarted, the first aircraft being delivered on 1 August 1917. As more and more came off the production line and were delivered to the various escadrilles, more and more complaints came back highlighting weaknesses still affecting the airframe. At one point, a directive stated that if a forward gunner was not carried, ballast was to take his place. Another warned of flying the aircraft in bad weather. By the end of 1917 most of the Type Ts had been withdrawn from active service, much to the relief of the crews.

Another Morane-Saulnier single-seat fighter appeared on the scene in place of the Type I, the Type V. Like the Type I, this was in effect a Type N with the more powerful 110-hp Le Rhône 9J engine and a number of small modifications. Twelve of the aircraft were built exclusively for the RFC, but none were accepted by the Aviation Militaire.

A slightly different version appeared at the end of 1916, the Type AC. It differed inasmuch as the wings were shoulder-mounted and had external bracing, which took away the central pylon that usually held the supporting wires. The wings were fitted with ailerons, which controlled the lateral movement of the aircraft instead of the usual wing warping. It also incorporated the all-moving tailplane that had been a feature of the Type P, together with a triangular fin. Very similar in design to the Bristol Bullet, the aircraft was accepted by the Aviation Militaire after tests and thirty of the aircraft were ordered. The SPAD 7 replaced it the following year.

One of the most successful of all the Morane-Saulnier aircraft built during the First World War was the Type AI. This was a small, single-seat monoplane fighter based on the design of the Type AF, a single-seat biplane fighter, which, although it was accepted by the Aviation Militaire, was not ordered by them.

The fuselage of the Type AI was constructed of a mixture of metal and spruce wood, and was longer than the Type AF. The forward section of the fuselage was constructed of metal, and the rear section was of spruce covered in fabric. The wing had a slight sweepback, and was constructed in one piece of wood. It was braced by two metal struts on either side of the fuselage, which in turn were braced by additional struts in mid-span. The landing gear was constructed out of metal tubes, and in an inverted 'W' configuration.

The first tests of the aircraft were so successful that the Aviation Militaire ordered 1,100 of the aircraft to be built and gave it a designation of MoS. 27 C.1. This was for the version fitted with a single synchronised Vickers machine gun, while the twin-gun version was designated MoS. 29 C.1, and over 1,000 were ordered. The success of the aircraft prompted the Aviation Militaire to equip entire escadrilles with it. Reports coming back from the Front Line pilots were very favourable, and all looked set for more of these aircraft to be built. Then, for no apparent reason the aircraft was withdrawn from Front line service. One of the probable reasons was that there were problems with the 150-hp Gnome engine. This was supported by reports coming back from escadrilles using the MoS 27 and 29 stating that they had to reduce the number of long-distance, high altitude flights because of the unreliability of the Gnome engine. There were also some references to weaknesses with the wing bracings, but nothing was ever officially said.

The 135-hp Le Rhône engine was fitted into some of the MoS 27s and 29s in an effort to solve the problem, but to no avail. This model was designated the MoS.30, and fifty-one of these were purchased by the USAS as fighter trainers. Odd ones were acquired by some other countries but production of the aircraft was cancelled. This was in effect the last of the production aircraft to be built by the Morane-Saulnier company in the First World War. There were some other models of which only single models were built, including the Types AN, ANL, ANR, ANS, BB and BH.

SPECIFICATIONS

Morane-Saulnier Type L

Wing Span:	36 ft 8 in (11.2 m)
Length:	22 ft 4 in (6.8 m)
Height:	12 ft 6 in (3.9 m)
Weight Empty:	866 lb (393 kg)
Weight Loaded:	1,492 lb (677 kg)
Max. Speed:	77 mph (125 km/h)
Engine:	One 80-hp Le Rhône 9C
Armament:	One synchronised Lewis machine gun

Morane-Saulnier Type LA

Wing Span:	35 ft 8 in (10.9 m)
Length:	23 ft 1 in (7.1 m)
Height:	12 ft 6 in (3.9 m)
Weight Empty:	882 lb (400 kg)
Weight Loaded:	1,433 lb (650 kg)
Max. Speed:	85 mph (138 km/h)
Engine:	One 80-hp Le Rhône 9C
Armament:	One synchronised Lewis machine gun

Morane-Saulnier Type N

Wing Span:	26 ft 6 in (8.1 m)
Length:	19 ft 1 in (5.8 m)
Height:	7 ft 2 in (2.2 m)
Weight Empty:	776 lb (352 kg)
Weight Loaded:	979 lb (444 kg)
Max. Speed:	89 mph (144 km/h)
Engine:	One 80-hp Le Rhône 9C
Armament:	One synchronised Lewis machine gun

Morane-Saulnier Type P

Wing Span:	38 ft 0 in (11.6 m)
Length:	23 ft 1 in (7.1 m)
Height:	11 ft 5 in (3.5 m)
Weight Empty:	954 lb (433 kg)
Weight Loaded:	1,609 lb (730 kg)
Max. Speed:	100 mph (162 km/h)
Engine:	One 110-hp Le Rhône 9JB
Armament:	One synchronised Lewis machine gun
	One Lewis machine gun in observer's cockpit

Morane-Saulnier Type BB

Wing Span:	28 ft 1 in (8.6 m)
Length:	22 ft 6 in (6.9 m)
Height:	8 ft 6 in (2.6 m)
Weight Empty:	1,082 lb (491 kg)
Weight Loaded:	1,678 lb (761 kg)
Max. Speed:	83 mph (134 km/h)
Engine:	One 110-hp Le Rhône 9J
Armament:	One synchronised Lewis machine gun
	One Lewis machine gun in observer's cockpit

Lt Harvey-Kelly with his B.E.2a, No. 347.

B.E.2a No. 217 being serviced.

B.E.2c No. 2594, *River Plate No. 2.*

B.E.2c under construction at the Daimler works.

B.E.2c carrying out firing tests of the Le Prieur rocket system.

Lts Ridley and Chabot of No. 4 Squadron in the cockpit of their B.E.2c.

B.E.2c stuck at the top of a tree while the pilot figures out a way to get down.

B.E.12 prototype.

Close-up of the engine section of a B.E.12.

F.E.2a on a training flight.

F.E.2b A5645 being prepared for take-off.

F.E.2b No. A5478, *Gold Coast No. 10*.

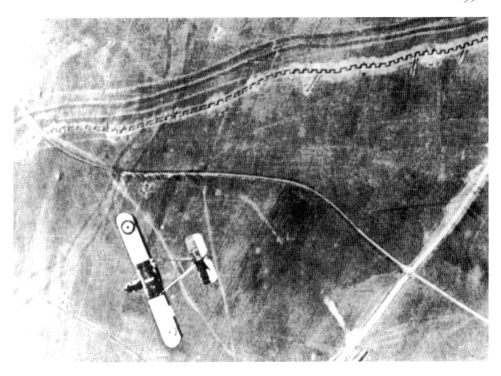

An F.E.2b on a reconnaissance flight over the Front.

F.E.2b No. 7666 after making a forced landing in someone's back garden.

R.E.8 No. A3598 of 15 Squadron RFC.

An Australian R.E.8 crew about to leave on a night-bombing mission.

Lts Hobbs and Chippendale of No. 15 Squadron RFC in their R.E.8.

R.E.8 No. A4267 of No. 52 Squadron RFC.

S.E.5a No. F927 of 29 Squadron RAF at Bickendorf.

S.E.5a pilot of 85 Squadron RAF at Saint-Omer, showing the unit's score.

S.E.5a of 141 Squadron at Biggin Hill.

S.E.5a under construction at the Wolseley Motor Co. plant in Birmingham. The aircraft are being fitted with 200-hp Wolseley Viper engines.

Salmson-Moineau S.M.1 of SOP 43.

Salmson 2 A2 of the 1st Aero Squadron, USAS.

Salmson 4 two-seat ground attack aircraft.

Commander Samson about to take off from HMS *Africa* in his Short S.27.

Short 827 in East Africa being prepared for take-off.

Short 184 about to launch from the slipway.

Short 310A dropping its torpedo during trials in the Solent.

Sopwith Camel No. B3811, powered by a 100-hp Gnome Monosoupape engine.

A side view of Sopwith Camel No. B5157.

Cockpit area of a Sopwith Camel, showing the twin machine guns.

Cockpit and instrument panel of a Sopwith Camel.

Société Anonyme des Établissements Nieuport

The development of one of France's foremost aircraft of World War One, the Nieuport, started life in a small back street workshop at Darracq. Édouard de Nieport started business designing and making magnetos and starter motors for car engines; this developed into producing them for aircraft engines. In 1909, Édouard Nieport decided to design and build his own engine and in order to test it, built an aircraft to his own design. Why the name Nieport was changed to Nieuport is not known, but it is thought that he changed the spelling of his name purely for business reasons.

One of the first aircraft to attract the attention of the Royal Flying Corps was the two-seater Nieuport Monoplane. The aircraft was powered by a 50-hp Gnome engine and was purchased by the RFC in September 1911, assigned to the Aeroplane Company of the Air Battalion and given the serial number B.4. On 19 June 1912, two more Nieuport Monoplanes were purchased, one being powered by a 70-hp Gnome engine, the other by a 100-hp Gnome engine. The aircraft were assigned to No. 3 Squadron, RFC, and numbered 254 and 255 respectively. With the arrival of the latest Nieuport Monoplanes, the B.4 was given the number 253.

In November 1912, after extensive flying, it was found that the fabric covering both the wings and fuselage of No. 253 needed replacing. In January 1913, it was found that the fabric once again needed replacing. The aircraft was crated and shipped off to the Royal Aircraft Factory, but the work was never completed and it was eventually scrapped. The other two, after being flown and tested at Farnborough, were also assigned to the Royal Aircraft Factory, where they too remained.

Just after the start of the First World War the RNAS purchased twelve Nieuport 6H seaplanes, specifically for use as trainers. The 6H was a two-seat monoplane with the wings fitted at the shoulders of the fuselage, and was powered by either an 80 or 100-hp Gnome engine. The floats were unusual in their design inasmuch as they had a thin, flat profile and had a 'stepped' bottom that enabled the aircraft to land safely in rough seas. The floats were approximately one-third the length of the fuselage, with an additional tail float suspended beneath the elongated fin and in front of the section of rudder under the fuselage.

The Nieuport 6H flying boat was operated by the French Aviation Maritime extensively in the Adriatic and Middle East, but never by the British.

The first of the Nieuports to see service with the British was the Nieuport 10 after the RNAS purchased twelve of the aircraft early in 1915. The development of the Nieuport 10 two-seater biplane had come about after demand for their monoplane had gone into a steep decline. Both the British and French favoured the biplane, considering them sturdier and more practical for reconnaissance purposes. Designed by Gustav Delage, the Nieuport 10 was a single bay sesquiplane; the upper wing was of conventional design, while the lower wing was literally half the length of the upper, and with a much narrower chord. The lower wing was braced to the upper wing by means of a V-shaped strut – one on either side.

The fuselage was of a standard box-like construction, made of pine and ash and covered with a linen fabric, with a rounded fairing on top. The tail section was constructed from metal tubes and covered with a linen fabric.

The prototype was powered by a single 80-hp Le Rhône engine, which gave the aircraft a top speed of 68 mph (110 km/h). Initially the observer/gunner sat in front of the pilot, but when the gunner had to stand up in order to fire the machine gun, it quickly became obvious that the pilot's view forward would be obscured. There were a number of other problems, including excessive engine vibration and an undercarriage track that was too narrow.

With the problems ironed out, the RNAS accepted the aircraft as they came off the production line and they were assigned to Nos 1, 3, and 4 Wings, RNAS. Although it was used primarily in a reconnaissance role, when flown as a single-seat fighter it proved to be a worthy adversary to the Germans.

As a result of the relative success of the Nieuport 10 when used as a single-seat fighter, the Nieuport 11, a single-seat fighter, was developed. The construction of the aircraft was similar to that of the Nieuport 10, inasmuch as it was a sesquiplane with a box-like fuselage with a rounded fairing on top, albeit of smaller dimensions. The track of the undercarriage had been widened, giving increased stability to the aircraft when landing and taking off.

The aircraft was found to be difficult to fly under combat conditions, but in the hands of a skilled and experienced pilot could more than hold its own against any German fighters. Unfortunately the life expectancy of a First World War fighter pilot was quite short, so there were not that many experienced fighter pilots around. What was required was a fighter aircraft that could be handled easily and safely by even the most inexperienced pilots.

The RNAS ordered eighteen Nieuport 11s, assigning them to Nos 1, 2 and 4 Wings. They were relatively successful, and consideration was given to transferring six of the aircraft to the RFC, but the move never took place.

The underpowered Nieuport 10 was regarded by the RNAS as useless as a reconnaissance aircraft, but the arrival of the Nieuport 12 powered by a 110-hp Clerget 9Z engine changed their minds. The design of the Nieuport 12 was almost an enlarged version of the Nieuport 10, and attracted the attention of both the RNAS and the RFC. They saw it as a two-seat fighter/reconnaissance aircraft, and after testing one, the RNAS ordered thirty with an additional fifty to follow when William Beardmore & Co. in England built the aircraft under licence. The first batch arrived early in 1916, and was assigned to Nos 1 and 2 Wings. In June 1916, Major-General Trenchard approached the Admiralty for help in strengthening the RFC in time for the Battle of the Somme. In an order issued by the Admiralty on 28 June 1916, it was requested that:

> Starting from 1 July, if possible, three Beardmore Nieuport two-seater, 110-hp Clerget machines per week, but not less that two per week up to a total of 20 machines. These machines will be supplied without guns. Army to make arrangements as to their transference from Messrs Beardmore, Dalmuir.

The first of the Beardmore-built Nieuport 12s was sent to the CFS Testing Flight at Upavon. The report that followed the intensive testing that the aircraft was subjected to was dismal, saying that in the opinion of the Test Flight, even with extensive modifications, they considered it unfit for overseas service. Despite the damning report, ten of the aircraft were immediately dispatched to No. 46 Squadron, RFC, at Saint-Omer, France. The squadron then moved to Droglandt, where it was used until it was replaced by Sopwith Pups some months later.

A further twenty Nieuport 12s were delivered to the RFC over the next few months, and were assigned to various training units and squadrons getting prepared for operations. A number of Nieuport 12s were fitted with the 110-hp Le Rhône 9J engines and given the designation Nieuport 20. At the end of August 1916, two of the Nieuport 20s were delivered to the RFC and immediately underwent extensive testing at Villacoublay. Interestingly enough, the French Aviation Militaire never accepted the aircraft, and the thirty of these aircraft that were delivered to the RFC were specially constructed to RFC specifications.

Delivery of the aircraft was painfully slow, and by the end of March 1917 only twenty-one of the thirty ordered had been delivered.

At the beginning of 1916, a development of the Nieuport 11 had appeared – the Nieuport 16. Both the RNAS and the RFC placed orders for the aircraft, but just before the Battle for the Somme commenced the first three Nieuport 16s, which had been destined for the RNAS, were diverted and given to the RFC. This was followed by a further seventeen, which was the total ordered, leaving the RNAS with almost no effective fighter aircraft. One of the exponents of the Nieuport 16 was Lieutenant Albert Ball. Ball was later to become a top fighter ace, and was one of the few aviators in the First World War to be awarded the Victoria Cross.

As the Nieuport 16s were gradually replaced, they were sent to Scout School at Saint-Omer and used for training purposes.

As the popularity of the Nieuport aircraft began to take hold, the company decided to set up a factory and build their aircraft under licence. The first aircraft to be produced here was the Nieuport 17. The design of the Nieuport 17 differed from the 16 inasmuch as, although retaining the sesquiplane wing design, the lower wing was almost the same length but was considerably narrower. Ailerons were fitted to the top wing only. The fuselage was constructed in the usual box shaped configuration, but had rectangular cross-section frames braced with wire covered in linen fabric and strengthened with plywood panels. The longerons in front of the cockpit were made of ash, while the rear section longerons were made of spruce. The engine supports were made of tubular steel, while at the other end the tail section was also constructed of light steel tubing and covered in linen fabric. The undercarriage was supported by V-legs made of aluminium and supported by a steel tube cross member all sprung by rubber shock absorbers.

A number of different armaments were used on the Nieuport 17, including twin Vickers machine guns mounted on the top wing, a synchronised machine gun fixed to the centreline of the forward fuselage and four Le Prieur rockets mounted either side of the fuselage on the main struts.

The RNAS purchased three of the aircraft and assigned them to No. 3 Wing, RNAS, but within months they had been transferred to No. 1 Squadron, RFC. In late July, the ten Nieuport 17s ordered by the RFC began arriving. This was followed by an additional order in October 1916 for a further fifty, of which thirty-nine were delivered by the end of the year. The tests of the Le Prieur rockets were causing some concern among some of the pilots. The strut-mounted tubular launchers were causing some of the struts to collapse or twist out of shape. In one incident, 2nd Lieutenant Edward (Micky) Mannock was flying his Nieuport 17 when, on launching the rockets attached to the wing struts, the lower wing separated from the strut. He managed to fly the aircraft back to his base, but on landing the aircraft turned over. Mannock was unhurt, but the aircraft was badly damaged. The struts were strengthened, but the seeds of doubt had been sown, and although trials with the Le Prieur rockets continued, very few were ever fired in combat.

At the beginning of 1917, with losses of Allied aircraft climbing rapidly, another sixty Nieuport 17s were ordered by the RFC. To help maintain the British squadron strengths, the French military released 100 of their Nieuport aircraft, including a number of Nieuport 23s, and handed them over to the RFC. By the middle of 1917 however, the number of Sopwith Camels being produced by various companies had risen dramatically, and they quickly replaced the Nieuport 17s and 23s of Nos 1, 11, 29, 40 and 60 Squadrons of the RFC.

The RNAS during this period were still purchasing Nieuport aircraft and five Nieuport 21s were assigned to training squadrons, but never saw combat. One of the variants of the Nieuport 17 was the Nieuport 24, and that only differed from the Nieuport 17 in having a 120-hp Le Rhône engine fitted and a fully faired fuselage. Two prototype models were built and flown by French ferry pilots to No. 2 Aircraft Depot. On arrival, they complained bitterly about the aircraft's poor lateral control. The aircraft were tested by British pilots who confirmed the findings of their French counterparts. Four more of the aircraft were in the pipeline, and all six aircraft were relegated to Scout School.

Further investigation found that the cause of the poor lateral control was the canvas strips that covered the aileron hinge gaps. Once these had been removed, the problems with lateral control disappeared and the aircraft were returned to front line operations, seeing service in both France and the Middle East.

The last of the variants to see action was the Nieuport 27, which superseded the Nieuport 24. The aircraft was almost identical to the Nieuport 24, the only difference being the undercarriage, which had a divided axle, and each wheel had rubber cords fitted to articulated axles. In addition, the 27 had an internally mounted tailskid. There were some other minor differences, such as thicker V-struts and a slightly broader chord on the wings. In August 1917, the RFC replaced their now ageing Nieuport 17s and 23s with a total of seventy-one Nieuport 27s. They were assigned to Nos 1 and 29 Squadrons and saw service throughout France. Four saw service in Palestine in January 1918.

SPECIFICATIONS

Nieuport 6H-Seaplane

Wing Span:	43 ft 4 in (13.2 m)
Length:	28 ft 6 in (8.7 m)
Height:	8 ft 6 in (2.6 m)
Weight Empty:	1,201 lb (545 kg)
Weight Loaded:	1,753 lb (795 kg)
Max. Speed:	68 mph (110 km/h)
Engine:	One 80-hp Gnome
	One 100-hp Gnome
Armament:	None

Nieuport 10

Wing Span:	25 ft 9 in (7.9 m)
Length:	22 ft 9 in (7.0 m)
Height:	8 ft 6 in (2.6 m)
Weight Empty:	882 lb (400 kg)
Weight Loaded:	1,433 lb (650 kg)
Max. Speed:	71 mph (115 km/h)
Engine:	One 80-hp Le Rhône 9C
Armament:	One Lewis machine gun

Nieuport 11

Wing Span:	24 ft 6 in (7.5 m)
Length:	18 ft 0 in (5.5 m)
Height:	8 ft 2 in (2.4 m)
Weight Empty:	705 lb (320 kg)
Weight Loaded:	1,058 lb (480 kg)
Max. Speed:	100 mph (162 km/h)
Engine:	One 80-hp Le Rhône 9C
Armament:	One Lewis machine gun

Nieuport 12 & 20

Wing Span:	29 ft 5 in (9.0 m)
Length:	23 ft 1 in (7.1 m)
Height:	8 ft 10 in (2.7 m)
Weight Empty:	1,212 lb (550 kg)
Weight Loaded:	1,819 lb (825 kg)
Max. Speed:	90 mph (146 km/h)
Engine:	One 110-hp Clerget 9Z (Nieuport 12)
	One 110-hp Le Rhône 9J (Nieuport 20)
Armament:	One free-moving Lewis machine gun
	One fixed forward-firing Vickers machine gun

Nieuport 16

Wing Span:	24 ft 7 in (7.5 m)
Length:	18 ft 4 in (5.6 m)
Height:	7 ft 10 in (2.4 m)
Weight Empty:	826 lb (375 kg)
Weight Loaded:	1,212 lb (550 kg)
Max. Speed:	102 mph (165 km/h)
Engine:	One 110-hp Le Rhône 9J
Armament:	One synchronised/flexible mounted Lewis machine gun
	Eight Le Prieur rockets

Nieuport 17

Wing Span Upper:	26 ft 6 in (8.1 m)
Wing Span Lower:	25 ft 6 in (7.8 m)
Length:	19 ft 0 in (5.8 m)
Height:	7 ft 10 in (2.4 m)
Weight Empty:	826 lb (375 kg)
Weight Loaded:	1,234 lb (560 kg)
Max. Speed:	102 mph (165 km/h)
Engine:	One 110-hp Le Rhône 9Ja
Armament:	One synchronised/flexible mounted Vickers machine gun
	Eight Le Prieur rockets

Nieuport 24

Wing Span Upper:	26 ft 6 in (8.1 m)
Wing Span Lower:	25 ft 6 in (7.8 m)
Length:	19 ft 0 in (5.8 m)

Height: 7 ft 10 in (2.4 m)
Weight Empty: 782 lb (355 kg)
Weight Loaded: 1,206 lb (547 kg)
Max. Speed: 109 mph (176 km/h)
Engine: One 130-hp Le Rhône 9Jb
Armament: One synchronised/flexible mounted Vickers machine gun

Nieuport 27

Wing Span Upper: 26 ft 9 in (8.2 m)
Wing Span Lower: 25 ft 6 in (7.8 m)
Length: 19 ft 0 in (5.8 m)
Height: 7 ft 10 in (2.4 m)
Weight Empty: 837 lb (380 kg)
Weight Loaded: 1,206 lb (535 kg)
Max. Speed: 109 mph (179 km/h)
Engine: One 130-hp Le Rhône 9Jb
Armament: One synchronised/flexible mounted Vickers machine gun

Norman Thompson Flight Company
(White & Thompson Company)

One of the lesser-known flying boat manufacturers of the First World War was the Norman Thompson Company, which despite only being small, produced some of the best flying boats of the era. The company had started life in 1909, when Norman Thompson entered into a partnership with Douglas White to create an aircraft manufacturing company known as White & Thompson Ltd at Middleton, near Bognor (later Bognor Regis), and built Curtiss seaplanes under licence.

In 1914, they entered one of their flying boats, the White & Thompson Seaplane No. 2 (which was based on the American Curtiss design), in the *Daily Mail* Circuit of Britain Race, but the race was cancelled because of the outbreak of the war. The White & Thompson No. 2 was taken over by the RNAS and used for training purposes.

At the beginning of 1915, a landplane was built by the White & Thompson Company, called the *Bognor Bloater*. How it acquired the strange name is a mystery because the *Bloater* was a slim, two-bay biplane with the pilot and observer sitting in tandem. Powered by a single 70-hp Renault engine, ten of these aircraft were built for the RNAS and were assigned to coastal air stations at Killingholme, Great Yarmouth and Eastbourne. They were used for communication experiments and in various forms of training.

The White & Thompson Company were given a contract to build eight White & Thompson Type 2 flying boats, one of which was fitted with dual controls, and powered by a 120-hp Austro-Daimler engine. The hulls of these flying boats, built by S. E. Saunders of Newport, Isle of Wight, were constructed for side-by-side seating and made of a single-step design of mahogany Consuta plywood round an ash and spruce frame. The wings were of Royal Aircraft Factory (R.A.F.) No. 6 design, and the basic design of the aircraft was based on the Curtiss flying boat. This was followed by the White & Thompson Type 3, an improved version of the Type 2 powered by a 150-hp Hispano-Suiza engine. This was to be the forerunner of the very successful Norman Thompson N.T.2b, which appeared in November 1915. Eight production Type 3s were assigned to the RNAS, and were used extensively on anti-submarine duties.

The White & Thompson Company, in the meantime, had dropped the Curtiss contract when Captain Ernest Bass, an American, acquired an interest in the company. He was one of those instrumental in changing the company name to the Norman Thompson Flight Company on 4 October 1915.

The first seaplane to come out of the newly formed Norman Thompson company was a single-engined, two-seat flying boat designed by F. P. H. Beadle. This small flying boat was first tested in September 1917 and although the initial results were favourable, the final tests were unsatisfactory as far as performance went.

The S. E. Saunders Company built the Norman Thompson N.T.2b under licence on the Isle of Wight as did the Supermarine Aviation Works, as well as the parent company. Fitted with the 200-hp Sunbeam Arab engine, the N.T.2b had a top speed of 85 mph and a service ceiling of 11,400 feet. A derivative, the N.T.2a, was produced later in the war, but only the one was built. It was a tandem, two-seat seaplane that had a tadpole-shaped hull and wings that folded forward for ease of storage on board ships. It was powered by a 200-hp Hispano-Suiza pusher engine, but during trials the hull was damaged and by time the repairs had taken place and new trials commenced, the Armistice arrived.

A new model appeared at the end of 1917, the Norman Thompson N.T.4. This was a twin-engine aircraft built on very similar lines to those of the Curtiss H.4 seaplane. The main difference was that the N.T.4 had pusher engines as opposed to the tractor engines on the Curtiss. The first ten N.T.4s off the production line were powered by 150-hp Hispano-Suiza engines; the remaining models built were powered by 200-hp Hispano-Suizas and were designated N.T.4as. Because of their likeness to the Curtiss H.4 seaplane, they acquired the name of 'Small Americas' and this was to cause a certain amount of confusion. They were armed with a single Lewis gun mounted on a Scarff ring, and provision was made for bomb racks beneath the lower wing. One model was experimentally fitted with a 2-pounder Davis gun mounted in the bows, but the trials came to nothing.

Nineteen N.T.4as were ordered, but because of the problems experienced with the 200-hp Hispano-Suiza engines there were no further orders, and the project was cancelled.

Although the contribution made by the Norman Thompson Flight Company was small when compared with the other aircraft manufacturers, they still managed to produce seaplanes that helped control and safeguard the seaways around Britain.

SPECIFICATIONS

White & Thompson Type 2

Length of Hull:	24 ft 0 in (7.3 m)
Overall Length:	27 ft 6 in (8.3 m)
Wing Span:	45 ft 0 in (13.7 m)
Weight Empty:	Not Known
Weight Loaded:	2,400 lb (1,088 kg)
Engine:	One 120-hp Beardmore
	One 150-hp Hispano-Suiza
Maximum Speed:	65 mph (104 km/h)
Armament:	None Fitted

White & Thompson *Bognor Bloater*

No details available

Norman Thompson N.T. 2b

Length:	27 ft 4½ in (8.2 m)
Wing Span Upper:	48 ft 3½ in (14.6 m)
Wing Span Lower:	28 ft 6½ in (8.6 m)
Height:	10 ft 8 in (3.2 m)
Weight Empty:	2,321 lb (1,052 kg)
Weight Loaded:	3,169 lb (1,437 kg)
Maximum Speed:	85 mph (136 km/h)

Engine:	One 160-hp Beardmore
	One 200-hp Sunbeam Arab
	One 200-hp Hispano-Suiza
Armament:	None Fitted

Norman Thompson N.T.4/4a

Wing Span:	78 ft 7 in (23.9 m)
Length:	41 ft 6 in (12.6 m)
Height:	14 ft 10 in (4.5 m)
Weight Empty:	4,572 lb (2,073 kg)
Weight Loaded:	6,469 lb (2,934 kg)
Maximum Speed:	95 mph (152 km/h)
Ceiling:	11,000 feet (3,352 m)
Engines:	Two 150-hp Hispano-Suizas (N.T.4)
	Two 200-hp Hispano-Suizas (N.T.4a)
Armament:	One Lewis machine gun mounted on a Scarff ring
	Provision for bomb racks beneath the lower wing

The Royal Aircraft Factory

The Royal Aircraft Factory started life in 1906 at Farnborough, and was originally known as the 'Balloon Factory'. The balloon had been used by the military for some years and in June 1903, after the recent war in South Africa, a committee was set up to look at the future of using the balloon in a military context. The balloon establishment at the time was situated at Aldershot, and was part of the Corps of Royal Engineers. During an enquiry, where evidence was taken from two infantry generals who were involved in the war and a number of officers who had served in balloon sections in South Africa and the Sudan, it was decided that the Army should have an airship, and that balloon training should come under the control of one section of the Army. It was also decided to move the unit to a more central site, and Farnborough was the chosen place. It was to stay here in various forms for the next 100 years.

The Balloon School, as it became known, started to concentrate on various type of aeronautics as the years went on, although primarily it trained balloonists for the British Army. There were a number of civilians at the school, including Samuel Franklin Cody, whose work with man-carrying kites was legendary. In 1909, a civilian by the name of Mervyn O'Gorman was appointed Superintendent of the Balloon Factory, and he immediately set about recruiting specialist engineers with the intent of producing aircraft. Frederick M. Green, an engineering designer who had worked for the Daimler Company, joined him. Green then recruited a young designer by the name of Geoffrey de Havilland, who had just designed and built his own aeroplane. De Havilland arrived at the factory with his aeroplane and immediately set to work as both designer and test pilot. The Balloon Factory purchased de Havilland's aircraft for the sum of £400, and put it with a selection of other aircraft they had purchased. One of the Balloon School's aircraft, the Blériot XII tractor, had been badly damaged in an accident, and O'Gorman was granted permission from the War Office to rebuild the aircraft.

In 1911, the Balloon Factory was renamed 'The Army Aircraft Factory', although the Balloon School remained as an entirely different unit. In the same year, the Duke of Westminster sent the wreckage of his Voisin pusher biplane to the factory for repair. It was reconstructed and emerged from the factory as a B-class aeroplane. The class classification had been determined in line with other differing designs in the following manner:

Class B: Aircraft like the Avro, Antoinette, Blériot and Breguet whose main wings are preceded by the propeller and followed by a smaller plane, which is more lightly loaded.

Class F: Aircraft like the Bristol Boxkite, Farman or de Havilland designs whose main wings are followed by a smaller plane more lightly loaded, but with the propeller between the main wings and the tailplane.

Class S: Aircraft like the Santos-Dumont and Valkyrie, designs whose main wings are preceded by a small plane which is intensely loaded and succeeded by the propeller.

In June 1911, the rebuilt Blériot XII emerged from the workshops looking nothing like the original aircraft; in fact, the only original thing left on the aircraft was the 60-hp E.N.V engine. Known as the S.E.1, this was the first aircraft to be designed and built by the Royal Aircraft Factory, albeit using the components of another aircraft. This was to be followed at the end of the year by the emergence of the B.E.1 (Blériot Experimental), which was in reality a reconstruction and re-design of the Voisin pusher biplane that had been sent to the factory for repair, and had then been given to the factory by the Duke of Westminster.

Geoffrey de Havilland's aircraft too had been reconfigured, and was re-designated the F.E.1. The first flights of the F.E.1 were troublesome and a number of modifications had to be made. Then, on 2 August 1911, Geoffrey de Havilland took Lieutenant Theodore Ridge, the Assistant Superintendent of the factory, for a flight in the F.E.1. Ridge had recently learned to fly and was allowed to take the controls for a series of short hops. On 15 August, he flew the F.E.1 once again and on landing had a minor accident, which was quickly repaired. Growing in confidence, he decided to take the S.E.1 for a test flight, despite being told that it was an extremely difficult aircraft for a novice to fly. Attempting a tight turn in the aircraft caused it to go into a spin from which he could not recover, and the aircraft crashed into the ground. Ridge died from his injuries and the aircraft was wrecked beyond repair.

With the information gathered from redesigning and rebuilding the Voisin and the Blériot, the Royal Aircraft Factory decided to build an aircraft entirely of their own design. Geoffrey de Havilland carried out the majority of the design work under the watchful eye of Frederick Green, the chief designer. The B.E.1 was a two-bay biplane powered by a 60-hp V-8 water-cooled Wolseley engine. The upper wing was slightly larger than the lower and lateral control was achieved by warping the upper wing. The fuselage was built in two sections joined just behind the cockpit, and was constructed using spruce longerons crossbraced with ash timbers. Above the engine a large radiator was mounted vertically, which restricted the pilot's view considerably. The undercarriage consisted of long curved skids, to which two wheels were attached by means of a V-shaped steel tube assembly, which was in turn was attached by steel tubes to the underside of the fuselage.

The first flight of the B.E.1 took place on 4 December 1911 with Geoffrey de Havilland at the controls. There were a number of minor problems, all of which were easily solved, and by the end of December a total of ten flights had been made, some with passengers. During January a number of modifications were made, including the re-rigging of the wings to give them an angle of one degree on each plane, and the cutting down of the propeller tips in an effort to bring the engine speed up to 1,200 rpm. After extensive testing, the aircraft was handed over to Captain Burke of the Air Battalion on 11 March 1912. The engine continued to be troublesome, so in June it was returned to the factory and the engine was replaced with the 70-hp Renault engine. This considerably improved the aircraft's performance, and the pilot's view became less restricted.

A second model in the series, the B.E.2, made its appearance on 1 February 1912, and was almost identical to the first model with the exception of the engine, which was the 70-hp Renault V-8, and the wings, which were of equal span. The initial trials went without mishap, and on 5 February, Geoffrey de Havilland demonstrated the aircraft to the Advisory Committee for Aeronautics, but after the flight it was discovered that it had cracked an engine flywheel. The B.E.2 second model was grounded for the next three weeks while the engine was stripped down and repaired.

The aircraft went through a series of tests and a number of trials were carried out, one of them concerning the installation of a wireless set in the aircraft. Tests were carried out on a wireless-controlled artillery trial, and the reports that came back were extremely favourable. In April 1912, the third B.E in the series was produced, the B.E.3. It differed from the previous two models because although it had the same wing structure, the B.E.3 had a very pronounced forward stagger. The construction of the fuselage was almost identical to the B.E.1 and 2, the only difference being that the section in front of the pilot was shaped in the same way as the 50-hp Gnome engine that powered it. The rear section of the fuselage tapered down to a large tail section and an ear-shaped rudder.

The first flight took place on 3 May 1912, was flown by Geoffrey de Havilland and was a complete success. It was so successful, in fact, that a number of flights took place on that day with passengers. One incident two days later, when the tip of the propeller struck the ground on landing, caused the undercarriage to be redesigned. The trials carried out afterwards showed no further problems. Then the B.E.4 appeared, which was again almost identical to the three previous models, but was fitted with a 70-hp Gnome radial engine. This was followed by the B.E.5, which was initially powered by a 60-hp ENV water-cooled engine, but the engine was changed to a 70-hp Renault, making it identical to the B.E.1.

In August 1912, the Military Aeroplane Competition took place at Larkhill and the Royal Aircraft Factory decided to enter their B.E.2. However, one of the judges was found to be Mr Mervyn O'Gorman, Superintendent of the Royal Aircraft Factory, making the B.E.2 entry into the competition ineligible. It was decided to use the B.E.2 at the trials as a general runabout and let it enter some of the trials to make up the numbers. Then a problem arose, when, after S. F. Cody had been declared the winner, it was discovered that the B.E.2 had in effect obtained better results and performed better all round than any other aircraft in the competition, including the winner.

The War Office decided that despite Cody's aeroplane being the winner of the competition, they would place an order for the B.E.2. In an effort to encourage the growth of aircraft manufacturers, with the war clouds gathering in Europe, additional orders for the B.E.2a, as it was now designated, were placed with Handley Page Ltd., Coventry Ordnance and Armstrong Whitworth & Co. as well as with the Royal Aircraft Factory. A number of modifications were made to later production models, which included making the wings of equal span and designing and fitting a new tailplane. A revised fuel system placed the fuel tank inside the fuselage, behind the engine and in front of the pilot's cockpit, with the main pressure tank remaining beneath the pilot's seat.

The first B.E.2a rolled off the production line on 12 January 1913 and was assigned to No. 2 Squadron RFC at Farnborough, where it joined the B.E.1. The B.E.2 remained at the Royal Aircraft Factory, where it was used for experimental work and for testing modifications. A number of B.E.2as were assigned to the RNAS for training purposes.

In June 1912, Edward Busk joined the company and set about designing the next generation of the B.E.2a. What he produced was the B.E.2b, which had a much stronger wing structure than that of the 2a and was considerably more stable, but was identical in specification. Powered by a 90-hp R.A.F.1a engine, the 2b had a top speed of 86 mph and an endurance of three hours.

As with the B.E.2a, manufacture of the 2b was given to various companies including Armstrong Whitworth, Whitehead Aircraft Co. and Jonques Aviation. With production of the B.E.2b well under way, Busk started on the development of the B.E.2c, which in reality was no more than a modified B.E.2a, powered by a 70-hp Renault engine. The tail section was replaced by a rectangular tailplane which was fitted between the longerons of the fuselage, rather than on top of the fuselage.

A number of other modifications were made which increased the stability of the aircraft and Major Sefton-Branker, the officer in charge of RFC supplies, demonstrated this to good effect. He had been invited to Farnborough to test the aircraft himself, and during a flight from Farnborough to Netheravon was able to write a report on the countryside over which he was flying without having to touch the control column. Only when he was about to land did he find it necessary to take over the controls. The RFC had now acquired the ideal observation platform, and Major Sefton-Branker was quick to realise this. Other service pilots flew the B.E.2c and all commented on its stability in the air, giving it the nickname 'Stability Jane', which was later changed to 'Quirk'.

During this period, a two-seat seaplane appeared – the H.R.E. (Hydro Reconnaissance Experimental) 2. It had been initially designed as a landplane, but then it was decided to fit floats for the Naval Wing of the RFC and tests were carried out. These amounted to nothing and the aircraft was reverted back to a landplane, which was still in service at the outbreak of war. Only the one was built.

A second prototype B.E.2c was built, this time powered by the 90-hp R.A.F.1a engine. Then tragedy struck on 5 November 1914, when Edward Busk, the plane's designer, was carrying out a test flight in the aircraft. A leak from the petrol tank caught fire and within seconds, flames had engulfed the aircraft. The B.E.2c crashed on Laffan's Plain, killing Busk.

With the outbreak of war, the production lines for the B.E.2c went into top gear. The advantage the Royal Aircraft Factory had over the other manufacturers was that they were geared up for mass production. Car, furniture, carriage makers and agricultural machinery manufacturers were being brought into the production lines, because they had the necessary skilled tradesmen. As the war progressed, so did the development of the aircraft and in June 1915 another variation of the B.E. series appeared, the B.E.2d. This model was fitted with dual controls, and the main fuel tank was moved to a position between the pilot and the observer's cockpit. Not long after production of the B.E.2d had started, the B.E.2e had superseded it. The production lines were stopped, and the ones already built were sent to training establishments.

The B.E.2e had an increased upper wingspan and a shorter lower wingspan, giving the aircraft a large overhang. The bracing of this outer section of wing was carried out by removing the outer pair of interplane struts and bracing it from inverted 'V' kingposts that were positioned above the remaining pair of struts. The tail section came from the B.E.2c. It was powered by a 90-hp R.A.F.1a engine, which gave the aircraft a top speed of 97 mph. The next model that appeared was the B.E.2f and that was in fact a hybrid, using the fuselage from a B.E.2c with the modified wings of a B.E.2e. It was decided that if the fuselage of the B.E.2d were used with the wings of the B.E.2e, they would be given the designation B.E.2g.

In the middle of 1915, with the B.E.2c in the front line carrying out numerous reconnaissance missions, a faster upgraded version was needed. With this in mind, it was decided to design a long-range single-seat reconnaissance/bomber using a converted B.E.2c as the prototype. The observer's cockpit was removed and faired over, and the space used to accommodate a larger fuel tank. The twin-skid type undercarriage was replaced with a substantially stronger 'V' type and a 140-hp V-12 R.A.F.4a engine was fitted. It was given the designation B.E.12, and the initial test flights were excellent. As Mervyn O'Gorman pointed out to the War Office, it was essentially a B.E.2c, and any pilot familiar with this aircraft could easily fly the B.E.12. This, of course, dispensed with any need for familiarisation flights and the aircraft could be put straight into squadron service.

Camera mountings were fitted on the starboard side of the fuselage on the earlier models, but no armament. Later models were fitted with a belt-fed Vickers machine gun, together with Vickers-Challenger synchronisation gear. Despite the fact that the B.E.12 was not exactly a new design, the production models that were being built by the Daimler and Standard Motor Companies were very slow in coming off the production line, and the first of these arrived at Farnborough in March 1916. The reason given for this was that there were problems with the R.A.F.4a engine. By this time, of course, the whole nature of aerial warfare had changed and the need for fighters was far greater than the need for reconnaissance aircraft, so the B.E.12 was assigned to fighter squadrons, for which it was totally unsuitable because of its lack of manoeuvrability. Within months, and after the loss of a number of the aircraft, the B.E.12 was returned to its original role of photo-reconnaissance/bomber.

The appearance of an improved model, the B.E.12a, was short-lived, although orders were placed for fifty of them to be built by Daimler and the Coventry Ordnance Works. This was superseded by the B.E.12b, which was powered by a 200-hp Hispano-Suiza engine and fitted with twin Lewis machine guns mounted above the top wing and operated by means of a swivel mechanism. An order for 100 of these aircraft was placed with the Daimler Company, but very few of them were ever completed, as the Zeppelin menace, for which they had been earmarked, had all but disappeared.

The B.E. series of aircraft produced by the Royal Aircraft Factory operated in every theatre of the war, and was used extensively by the Australian Flying Corps in the Middle East to great effect. Despite the earlier shortcomings, the BE acquitted itself well throughout the conflict and after the war in the civil aviation world.

F.E. SERIES (FARMAN EXPERIMENTAL)

Before the Royal Aircraft Factory came into being, it was known as the Army Aircraft Factory and it was with this company that Geoffrey de Havilland was to make his name as both designer and test pilot. When he arrived at the company, he brought with him his own aircraft that he had designed and had built by the Iris Motor Company. The factory purchased the aircraft for £400 and modifications were made to improve the speed and stability. Given the designation of F.E.1, a number of test flights were carried out and some re-construction work carried out, but on one of the test flights it crashed and was badly damaged. The wreckage was rebuilt and the aircraft re-designated the F.E.2, and incredibly it was flown the day after the crash. The modifications made could not have been that extensive, and so it must have been almost identical to the original.

Extensive tests were carried out with the F.E.2, using the aircraft as a flying test bed for new designs. On one test a Maxim machine gun was fitted in the front cockpit, but there are no records regarding any firing tests being carried out.

Another F.E.2 was produced during the summer of 1915. It was a completely re-designed version with fully enclosed cockpit nacelles, and was powered by a 70-hp Renault air-cooled engine. The main gravity-fed cylindrical fuel tank was situated behind the pilot's head and shoulders. The equal-span wings were based on those of the B.E.2a, but were longer and had been modified to help support the steel tube tailbooms, above which were fitted the horizontal tail surfaces. During trials at Wittering, the aircraft spun into the ground killing the passenger, Ewart T. Haynes, but the pilot, Roland Kemp, survived with just a broken leg.

The information gathered from this design, and from the trials, resulted in a most unusual model, the F.E.3. It also carried the designation A.E.1 – Armed Experimental. Although fitted with the undercarriage of the F.E.2, the cockpit and engine nacelle were of a completely new design. Powered by a 100-hp Chenu engine, which was mounted close to the front of the aircraft, and with a large circular hole in the nose for additional air-cooling, it had a shaft that passed under the pilot's seat, which drove the chains that turned the four-bladed propeller. One of the most striking features of the aircraft was the tail section that was attached to a single boom, unlike other models that had four booms supporting the tail unit. The tail unit was braced with wires attached to the upper wings and the undercarriage, but despite the ingenuity behind the design the tail section was found to be less rigid than the four-boom design. After a number of test flights by Geoffrey de Havilland and Roland Kemp, both of whom criticised the design, a four-boom support section was installed. The one-pounder gun developed by the Coventry Ordnance Works that had been destined for the F.E.3 was never installed; instead, trials were carried out with a single Lewis machine gun. The F.E.3 never went farther than the prototype and the design was re-developed, producing the F.E.2a.

With the war now firmly under way, production of the F.E.2a began after an order from the War Office for twelve of the aircraft. The first production model was ready for the Aeronautical Inspection Department (AID) at the end of January 1915. The first initial test flight showed that the aircraft was greatly underpowered and the 100-hp Green engine was replaced by the 120-hp Austro-Daimler, which was being built under licence by the Beardmore Company. The fitting of the 120-hp Beardmore engine, as it was now called, necessitated in major modifications of the engine nacelle, as the engine was almost fully enclosed. It needed larger air scoops to cool the radiator and a streamlined gravity tank was fitted under the upper section. With the new engine fitted and the modifications made, the test flights were very successful.

A problem arose when it was realised that the 120-hp Beardmore engine was also powering the R.E.5, which was already in production. The engine became in short supply, and so the building of the F.E.2a was not hurried, and it wasn't until May that the next model appeared. Number ten of the twelve ordered did not appear until October, and was assigned to No. 16 Squadron, RFC, the previous nine having been assigned to No. 6 Squadron, RFC.

The F.E.2a was armed with a single Lewis machine gun, mounted on a swivelling pillar that was fixed to the floor of the cockpit in front of the pilot. The gunner's position was extremely vulnerable because when the gunner/observer stood up to fire the machine gun, almost three-quarters of his body was above the edge of the cockpit. This was highlighted on many occasions when the aircraft was being thrown about during a dogfight, and the gunner/observer had to hold on for dear life to prevent himself being thrown out, despite being anchored by a safety cable.

The F.E.2a was an extremely lively aircraft, and more than capable of holding its own in a dogfight. On one occasion, Oberleutnant Max Immelmann led a Jasta from Flieger Abteilung 9 (FA.9) of seven Fokker E.IVs against two F.E.2as from No. 25 Squadron, RFC. During the dogfight, one of the F.E.2as was shot down. The other, flown by 2nd Lieutenant G. R. McGubbin with his gunner/observer Corporal J. H. Waller, fought ferociously and shot down the legendary Max Immelmann, which was a massive blow to the morale of the Germans.

A modified F.E.2a, the F.E.2b, appeared at the end of 1915 with its modified 'V' undercarriage, disposing of the need for the nosewheel section. This was the most prolific of all the F.E. models. Because of the number ordered, other manufacturers like G. & J. Weir, Boulton & Paul, Ransomes, Sims & Jeffries, Garratt & Sons, Alex. Stephen & Sons and Barclay, Curle had to be brought in to keep up with the demand. For a couple of the manufacturers, this was the first time they had ever built an aircraft. Bolton & Paul was one of these, but ultimately went on to make fighter aircraft of its own.

Initially the F.E.2b had a flight endurance of 2½ hours, but reconnaissance duties realistically required at least 3½ hours, so a request was put in for an additional 8-gallon fuel tank to be installed. It was later realised that even this would not be sufficient, so more powerful engines were installed and an additional 18-gallon tank was fitted under the pilot's seat.

A number of modifications were carried out using the F.E.2b as an experimental platform. One experiment concerned the fitting of a 6-foot rod to the nose of the aircraft with wires running from the tip of the rod to the tips of both lower wing tips. This had come about after a squadron aircraft had run into a balloon cable and had crashed. The idea was to see that if the aircraft ran into a balloon cable, the cable would slide along the wire stretched to the wingtip and slip away. An experiment was carried out and the collision caused the aircraft to go into a spin from which the pilot, Captain Roderick Hill, only just managed to recover. The idea was not adopted.

Other experiments were carried out using twin Lewis machine guns with a small searchlight, powered by a small wind-powered generator mounted just below the cockpit nacelle. Even flotation trials were carried out using air bags fitted to the underside of the cockpit nacelle after a proposal for a seaplane version.

The first of the F.E.2bs was fitted with a single Lewis machine gun in the observer's position, carried on a horizontal rail with a Mk I mounting. A number of trials were carried out with a variety of mountings, but it was decided that the Anderson mounting (Mk I) was to be the standard one. This was a fixed pillar that was installed centrally on the front edge of the observer's cockpit. Later versions had the pillar attached to a universal joint that was fixed to the floor of the cockpit. This enabled the Lewis machine gun to be moved in a variety of positions while still being held rigid. Another version allowed the observer to fire rearwards over the top of the upper wing. This of course meant that the observer/gunner had himself to be anchored, by means of a safety cable.

The F.E.2c night version, where the cockpit positions were switched, the pilot being in front and the observer/gunner behind, followed the F.E.2b. Only seventeen of these models were eventually built or modified.

The F.E.2d model reverted back to the pilot sitting behind the observer/gunner, but some models were fitted with two Lewis machine guns, one mounted on a swivel pillar pointing forwards, the other fitted to a device called the Anderson arch which allowed for firing behind and above. This aircraft was powered by a 250-hp Rolls-Royce Mk I engine, and the initial order from the war office was for forty. The prototype was first flight tested on 7 May 1916 and although superior in speed and climb rate, it was found to be considerably slower to manoeuvre, was heavy on the controls and nose heavy, which caused a number of problems when landing. The problem was that these anomalies came about when the aircraft was in full production, and the first batch that had been ordered was completed at the end of August. The first thirty were fitted with the 250-hp Rolls-Royce Mk I, the remaining ten with the Mk.III engine.

Originally, the F.E.2d was produced as a stopgap to replace the F.E.2bs that were being lost or damaged in combat. The first of the F.E.2ds to be delivered to France unfortunately landed up in the hands of the Germans almost intact. The pilot, 2nd Lieutenant S. C. T. Littlewood, together with his passenger, Lieutenant D. Lyall Grant, flew over the Channel and got lost. Spotting an airfield below them they dropped down and landed, only to find they had landed on the airfield belonging to Flieger Abteilung (Fl.Abt.) 292. On landing the aircraft displayed its nose heaviness and stood on its nose, sustaining a little damage. Unfortunately, no damage was sustained by the new 250-hp Rolls-Royce engine, giving the Germans access to the latest aero engine. Both officers were taken prisoner.

The F.E.2d managed to get to France intact, and thirteen of them were assigned to No. 20 Squadron on 1 July 1916, the only unit to be flying the aircraft at the time. It fell to the squadron to carry out trials with the aircraft under combat conditions, and a number of recommendations were made. One of these was that the wing panels were to be internally cross-braced with swaged tie-rods, instead of piano wire as in the F.E.2b. Also, the undercarriage was to be altered to incorporate the modified oleo Trafford Jones undercarriage. The officer commanding No. 20 squadron, RFC, Major W. H. C. Mansfield, when asked for an assessment of the F.E.2d, commented:

I consider the F.E2d a most efficient machine for an Army Wing whose principal duties are long reconnaissance, patrols, and escort duty; it has not been used for Artillery work. As fighting machine it is in my opinion only been beaten by the Nieuport Scout; it can out fly a de Havilland (D.H.2) and is the only machine in this Brigade which can dive with engine all out at really steep angles.

It is open to improvement as regards the radiator, which is far too large, and the undercarriage; this latter I believe can be converted into a simple 'V' without a front wheel and should be a marked improvement.

The Rolls-Royce engine is running well and has not shown any serious mechanical troubles as yet. Plugs and air pressure being the only difficulties encountered.

The best testimonial this machine can receive is the fact that enemy machine will never engage it if they can possibly avoid it.

Using the same radiator that was used on the F.E.2b and mounting it externally solved the problem with the overheating of the radiators.

Initially, the F.E.2d had just been intended to replace the lost and damaged F.E.2bs, but such was the response of the pilots who flew the aircraft in combat that it was decided to press on with production, and a total of eighty-five of the aircraft were built by the Royal Aircraft Factory. The Bolton Paul factory that was making the F.E.2b under licence converted some of those models to the F.E.2d. A small number also found their way to training units: fourteen in 1916, a further twenty-three in 1917 and just three in 1918. There was even talk about producing a seaplane version, but nothing ever came of it.

Another version, the F.E.2e, appeared at the same time. This one was powered by a 230-hp Siddeley Puma engine, giving it a top speed of 93 mph. The F.E.2f and g models were test beds for different engines, the 200-hp RAF 3 and 5b. Various modifications were developed, and trials were carried out using different types of bomb racks, searchlights, cameras and single-seat fighters. The final variant was the F.E.2h that was powered by a 230-hp Siddeley Puma engine.

What developed from the various variants was a single-seat fighter, the F.E.8, a biplane with equal-span wings fitted with a 100-hp Gnome Monosoupape nine-cylinder rotary pusher engine. The design of the F.E.8, unknown to its team of designers headed by John Kenworthy, was almost identical to that of the de Havilland Airco D.H.2. Critics in the aviation press immediately jumped on the band-wagon and condemned the F.E.8, saying that it was no more than a copy of the D.H.2. Nothing could be further from the truth. No one knew of the existence of the D.H.2 until it was unveiled almost six months after design work had started on the F.E.8. What it showed was that both teams of designers had realised the need for a fighter and had chosen similar designs, oblivious to one another.

One of the reasons that both designers had chosen a pusher engine was that there was no reliable synchronisation gear available. However, the field of fire it gave the observer/gunner was far better than had there been one available. The tail boom support on the F.E.8 was almost the same as that on the F.E.2, the only difference being that the tail booms met at the tailplane spar and not at the rudderpost. Other tail boom designs and configurations had been tried and experimented with, but none were as satisfactory as the one fitted to the F.E.2.

The wings of the F.E.8 were of conventional construction, wooden spars and ribs covered in fabric. The outer section of the wings had a five-degree dihedral, whereas the centre section had none. The ailerons were fitted with rubber bungees to return them to their normal position after use, instead of the spanwise balance cables used in previous models. The tailplane angle of incidence could be altered on the ground by moving the strut between the tail booms that was fitted in front of the elevator's leading edge. This was achieved by having a series of holes drilled in the strut into which the fixing bolts were placed; whatever hole was selected altered the angle of incidence.

There was only one gun fitted, and that was a single Lewis machine gun mounted on a swivel with the muzzle pointing through a small dish-shaped hole in the nose of the aircraft. Control of the gun was through a series of linkages to a spade-like grip close to the pilot's hand.

Two prototypes were built, and the first one flew on 15 October 1915 with test pilot Frank Gooden at the controls. The first flight lasted just ten minutes with no problems reported; the second, two days later, was a much more detailed flight which lasted 1½ hours. Again there were no major problems, and after another two test flights the prototype was flown to the Central Flying School for evaluation and service trials. This time the Lewis machine gun was fitted; up to this point, it had been left out. The trials were very successful and the pilots that flew the aircraft were pleased with the way it handled and the ease of landing. A small number of modifications were recommended:

1. The back of the pilot's seat should be straighter.
2. The gun mounting should be raised a further six inches, as it was difficult to reload. This would bring the pistol grip in line with the top of the control lever.

The overall test results were excellent and the aircraft was flown back to Farnborough by another test pilot, B. C. Hucks. The flight took place on 15 November 1916, and as the aircraft landed it crashed, for some inexplicable reason. After the tests it had been through, this could only be put down to pilot error. Fortunately, the second prototype was almost finished, and flight trials commenced on 6 December 1915 with test pilot Frank Gooden at the controls. On 19 December, Frank Gooden flew the F.E.8 to France to be evaluated by front line pilots from No. 5 Squadron, RFC. On arrival Frank Gooden discovered that the squadron also had a D.H.2, the aircraft some thought the F.E.8 had been based upon. Its pilot, Lieutenant Frederick J. Powell, was given the job of evaluating the F.E.8, which placed him in the unique position of having flown and evaluated both aircraft. In his report, he stated:

Every detail of the F.E.8 was so far advanced from the rather Heath-Robinson D.H.2.

It wasn't all good for the F.E.8, as Lieutenant Powell criticised the gun sight as being inaccurate and found the gun mounting needed to be raised considerably; both of these criticisms had been voiced by pilots at the Central Flying School. The propeller spinner was, in Powell's opinion, unsafe as it sometimes caused a severe vibration. When it was removed, after one flight, all subsequent flights were vibration free. His comments were taken on board by Frank Gooden and relayed to the designers and engineers back at Farnborough, who set about making the modifications.

The aircraft, however, stayed with the squadron and was flown on a number of sorties. During one of these sorties, Powell spotted an Aviatik on a reconnaissance mission and slid beneath it from behind. He then realised he was too close, and in order to get a shot off at the underside of the Aviatik, he would have to raise the nose of the F.E.8 dramatically and that would put him in danger of colliding with the enemy aircraft. Powell pulled away, and as he did so the German observer/gunner spotted him and opened fire, riddling his fuel tank. The engine shut down and Powell had to glide back, but only managed to make it back as far as a field which was close to the airfield. The fuel tank from the first prototype, which had crashed returning from testing, was then flown out to replace the damaged one.

Another time the engine failed and had to be replaced, so a Gnome Monosoupape engine was 'borrowed' from a Vickers F.B.5. Lieutenant Powell was then told that the squadron could not keep both the F.E.8 and the D.H.2, so Powell selected the F.E.8 quite happily. The D.H.2 was then given to the Commander of C Flight to use as his own personal aircraft.

The demand for the F.E.8 caused it to be built under contract with other manufacturers, and one of these was the Darracq Motor Engineering Co. Ltd of Fulham, who had only ever built motorcars; the building of the F.E.8 was their first experience of building an aircraft. This became obvious after production had started, as it was so slow that the initial 100 aircraft ordered were reduced to fifty and the remaining fifty were given to Vickers Ltd, an experienced aircraft manufacturer. The War office ordered an additional twenty-five, which were to be built by the Royal Aircraft Factory itself. The order was never completed after MP Noel Pemberton-Billing had accused the RFC and the Royal Aircraft Factory of sending pilots to their death in outdated, outclassed and inferior aircraft. His accusations brought about an enquiry into the role played by the Royal Aircraft Factory in developing aircraft. The enquiry, although it found no basis for such an accusation, severely restricted the aircraft's development and damaged the company's reputation.

The first production models arrived for squadron service in France on 15 June 1916, complete with spinners that were removed before being assigned. Lieutenant Powell, in his report, had criticised the use of the spinner and had recommended that they be removed. Further aircraft, when delivered, came without the spinner. The first squadron to be completely equipped with F.E.8s was No. 40 Squadron, RFC, under the command of Major Robert Loraine. The squadron formed up at Gosport and was immediately shipped off to France to take part in the Battle of the Somme, which was at its height.

Problems were soon discovered with the rubber bungees that returned the ailerons to their normal position after use. It was discovered that they were perishing after being subjected to sunlight for long periods, and so they were replaced by spanwise balance cables. This modification could, fortunately, be carried out in the field by the ground crews. A gravity fuel tank was also installed after pilots claimed that after a long flight, the pressure in the tank was insufficient for the fuel-feed system unless it was hand pumped.

Then it was found that after a couple of months in service, the duraluminium elevator ribs in the tail surface had begun to corrode and in some cases had become detached, which of course could have led to a fatal accident. It was found later that the cause was attributed to electrolytic corrosion, brought about by having two different types of metal in contact with each other. The ribs were replaced with wooden ones until the problem could be resolved.

By the beginning of 1917 the F.E.8 was being superseded by new fighters, and the additional order for a further 120 of the aircraft from the Darracq Company, to be delivered by March 1917, was cancelled. What aircraft remained were withdrawn from squadron service and assigned to various advanced flight training schools. After such a bumpy start, the F.E.8 had shown itself to be an exceptional aircraft for the short period of time that it was involved in the war.

The arrival of the R.E.8 appeared to hold the promise that the new model would be a successful replacement for the B.E.2, but initially it turned out to be one of the most dangerous aircraft to be added to the RFC's inventory of aircraft. During one month, thirty pilots and observers were lost during training before the aircraft was even assigned to squadrons at the front.

The first of the two prototype R.E.8s (Reconnaissance Experimental 8) flew on 16 June 1916 with test pilot Frank Godden at the controls. It had a 140-hp R.A.F.4a engine with a two-bladed propeller. The second prototype took to the air on 5 July, this time fitted with a four-bladed propeller giving an improved performance, in particular when carrying a heavier payload. It was armed with a synchronised, forward-firing .303 Vickers machine gun and a Lewis machine gun mounted on a Scarff ring in the observer's cockpit. It was a more stable aircraft than the B.E.2, although modifications had to be made to improve stability before it could gain acceptance by pilots used to flying the B.E.2e. The modifications to the production version made it ideal for artillery spotting, but gave it little chance of out-manoeuvring enemy fighters. It also had a tendency to spin out if subjected to a violent manoeuvre and would burst into flames on crashing, giving it a reputation for being a 'flying coffin'. The fact that the fuel tanks were mounted directly behind the engine without a firewall between did not help. It was rumoured that some pilots put Pyrene instead of petrol in the reserve tanks. Pyrene is made from coal tar and is less combustible than petrol.

The design of the aircraft produced a long, scoop-like nose, a slim fuselage and very heavy aileron struts. Pilots found it very easy to fly and it was used mostly for observation missions. These were usually long flights carried out in cramped conditions, which added to the problems for the pilot. However, the small cockpits afforded both the pilot and the observer excellent views of the ground.

Most of the production R.E.8s were powered by the 150-hp Royal Aircraft Factory air-cooled 12-cylinder in-line engine, though some received the 200 hp R.A.F. 4d engine, and a small number were fitted with a Hispano-Suiza engine. A shortage of

Hispano-Suiza engines and Rolls-Royce aero engines resulted in the R.A.F. 4 remaining the standard engine. The propeller of the R.A.F. 4 engine was inclined upwards to improve the takeoff and landing run. This created a 'broken back' appearance to the fuselage, giving the illusion that the tail sloped upwards. The twin exhausts protruded over the upper wing to carry the fumes clear of the crew. As with the B.E.2e, the long extensions on the upper wing were reputed to be liable to collapse if the aircraft dived too sharply.

Despite the many criticisms, a total of 4,077 R.E.8s had been produced by the end of the war by the Royal Aircraft Factory, Austin Motors, Standard Motors, Siddeley-Deasy and the Coventry Ordanance Works.

The first production aircraft reached France in November 1916. At first, pilots converting from the B.E.2e had problems with the R.E.8's more sensitive controls, resulting in a number of accidents. The R.E.8 was then grounded while a larger tailfin was designed and fitted. The modified type proved to be more acceptable but the intial results were not encouraging. On 13 April 1917, a patrol of six R.E.8s from No. 59 Squadron was met by aircraft from Jasta 11and all the R.E.8s were shot down within five minutes. On that day in April, 59 Squadron lost ten pilots and observers, all flying R.E.8s.

As a result of improved pilot training and tactics, the casualty rate in R.E.8 squadrons dropped from the levels of that disastrous 'Bloody April'. The R.E.8 became a popular aeroplane with observation crews, and it was deemed to be very satisfactory for the tasks demanded of it, and was even regarded with some affection, gaining the nickname 'Harry Tate' (after a popular music hall artist of the time).

Eighteen Royal Flying Corps squadrons were equpped with the R.E.8 by 1917 and nineteen squadrons in 1918. Belgium was the only country other than Britain to operate the R.E.8, receiving twenty-two in July 1917. A small number of R.E 8s were fitted with the Hispano-Suiza engine and given the designation the R.E.8a, but none ever saw action. By November 1918, the R.E.8 was regarded as completely obsolete and was quickly retired after the Armistice.

With the war still raging on the Western Front, a new British fighter aircraft was required to take on the Albatros fighter of the German Army Air Service. Major-General Sefton Brancker visited the Royal Aircraft Factory in April 1916, and invited them to submit a design for a new single-seat fighter to be fitted with the Hispano-Suiza engine. The company's designer H. P. Folley got to work, and by July he had completed the basic design of the S.E.5. Three prototypes were ordered, and the first was completed by November 1916. The airframe was of the conventional design, four spruce longerons with spruce vertical struts and cross members covered in fabric. All the joints had steel fittings into which steel tie rods were screwed, bracing each bay of the frame. The single-bay, equal length wings were of conventional construction. The upper wing section was constructed of spruce, as were the ribs, and covered in plywood. Compression struts were actually solid spruce wing ribs, and false ribs were used to strengthen the leading edge. The interplane struts were also made of spruce and were shaped to a streamlined cross-section.

Powered by a 150-hp Hispano-Suiza engine, the S.E.5, as it had been designated, made its first flight on 22 November 1916, flown by test pilot Frank Gooden. The following day Captain Albert Ball flew the aircraft for ten minutes and disliked it intensely, although he could find nothing wrong specifically with the aircraft.

The second prototype was ready for its first flight the following week after a number of modifications, which included the fitting of a modified fuel system with an over-wing gravity tank, the fitting of a fixed Vickers machine gun with the Constantinesco C.C. synchronised mechanism and an over-wing Lewis machine gun. The S.E.5 carried out its first test flight on 4 December, and on Christmas Eve Frank Gooden flew the aircraft to France for evaluation by front line pilots, which resulted in a number of minor modifications being made. Then tragedy struck on 26 January 1917, when on another test flight of the S.E.5, the port wings folded at 1,500 feet and in the subsequent crash Frank Gooden was killed. In the subsequent aircraft post-mortem, extensive structural modifications were made to the wings of the S.E.5.

The third prototype, powered by a 150-hp Hispano-Suiza engine, had been flight tested by Gooden only days previously and underwent the modifications to the wings required. Following tests cleared the aircraft and it was put into production, the first one coming off the production line on 1 March 1917. The first model was taken to Martlesham Heath, where it was subjected to a rigorous testing procedure and was found to have a considerably inferior performance to the prototypes. Despite this the production continued, and the first twenty-four S.E.5as, as they were now designated, were completed by 30 March.

Almost all the first batch were assigned to No. 56 Squadron and among the flight commanders was Captain Albert Ball, whose dislike of the S.E.5 had not diminished in any way. On receiving his aircraft, the first things he did were to remove the large windscreen, replace the Vickers machine gun with a Lewis gun and have his ground crew build a new type of leading-edge gravity tank into the centre-section of the upper wing. Brigadier-General Brooke-Popham, who visited the squadron the day after Ball had had the modifications made to his aircraft, took on board Ball's modifications and his reasons for doing so, and ordered the remaining aircraft to be modified in the same manner.

The next order, for fifty, was made in December 1916 and deliveries of the second batch began in the April of 1917. The wings were shortened in order to strengthen them, as were the levers on the ailerons. The 200-hp Hispano-Suiza engine powered the latest model. In January 1917 large-scale production took place, and major contracts were given to the Vickers and Martinsyde companies in the shape of 200 aircraft each, with deliveries expected by the summer. Then news was received regarding the 200-hp Hispano-Suiza engine. Problems were being experienced with lubrication, and then it was discovered that the reduction gears and airscrew shaft had not been hardened properly. This was supported by a message from Colonel Duval, Chef du Service Aéronautique au Grand Quartier Général, who said that the majority of his aircraft that were fitted with the 200-hp Hispano-Suiza engine were grounded two days out of three because they were unserviceable. Spares for the engines were becoming so scarce that some of the squadrons, both British and French, had to resort to cannibalising some of the other engines in order to keep their aircraft flying.

The 200-hp Sunbeam Arab engine was considered as an alternative, but that proved to be almost as unreliable, as was the supply. Such was the delay that by January 1918, over 400 S.E.5a aircraft were being held in stores awaiting a suitable engine. In November the number of squadrons still flying the S.E.5a had been reduced to three. This was increased to five by December, but still there were problems with the engine and, increasingly, with steel-tubing undercarriage struts. The latter problem was resolved by strengthening the struts, and the aircraft continued to gain a reputation for itself.

At the beginning of 1918, one of the S.E.5as was modified by redesigning the nose section so as to reduce drag, and the front radiator was removed and replaced with an angled underslung radiator that could be retracted for gliding. Known as a sesquiplane, it was powered by a modified Aries-built 200-hp Hispano-Suiza engine that had had its reduction gear removed to provide a lower thrust line when a larger spinner was fitted. The upper wing was increased both in span and in chord, while the lower wings were reduced by the same margin. Redesignated the S.E.5b, the aircraft made its first flight on 8 April 1918 and, despite its racy looking appearance, there was no difference in the overall performance. A later model in 1919, after the war in Europe had ended, was redesignated the S.E.5c and again showed no improvement in the performance.

At the end of 1917, over 800 S.E.5 and 5as had been built and assigned to just five squadrons, Nos 40, 41, 56, 60 and 84. Two further squadrons, Nos 24 and 68, were in the process of being equipped when they were withdrawn and replaced. The S.E.5, despite its problems, was a great asset to the Royal Flying Corps during the relatively short period it saw action, and it accounted for many German aircraft.

SPECIFICATIONS

B.E.1

Wing Span Upper:	36 ft 7½ in (11.8 m)
Wing Span Lower:	34 ft 11½ in (10.6 m)
Length:	29 ft 6½ in (9.0 m)
Height:	10 ft 2 in (3.1 m)
Weight Empty:	Not known
Weight Loaded:	Not known
Maximum Speed:	59 mph (94 km/h)
Engine:	One 60-hp Wolseley
Armament:	None Fitted

B.E.2/2a/2b

Wing Span Upper:	36 ft 11 in (11.2 m)
Wing Span Lower:	34 ft 11½ in (10.6 m)
Length:	28 ft 4 in (8.6 m)
Height:	10 ft 8 in (3.3 m)
Weight Empty:	1,100 lb (499 kg)
Weight Loaded:	1,600 lb (723 kg)
Maximum Speed:	74 mph (118 km/h)
Engine:	One 70-hp Renault
Armament:	None Fitted

B.E.2c

Wing Span:	37 ft 0 in (11.3 m)
Length:	27 ft 3 in (8.3 m)
Height:	11 ft 1½ in (3.4 m)
Weight Empty:	1,370 lb (621 kg)
Weight Loaded:	2,142 lb (972 kg)
Maximum Speed:	86 mph (138 km/h)
Engine:	One 90-hp R.A.F.1a
Armament:	None Fitted

B.E.2e

Wing Span Upper:	40 ft 6 in (12.3 m)
Wing Span Lower:	30 ft 6 in (9.3 m)
Length:	27 ft 3 in (8.3 m)
Height:	11 ft 9 in (3.6 m)
Weight Empty:	1,431 lb (649 kg)
Weight Loaded:	2,100 lb (953 kg)
Maximum Speed:	88 mph (139 km/h)
Engine:	One 90-hp R.A.F.1a
Armament:	None Fitted

B.E.12

Wing Span:	37 ft 0 in (11.3 m)
Length:	27 ft 3 in (8.3 m)
Height:	11 ft 1½ in (3.4 m)
Weight Empty:	1,635 lb (741 kg)
Weight Loaded:	2,553 lb (1,158 kg)
Maximum Speed:	102 mph (163 km/h)
Engine:	One 140-hp R.A.F.4a
Armament:	One forward firing synchronised Lewis machine gun
	Twin Lewis machine guns mounted on upper wing (B.E.12b)

F.E.2

Wing Span:	42 ft 0 in (12.8 m)
Length:	30 ft 0 in (9.1 m)
Height:	12 ft 7½ in (3.8 m)
Weight Empty:	1,012 lb (459 kg)
Weight Loaded:	1,865 lb (846 kg)
Maximum Speed:	75 mph (120 km/h)
Engine:	One 70-hp Renault
Armament:	One forward firing Lewis machine gun

F.E.2a

Wing Span:	47 ft 9 in (14.5 m)
Length:	32 ft 3 in (9.8 m)
Height:	12 ft 7½ in (3.8 m)
Weight Empty:	1,993 lb (904 kg)
Weight Loaded:	2,690 lb (1,220 kg)
Maximum Speed:	75 mph (120 km/h)
Engine:	One 100-hp Green
Armament:	One forward-firing Lewis machine gun

F.E.2b

Wing Span:	47 ft 9 in (14.5 m)
Length:	32 ft 3 in (9.8 m)
Height:	12 ft 7½ in (3.8 m)
Weight Empty:	2,105 lb (955 kg)
Weight Loaded:	2,967 lb (1,386 kg)
Maximum Speed:	80 mph (128 km/h)
Engine:	One 120-hp Beardmore
Armament:	One forward-firing Lewis machine gun

F.E.2d/e/f/g/h

Wing Span:	47 ft 9 in (14.5 m)
Length:	32 ft 3 in (9.8 m)
Height:	12 ft 7½ in (3.8 m)
Weight Empty:	2,105 lb (955 kg) (d)
	2,280 lb (1,034 kg) (e)
Weight Loaded:	2,967 lb (1,386 kg) (d)
	3,355 lb (1,522 kg) (e)

Maximum Speed: 88 mph (141 km/h) (d)
                    93 mph (149 km/h) (e)
Engine: One 160-hp Beardmore (d)
                    One 200-hp Siddeley Puma (e)
                    One 200-hp RAF3 (f, g)
                    One 230-hp Siddeley Puma (h)
Armament: One forward-firing Lewis machine gun

F.E.8

Wing Span: 31 ft 6 in (9.6 m)
Length: 23 ft 8 in (7.2 m)
Height: 9 ft 2 in (2.8 m)
Weight Empty: 895 lb (406 kg)
Weight Loaded: 1,346 lb (611 kg)
Maximum Speed: 95 mph (128 km/h)
Engine: One 100-hp Gnome Monosoupape rotary
Armament: One forward-firing Lewis machine gun

R.E.8

Upper Wing Span: 42 ft 7 in (12.17 m)
Lower Wing Span: 32 ft 7 in (9.17 m)
Length: 27 ft 10½ in (8.5 m)
Height: 11 ft 4½ in (3.5 m)
Weight Empty: 1,803 lb (817 kg)
Weight Loaded: 2,869 lb (1,301 kg)
Maximum Speed: 103 mph (165km/h)
Engine: One 140-hp R.A.F.4a
Armament: One forward firing Lewis machine gun
                    One Lewis machine gun on Scarff ring in observer's cockpit

S.E.5

Wing Span: 27 ft 11 in (8.5 m)
Length: 20 ft 11 in (6.4 m)
Height: 9 ft 6 in (2.9 m)
Weight Empty: 1,280 lb (581 kg)
Weight Loaded: 1,850 lb (839 kg)
Maximum Speed: 128 mph (205 km/h)
Engine: One 150-hp Hispano-Suiza
Armament: One forward firing Lewis machine gun

S.E.5a

Wing Span: 26 ft 7 in (8.1 m)
Length: 20 ft 11 in (6.4 m)
Height: 9 ft 6 in (2.9 m)
Weight Empty: 1,406 lb (638 kg)
Weight Loaded: 1,940 lb (880 kg)
Maximum Speed: 134 mph (214 km/h)
Engine: One 200-hp Wolseley Viper
Armament: One forward-firing Lewis machine gun

Salmson-Moineau Company

Salmson was known more for its engine manufacturing than for its aircraft. The aircraft side of the company was developed by its chief designer René Moineau, after a request by the Aviation Militaire for a three-seat reconnaissance aircraft. What he created was the S.M.1, a large biplane powered by a single 240-hp Salmson 9A2c engine which was mounted traversely within the fuselage. This, through a very complicated series of gearboxes and shafts, turned two propellers that were mounted inboard of each wing. Two radiators were mounted either side of the nose, in which the gunner was situated. The pilot's cockpit was situated just behind a cut-out in the trailing edge of the upper wing, and in front of the rear gunner/observer. Both gunners had APX 37 mm cannons mounted on rings, which gave them an excellent field of fire.

The wings were of unequal span, were made of wood and had square tips. Only the upper wings had ailerons fitted. The landing gear was of a tricycle configuration made of steel tubing, but the pilots were told that they were not to use the nosewheel in the landing sequence as it would probably cause the aircraft to flip over. The nose gear was there simply to stop the aircraft from nosing over when taxiing.

The first tests were carried out at Villacoublay, and were successful enough for an order for 100 of the aircraft to be built. By the end of the war, a total of 155 had been built and assigned to various Escadrilles. It was soon discovered however that, despite the successful tests, when put on the front line under battle conditions, it was markedly inferior to the Sopwith 1½-Strutter. The very complex engine transmission was the cause of numerous engine breakdowns and a constant headache for the mechanics.

After a number of accidents and engine and transmission failures, it was quickly realised that the S.M.1 had a limited operational use, and those that were still able to fly were returned to aircraft parks as emergency spares. Two of the aircraft were sold to the Imperial Russian Air Service, but they too found it to be more trouble than it was worth.

In an attempt to improve on the model, a two-seat version was built with an additional engine fitted in the nose. Tests showed that there were very serious problems with the engine cooling system, and only the one aircraft was built.

Meanwhile, the company were engaged in building the Sopwith 1½-Strutter under licence and when the Aviation Militaire put out a requirement for a two-seat reconnaissance aircraft, they put forward a design they had been working on – the Salmson 2 A2. This was a two-seat, equal span, two-bay reconnaissance aircraft powered by a 230-hp Salmson 9Za engine.

Ailerons were fitted on both upper and lower wings, which had hollow spars of spruce. The ribs were constructed out of plywood and covered in poplar underneath with doped fabric on top. The two wings were attached by means of struts, while the upper wing was secured to the fuselage by two cabane struts.

The fuselage was constructed by means of four ash longerons that were covered in aluminium at the fixing points and reinforced with plywood formers strengthened by a latticework of piano wire. The tail section consisted of a rudder and a vertical stabiliser that was connected to the fuselage by two vertical aluminium tubes. The twin fuel tanks, each holding 100 litres, were mounted in the fuselage.

The robust undercarriage consisted of six struts, three each side, one strut connected to the engine mount, the other two to the rear spar. The axle was articulated and wrapped in a bungee cord in an attempt to absorb the shock on landing.

Armament consisted of three machine guns: one synchronised Vickers 7.7 mm and two flexible 7.7 mm Lewis guns in the rear observer's cockpit. Initially there was no provision for the aircraft to carry bombs, but as the war progressed, a small number had modifications carried out to enable them to carry 207 lb (230 kg) of bombs.

Tests were carried out, and the results prompted the Aviation Militaire to place an order for 200 of the aircraft, quickly followed by further orders. Such was the demand for the aircraft that the firms of Latécoere, Desfontaines and Hanriot were licensed to build the aircraft. A total of 3,200 Salmson 2 A2s were built, over 700 of which were purchased by the United States Army Air Service.

Remarkably there were very few variants of the Salmson 2 A2, and throughout the war this was one of the most reliable of all the French aircraft built during this period.

A later version was the Salmson 3 C1, which had been designed as a single-seat fighter. Only the one was built after test pilots complained of the poor visibility because of the low seating and reported that it was extremely tiring to fly – not the best recommendation for a front-line fighter aircraft.

Another model appeared around the same time, the Salmson 4. This was in effect an enlarged version of the Salmson 2 with an increased wing span and additional wing struts. Twelve of the aircraft were initially ordered, but the end of the war halted the production lines and no more were built.

The Salmson 5, which appeared at the beginning of 1917, was intended to be used for artillery spotting and was based on the design of the Salmson 2 A2. After extensive testing it was decided that it was in fact inferior to the 2 A2, and only the one was built.

The findings from the flight tests of the Salmson 5 helped create the Salmson 7, a two-seat reconnaissance aircraft. This was also based on the design of the 2 A2, but with a number of modifications. One of these was to move the pilot and the observer back-to-back in the same cockpit, which made communication between them easier, and solved a problem that had been apparent in the earlier models.

The tests were a complete success and an initial order for fifty was awarded to the company, but only twenty of the aircraft were built and delivered to the Aviation Militaire. It had been intended to build over a thousand of the aircraft and equip a large number of the escadrilles, but the Armistice came about and production was halted.

SPECIFICATIONS

Salmson-Moineau S.M.1

Wing Span:	17.47 m
Length:	10.00 m
Height:	3.80 m
Weight Empty:	1,680 kg
Weight Loaded:	2,050 kg
Engine:	240-hp Salmson 9A2c

Armament: Two APX 37 mm cannons, one in the nose and one in
                         the rear position

Salmson-Moineau S.M.2

Same specifications as for the S.M.1, but with the addition of another Salmson 9A2c
placed in the nose of the aircraft while still retaining the laterally mounted engine.

Salmson 2 A2

Wing Span: 11.75 m
Length: 8.50 m
Height: 2.90 m
Weight Empty: 780 kg
Weight Loaded: 1,290 kg
Engine: 230-hp Salmson 9Za
Armament: One synchronised Vickers 7.7 mm machine gun
                         Two 7.7 mm Lewis machine guns mounted on a ring in
                         the rear cockpit

Salmson 4

Wing Span: 15.20 m
Length: 8.80 m
Height: 2.96 m
Weight Empty: 1,410 kg
Weight Loaded: 1,935 kg
Engine: 260-hp Salmson 9Z
Armament: None

Salmson 5

Wing Span: 12.20 m
Length: 7.80 m
Height: 2.90 m
Weight Empty: 1,410 kg
Weight Loaded: 1,935 kg
Engine: 230-hp Salmson 9Za
Max speed: 169 km/h
Armament: None

Salmson 7

Wing Span: 12.34 m
Length: 8.80 m
Height: 2.90 m
Weight Empty: 1,410 kg
Weight Loaded: 1,935 kg
Engine: 230-hp Salmson 9Za
Max speed: 189 km/h
Armament: None

Tommy Sopwith in his Howard-Wright biplane.

Sopwith Bat Boat No. 1.

Sopwith tractor biplane built for the Gordon Bennett Race.

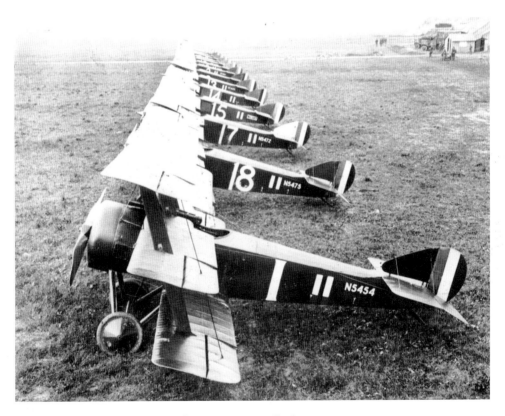

Sopwith Triplanes of No. 1 Squadron RNAS at Bailleul.

Sopwith Snipe being started with a Hucks starter.

SPAD SA.2.

SPAD S.VII in RFC markings.

Georges Guynemer's SPAD S.VII, *Vieux Charles*, at Dunkirk.

SPAD XIII.

SPAD 14 floatplane.

SPAD 17 of Spa 3.

Tellier T.5 flying boat, fitted with two 250-hp Hispano-Suiza engines back to back.

Tellier T.6 with a 47-mm Hotchkiss cannon mounted in the nose.

Tellier T.7 'High Seas' flying boat.

Vickers FB.5 Gunbus straight off the production line.

Vickers FB.9 fighters.

Vickers FB.19, or E.S.I.

Vickers FB.24C.

Vickers FB.26A Vampire II.

Commander
Samson in his
Voisin of 3
Wing, RNAS.

Voisin 5.

Voisin 8 at the factory preparing for a test flight.

Voisin 8 powered by a Peugeot engine.

Voisin 10.

Wight Type A1 pusher being hoisted aboard HMS *Ark Royal*.

Wight-built AD100 at anchor in the Solent.

Wight-built AD 100 carrying out torpedo trials in the Solent.

Short Brothers

Of all the aircraft manufacturers in the world, none could have had such a life prior to entering the world of aviation than that of Horace Leonard Short. Born in 1872, one of three brothers, Horace Short suffered a serious head injury while an infant which brought on meningitis. The result was that he suffered from an abnormal brain development that gave an unusual shape to his head, but which also appeared to turn him into a genius. He also developed physically, which together with the ferocious appearance brought about by his disfigurement, could be off-putting to others, belying the charm he possessed. In 1890 he set out to see the world and visit his uncle in Australia, working his passage on a sailing ship. While on the trip he visited Samoa and met the author Robert Louis Stevenson. While visiting another of the islands close by, cannibals captured him, but his charm and great physical strength coupled with his unusual appearance and brilliant mind won them over, and they worshipped him as a god. Unfortunately, when he decided it was time to leave, the natives would not allow it and he had to steal one of the dugout canoes and paddle to another island to effect his escape.

On finally reaching Australia, Horace wrote home describing his adventures and then moved on to South America. Once there, he trekked up the Amazon and finally turned up in Mexico. In the meantime, one of his brothers, Eustace, had been sent to find him as their father had died, leaving the family penniless. Eustace found his brother running a silver mine in Mexico. He was already a legend among the locals, a man to be feared and one that the local bandits dared not attack. In 1896 Horace returned to England, a relatively wealthy man. His youngest brother Oswald had joined with Eustace to embark on a balloon making enterprise which Horace quietly observed without getting involved.

Over the next twelve years the two brothers produced a variety of balloons, until the arrival of the Wright Brothers and their aircraft, the *Wright Flyer*, altered their world. The American brothers carried out a number of demonstration flights in Europe, and it soon became clear to Eustace Short that the aeroplane was going to be the way forward, not the balloon. The two brothers approached Horace and persuaded him to join them, and so in November 1908 the company of Short Brothers was born. That same month Eustace Short was taken on a flight in the *Wright Flyer* by Wilbur Wright, and the following month he set about designing his own aircraft based on a similar design to that of the *Flyer*.

Wilbur Wright, in the meantime, had been inundated with requests from wealthy enthusiasts to either sell the *Flyer* or build one for them. Wright had no facilities in Europe to build any of the aircraft, but on the recommendation of his European agent, Griffith Brewer, it was suggested that the Short Brothers be allowed to build replicas of the aircraft under licence. This was agreed, and a contract for six of the aircraft, known as Short-Wright biplanes, came immediately from members of the Aero Club, the first of the aircraft to be produced in February 1909.

In 1908 the Royal Navy awarded Vickers a contract for Naval Airship No. 1, but after a disastrous moment when the airship was destroyed as it was being removed from its floating hangar, even before its first test flight, their thoughts turned to the use of aircraft. The Royal Aero Club offered to give free instruction to selected officers from the Royal Navy, and out of 200 applicants, four were selected: Lieutenants Charles Rumney Samson, Reginald Gregory, Arthur Longmore and Eugene L. Gerrard, RM (Gerrard had taken the place of Lt Wildman-Lushington RM, after the latter had become ill). Each student was trained for six months, at a cost of £20 plus any damage caused during the course. The first to qualify was Lt Samson in April 1911 and nine months later, flying a Short S.38, he carried out the first launch of an aircraft from the deck of a warship when he took off from the foredeck of HMS *Africa* while the ship was at anchor off Sheerness. In May 1912 he carried out a similar flight from the deck of HMS *Hibernia* while the ship was steaming at 15 knots off Weymouth, again in the Short S.38. During the next two years the Short Brothers developed the S-series of aircraft rapidly, carrying out numerous tests and trials with the RNAS.

When war broke out in August 1914, the Royal Navy was in the process of converting a tramp steamer into an aircraft carrier. As a stopgap, the Channel packets *Empress*, *Engadine* and *Riviera* were converted to take seaplanes and the S-series were ideally suited for these ships. These three seaplane-carriers were equipped with nine Short Brothers aircraft, three Short Folders on *Engadine*, two Type 135s and one Type 74 on *Riviera* and three Type 74s on *Empress*. They were to carry out an audacious raid on the Zeppelin sheds at Cuxhaven on Christmas Day, 1914.

The Short Brothers were already in production with another aircraft: the Short Type A, also known as the Short Type 166; this, however, was a land version. When the *Ark Royal* made its appearance in October 1915, all six aircraft were embarked on board and sent to Salonika. They were used for reconnaissance, artillery spotting and bombing missions and served well under the hostile conditions there, operating from the RNAS land base at Thasos.

A smaller version of the Type 166, the Short Type 827/830, appeared almost at the same time as the Type 166. The fuselage was of wooden construction, fabric covered and carried a crew of two. The two-bay wings were of unequal span, and fitted with oval steel tube wing struts. The Admiralty ordered twelve of these aircraft, six Type 827s and six Type 830s. The only difference between the two aircraft was the engine. The Type 827 was fitted with the 150-hp Sunbeam Nubian, while the Type 830 was fitted with the 200-hp Salmson water-cooled radial. The Type 827 proved to be one of the RNAS' most reliable aircraft and was still operational at the end of the war – a remarkable achievement for any aircraft manufacturer. Over 100 of the aircraft were built during this period: thirty at Rochester by Short Brothers; twenty at Parnall & Sons Ltd, Bristol; twenty at the Brush Electrical Engineering Co. Ltd, Loughborough; twenty at the Sunbeam Motor Car Co. Ltd at Wolverhampton; and twelve at the Fairey Aviation Co. Ltd, Middlesex. The twelve aircraft built by Fairey were the first aircraft the company had ever built; however, C. R. Fairey had worked for the Short brothers as works manager and assistant designer, so it wasn't exactly uncharted territory for the new company.

Two of the Short Type 827s were sent to take part in the action to destroy the armoured cruiser SMS *Königsberg*, which was holed up in the Rufiji Delta, but the action was over by the time they arrived. They were then sent to Mesopotamia, where they were converted to landplanes and used in reconnaissance and bombing missions against the Turkish Army.

In 1913, one of Short's seaplanes had been entered in the Circuit of Britain race, but had to be withdrawn because of trouble with the 100-hp Green engine. This was the cause of some consternation with the Short brothers, because they only entered their aircraft in races or competition if there were some experimental testing results to come from it. Then, in September 1914, Captain Murray Sueter, Director of the Air Department, invited a number of aircraft manufacturers, including Shorts, to submit proposals for a long-range seaplane. The aircraft had to be able to carry a 14-inch Whitehead torpedo, a crew of two with a wireless and be powered by a 225-hp Sunbeam engine. Horace Short immediately put forward a proposal based on the seaplane they had built for the Circuit of Britain race. The specifications were almost the same as the 1913 Circuit seaplane, but the Short Type 184, as it was called, was a strengthened version with three bay, equal-span folding wings for ease of storage and large sprung floats. The folding wings were an ingenious idea designed by Horace Short, inasmuch as the pilot, by means of a windlass in the cockpit, could carry out the whole folding, unfolding and locking operation quite easily. The locking and unlocking device was a splined and threaded spigot and socket that was activated by a quarter-turn, not unlike that of a breechblock on a field gun. When folded, a cross-shaft with up-turned ends engaged slots in the rear middle wing struts that were then rotated into a locking position by means of a lever in the cockpit, giving support to the wings.

The Admiralty was now quite desperate for this type of aircraft and placed an order for ten Short Type 184s even before the two prototypes had left the water. Orders were also placed with the Wight Company for ten of their Wight Type 840s, and with the Sopwith Company for ten of their Sopwith Type 860s. It was obvious from day one that the Short 184 was vastly superior to any of the other two types of seaplane, and they were delivered earlier than the others. The Admiralty, suitably impressed, ordered a further 130 of the aircraft, which meant that the orders had to be farmed out to other manufacturers as Short Brothers' Rochester factory was incapable of managing such a large order. Thirty of the aircraft were ordered from the Saunders Company from Cowes, Isle of Wight; twelve from Mann, Egerton & Co. Ltd. of Norwich; twelve from Westland Aircraft of Yeovil; twelve from the Phoenix Dynamo Co., Bradford; and twelve from Frederick Sage & Co., Peterborough. The remainder were built by Shorts at their Rochester factory.

One of the first reports of the Short Type 184 in action came when Flight Commander C. H. K. Edmonds took off from the Gulf of Xeros and, after crossing the Blair Peninsular, attacked and torpedoed an enemy transport off the coast of Gallipoli. The ship apparently had already been badly damaged by a torpedo from a submarine, and Edmonds' attack just finished it off. Five days later on 17 August, he was on patrol when he spotted three enemy transports steaming line astern and successfully torpedoed the middle one. During their time in the Middle East, the Short Type 184 showed that it was one of the most reliable of all the aircraft that were available at the time, and it carried out a variety of missions from reconnaissance to bombing to directing shellfire from ships at sea.

Slowly but surely, the number of Short Type 184s from the various manufacturers was starting to build the RNAS fleet of aircraft. The sinking of the liners *Lusitania* and *Arabic* by the U-20 and U-24 respectively caused the Admiralty to think of providing long-range reconnaissance patrols and the Short Type 184 filled the requirement exactly. One of the major problems faced by the pilots of the seaplanes was, of course, having to land in the sea, where conditions could be less than favourable. Take-offs and landings were restricted to fair seas, which restricted the number of patrols, especially in the winter months. Even in the Middle East there were restrictions, but these were caused by the hot climate.

Commander Samson, who had taken the seaplane carrier *Ben-My-Chree* to the eastern Mediterranean, Indian Ocean and the Red Sea, was having problems in getting airborne from the waters there. In an effort to overcome the problem, he had 16 feet removed from the lower wing and reduced the fin area on the tail section. Samson claimed to have increased the speed of the aircraft by six knots and significantly increased the rate of climb. Further tests were carried out and ten Short Type 184s being built by Mann, Egerton & Co. were modified with the shorter lower wing and the reduced tail fin, and given the designation Short 184 Type B.

Other modifications were made on a number of Short Type 184s, including converting one from the Rochester factory, into a single-seat bomber with the space where the front cockpit used to be taken up with nine 65 lb bombs. This was known as the Type D but only the one was ever built. A variety of different engines were tried, including the highly successful 250-hp Rolls-Royce Eagle IV, which increased the aircraft's performance but was never put into the production models. One model that appeared was the Short Dover Type 184, powered by a 260-hp Sunbeam engine fitted with a four-bladed propeller and fitted with larger floats. It was modified to cope with the rough seas and heavy swells that were almost always present around the Dover Patrol Stations at Cherbourg and Newhaven.

A total of 829 Short Type 184s were built, including 190 by the Brush Engineering Co. Ltd. They served in every theatre of war, including the Arctic Circle during the Archangel campaign, when they served aboard the seaplane carrier HMS *Pegasus*.

When, in 1915, the Admiralty invited proposals to meet their requirement for a long-range bomber capable of carrying six 112 lb bombs, one of the first to appear was the Short Bomber. The prototype was in reality a landplane version of the Short Type 184 seaplane, but with the crew positions reversed. The gunner's position was moved so that he was in front of the pilot, and when required to fire the pillar-mounted Lewis machine gun, which was mounted on the upper wing, he would stand on decking fixed on top of the fuselage. This was a very precarious position, especially if the bomber had to take sudden evasive action.

The prototype was a two-bay, unequal span version, but during tests it was found that the bomber could not lift a full bomb load as well as the crew of two. The wings were lengthened from 72 feet to 84 feet and although it could then take off with a full bomb load, it was found to be unstable. After further trials it was realised that the only way to cure the problem was to extend the fuselage and with this done, the bomber was able to conform to the required specifications. An order for seventy of the aircraft was placed by the Admiralty: fifty with Short Brothers, all to be powered by 250-hp Rolls-Royce Eagle engines, and twenty with the Sunbeam Motor Car Co., to be fitted with the 225-hp Sunbeam engines. The production models had three-bay wings and with the lengthened fuselage, the crew positions reverted back to their original positions, mainly because of the precarious position for the gunner and the advent of the Scarff ring.

The first of the bombers were assigned to No. 7 Wing, RNAS at Coudekerque and carried out their first raid on the night of 15 November 1916 against the submarine pens at Zeebrugge. A further fifteen were attached to 3 Wing, RNAS, and it was from this unit that the Independent Air Force grew – the catalyst of Bomber Command.

With the Battle of the Somme about to get under way, General Trenchard's need for bombers led him to request the Admiralty to assign some of their Short Bombers to the Royal Flying Corps. The Admiralty responded by transferring fourteen bombers to the RFC, but by now the Handley Page O/100 bombers had arrived, the need for more bombers had diminished and further orders of the Short Bomber were cancelled. Those that had been assigned to bomber wings carried out their role, but were gradually replaced by bigger and better bombers, relegating the Short Bomber to training squadrons.

The Short Type 184 had carried out its role as a reconnaissance/bomber satisfactorily, and although it had initially been put forward as a torpedo-carrying aircraft, it had never lived up to its expectations. This was mainly down to the insufficient power of the 250-hp Rolls-Royce engine. It was too much to ask an engine on only 250 hp to carry a 14-inch torpedo, two crew members and a full fuel load and perform satisfactorily. It was decided that an engine of at least 300-hp would be required, or a twin-engine aircraft, but after the Admiralty had had problems with the twin-engine, twin-fuselage Wight torpedo-carrying seaplane, the latter was dismissed. Horace and Oswald Short had been aware of the development of the 320-hp Sunbeam Cossack engine and decided to design an aircraft, based on the design of the Short Type 184. The result was the Short Type 310 seaplane.

There were a number of modifications, the main one being the redesigning and re-siting of the central exhaust manifold, which had a downswept stack that poured fumes into the cockpit, to an upswept stack that was canted to the portside. The 320-hp Sunbeam Cossack engine was fitted with a four-bladed propeller on the prototype, but two-bladed propellers were fitted on the production models.

In July 1916, the first prototype lifted off the water at Rochester, followed the following month by the second. The initial trials, flown by test pilot Roland Kemp, were very successful and were quickly accepted by the RNAS. They immediately dispatched them both to the RNAS seaplane base at Otranto, Italy, where torpedo trials were to be carried out. The first trials were relatively successful, but then tragedy struck when both Type 310s broke up in the air, killing both pilots. Initially it was thought that it was the sudden release of the heavy torpedo (810 lb), which caused the aircraft to suffer structural failure as the aircraft rebounded with loss of the weight. After extensive tests it was discovered that the rear float attachment was faulty, and a redesign that put the floats farther apart and additional bracings to the lower wings solved the problem. In addition, the following notice was painted on both sides of the fuselage:

The Removable Rear Crossbar Must Always be in Position before the Wings are Folded.

The first of the newly modified aircraft was given the designation Short Type 310-A4, the second was called the Short Type 310-B. The first batch of thirty, which were built at Rochester, were sent to RNAS Otranto, Italy and RNAS Kalafrana, Malta, and these were followed by a further forty-four. Demand for the aircraft meant that contracts to be placed with the Sunbeam Co. for a further fifty Type 310-A4s. By the end of the war, a total of 127 Short Type 310-A4s had been built. The option to build the Type 310-B was never taken up by the Admiralty.

Encouraged by the success of the Type 310-A4, two designs for a small, fast, two-seat scout seaplane were put forward by the Short Brothers, one from Horace Short, the other from his brother Oswald. Horace's design was based on that of the Type 310-A4, while the one from Oswald was of a different layout altogether, and had been developed using results from wind-tunnel tests. The Admiralty placed an order for one of each, both to be powered by the 200-hp Sunbeam Afridi engine and with the requirement that both designs would have to meet the Air Department's specification N.2A that covered all aircraft.

On 1 January 1917, the first of the new designs appeared: that developed by Horace Short. Given the designation Experimental Scout No. 1 – S.313, it was a single bay sesquiplane with a large staggered upper wing and a short lower wing. The fuselage was a stubby version of the one made for the Type 310-A4, and it was this that was to cause a major problem. The engine was mounted in an enclosed front section, covered with a motorcar-type bonnet that was hinged on the top with louvered slits down the side. The radiator tucked below the engine, and cooling air was taken in through an open front cowling and ejected through ducts mounted above the lower wing.

The first tests took place the following day, but there were problems. The insistence of the Admiralty that the aircraft should be of a compact design had caused the fuselage to be shortened considerably, so consequently the aircraft was found to be nose-heavy. So much so in fact, that test pilot Ronald Kemp could not get the aircraft to lift off the water. Modifications were hurriedly made, including inserting an extra bay in the rear fuselage section and increasing the tail arm by 2 feet. Re-designated Experimental Scout No. 2, it was soon discovered that although the modifications had solved the immediate problem, the performance figures were woefully below what were required and the project was abandoned.

Attention then focused on Oswald Short's design, designated Experimental Scout No. 3 – S.364, an aircraft with a slender fuselage and equal span wings with stiff trailing edges. Although the appearance of the aircraft was markedly different to that of Horace Short's Experimental Scouts Nos 1 & 2, the performance figures were equally as disappointing.

The first test flight showed the aircraft to be tail-heavy and very underpowered. It was decided to replace the engine with a 260-hp Sunbeam Maori I, and to compensate for the additional weight, larger floats were fitted. Despite the additional power, the bomb load was reduced to just two 65 lb bombs and when fitted with the additional weight of a Lewis machine gun mounted on a Scarff ring, the performance figures were totally unacceptable to the Admiralty. By this time, however, the use of the seaplane as a scouting aircraft had waned in favour of using deck-launched aircraft, as the aircraft carrier started to make its appearance.

The success of the Short Type 184 prompted the designers at Short's to come up with a replacement, a two-seat, long-range patrol seaplane as defined by Admiralty specification N.2B. Known as the Short N.2B, the design incorporated some of the designs from previous Short aircraft, such as the frontal honeycomb radiator fitted on the Experimental Scout No. 3 and the hinged engine cowling with slatted louvers like those on the Experimental Scout No. 1. Two prototypes were built, and both were found to be lacking in performance; in fact, one report stated that they were no better than the Short Type 184. The RNAS or the RAF accepted neither aircraft.

The Short brothers' contribution to the field of aviation in the First World War may not have been as extensive as they had wished, but their contribution during the Second World War was beyond question, and many a downed airman owed his life to the ruggedness of the Short flying boats that patrolled the seas.

SPECIFICATIONS

Short Type 166

Wing Span:	57 ft 3 in (17.4 m)
Length:	40 ft 7 in (12.3 m)
Height:	13 ft 6 in (4.1 m)
Weight Empty:	3,236 lb (1,467 kg)
Weight Loaded:	4,580 lb (2,077 kg)
Maximum Speed:	65 mph (104 km/h)
Engine:	One 200-hp Salmson
Armament:	Four 250 lb bombs

Short Type 827/830

Wing Span:	53 ft 11 in (16.4 m)
Length:	35 ft 3 in (10.7 m)
Height:	13 ft 6 in (4.1 m)
Weight Empty:	2,736 lb (1,241 kg)
Weight Loaded:	3,400 lb (1,542 kg)
Maximum Speed:	61 mph (98 km/h)
Engine:	One 150-hp Sunbeam Nubian (Type 827)
	One 200-hp Salmson radial (Type 830)
Armament:	One free-mounted Lewis machine gun
	Four 250 lb bombs

Short Type 184

Wing Span:	63 ft 6¼ in (19.4 m)
Length:	40 ft 7½ in (12.3 m)

Height:	13 ft 6 in (4.1 m)
Weight Empty:	3,703 lb (1,679 kg)
Weight Loaded:	5,363 lb (2,432 kg)
Maximum Speed:	89 mph (143 km/h)
Engine:	One 225/240/260-hp Salmson
Armament:	One free mounted Lewis machine gun
	Four 250 lb bombs
	One 14-inch Whitehead torpedo

Short Bomber

Wing Span:	85 ft 0 in (25.9 m)
Length:	45 ft 0 in (13.7 m)
Height:	15 ft 0 in (4.5 m)
Weight Empty:	5,000 lb (2,268 kg)
Weight Loaded:	6,800 lb (3,082 kg)
Maximum Speed:	77 mph (124 km/h)
Engine:	One 225-hp Sunbeam
	One 250-hp Rolls-Royce Eagle
Armament:	One free mounted Lewis machine gun
	Six 250 lb bombs
	One 14-inch Whitehead torpedo

Short Type 310-A4/B

Wing Span:	75 ft 0 in (22.9 m) (Type 310-A4)
	68 ft 6 in (20.85 m) (Type 310-B)
Length:	45 ft 9 in (13.9 m)
Height:	15 ft 0 in (4.5 m)
Weight Empty:	4,900 lb (2,222 kg)
Weight Loaded:	7,020 lb (3,185 kg)
Maximum Speed:	79 mph (127 km/h)
Engine:	One 320-hp Sunbeam Cossack
Armament:	One free mounted Lewis machine gun
	Six 250 lb bombs
	One 14-inch Whitehead torpedo

Experimental Scout No. 1/2/3

Wing Span:	46 ft 0 in (14.0 m) (No. 1)
	46 ft 0 in (14.0 m) (No. 2)
	39 ft 0 in (11.8 m) (No. 3)
Length:	31 ft 6 in (9.6 m) (No. 1)
	33 ft 6 in (11.8 m) (No. 2)
	28 ft 0 in (8.5 m) (No. 3)
Height:	15 ft 0 in (4.5 m)
Weight Empty:	Not Known
Weight Loaded:	Not Known
Maximum Speed:	92 mph (127 km/h)
Engine:	One 260-hp Sunbeam Maori
Armament:	One free mounted Lewis machine gun
	Two 65 lb bombs

Sopwith Aviation Company

The first Sopwith-built aircraft took to the air on 4 July 1912. A tractor biplane powered by a 70-hp Gnôme engine, the first flight was a complete success and was to set the standard for all the Sopwith aircraft that were to follow.

Tommy Sopwith stared this venture into the field of aviation by opening 'The Sopwith School of Flying of Brooklands, Weybridge, Surrey' in January 1912. Within months, the school had been inundated with applications for pilot training and was established as the premier flying school in England. Tommy Sopwith, ever the entrepreneur, went seeking new fields to explore, and started to design his own aircraft. One of his former pupils, Harry Hawker, joined him as test and demonstration pilot, Fred Sigrist built the aircraft to Sopwith's design, and the team set to work.

In 1914, the Sopwith Company were in the process of preparing their latest aircraft for the Circuit of Britain and the Gordon Bennett Trophy races when, on 4 August, war with Germany was declared. The airfield at Brooklands was placed under military guard almost immediately. The company was already in the process of building ten Type 860 and six Type 880 seaplanes for the Admiralty at their Kingston factories, and had just received an order for twenty-four Spinning Jennies (a landplane version of the Type 807 seaplane), and thirteen Tabloids. Twelve Type 807s, powered by 100-hp Gnome Monosoupape engines, were delivered to the RNAS at the beginning of the war. They saw service both on the Home Front and in the Dardanelles. The Spinning Jenny, on the other hand, was not the success hoped for, and was withdrawn from service by the end of 1915.

Just prior to the war, the company produced the Sopwith Three-Seater tractor biplane, which carried two passengers sitting side-by-side in the front cockpit and the pilot in a second cockpit behind. At the outbreak of war, it was adopted by both the Military and Naval Wings of the RFC and the RNAS as a two-seat reconnaissance aircraft. Of the six that went to the RNAS, two went with Commander C. R. Samson's Eastchurch Squadron to France, while the remaining four were assigned to the naval air station at Great Yarmouth to be used for reconnaissance duties over the North Sea and English Channel. It is not known what happened to those assigned to the RFC, but one imagines they were used for both reconnaissance and training purposes as they were not armed in any way.

One aircraft that did serve well at the very beginning of the war was the first flying boat to be built in Britain – the Sopwith Bat Boat. It had entered service with the RNAS at the beginning of 1913, and even took part in the Naval Review of July 1914; at the outbreak of war, it was assigned to seaplane patrols from Scapa Flow. Powered by a 100-hp Green engine, the seaplane had a top speed of 65 mph. It was replaced at the beginning of 1915, but had shown the value of using small seaplanes for reconnaissance patrols.

One of the problems the Sopwith Company faced was that a large proportion of their workforce was joining the services to fight in the war. Those who didn't go were issued with a special badge to show that their work was of national importance. When the British Expeditionary Force (BEF) left for France in August 1914, the Royal Flying Corps (RFC) followed them in a variety of aircraft, including four Sopwith Tabloids still in their crates. The Sopwith Tabloid was a simple little single-bay biplane with staggered wings of equal span with warping for lateral control. The undercarriage was unique inasmuch as initially, each wheel had its own half-axle; this was later replaced by a split-axle that made the whole thing considerably sturdier and reduced the number of landing accidents considerably.

On arriving in France, two of the Sopwith Tabloids were assembled and together with their pilots, 2nd Lieutenants C. G. Bell and N. C. Spratt, took part in the Battle of Le Cateau. The remaining two were later assembled and assigned to No. 3 Squadron, RFC. The two that had taken part in the battle were assigned to No. 4 Squadron, and it was while with this squadron that 2nd Lieutenant Spratt, flying his unarmed Tabloid, chased after a German bomber that had dropped three bombs on their camp. The speed and manoeuvrability of the little aircraft, according to one report 'put the wind up the Hun in no uncertain manner'.

The Royal Naval Air Service (RNAS) was also flying the Sopwith Tabloid, having purchased three of them after seeing the prototype flying. While the representatives of the Admiralty were at Brooklands watching the demonstration, they saw Sopwith's Tractor Biplane, which was being used as a general runabout. After seeing a demonstration of the aircraft, they purchased that as well and all four aircraft were sent to Eastchurch to join the other mixed bag of aircraft that the Navy had assembled there. The intention was to move between forty and fifty aircraft, fifty armoured cars and 300 marines to Dunkirk under the command of Commander C. R. Samson, RN. The aircraft were to be formed into three squadrons, Nos 1 to 3, consisting of a mixture of types of aircraft.

Toward the end of 1914, the RFC realised that the Tabloid was not really suitable as an operational aircraft and discarded it. Those that were airworthy were sold to the RNAS for the sum of £1,075 each. Its replacement was the Sopwith Schneider, whose production began at the end of November 1914. The first twelve produced differed very little from the early Tabloids, the similar bull-nosed cowling housing the same 100-hp Gnome Monosoupape engine. Control was achieved by wing warping on these early models, but later production models used ailerons and had an enlarged curved fin in place of the triangular one. A total of 160 Sopwith Schneiders were built for the RNAS, and two were used on experiments aboard the submarine *E-22*, but these came to nothing as the floats were found to be too flimsy for use in rough weather. Two-wheeled dollies were later fitted to strengthened floats, enabling the Schneider to take off from the decks of aircraft carriers. A number of the aircraft saw service in the Dardenelles, where they acquitted themselves admirably.

In the meantime, the design office at Sopwith had come up with a new model, the Land Clerget Tractor, or the Sopwith 1½-Strutter as it later became known. This was a small, compact fighter/reconnaissance aircraft that had a new innovation, a variable-incidence tailplane, which was controlled by the pilot. Air brakes were also fitted in the trailing portions of the lower centre section. The prototype took off on its first test flight at the Central Flying School (CFS) in January 1916. Powered by a 110-hp Clerget 9Z rotary engine, the aircraft attained a maximum speed of 105 mph. There were some concerns about the single-bay interplane bracing, the lack of flying wires under the lower wings and the aft position of the undercarriage wheels, but these amounted to nothing and the performance of the aircraft far outweighed the concerns.

The Admiralty immediately placed an initial order for fifty-two of the aircraft, to be followed some months later by an additional order for 100 more. The report of the first test flight was sent to the headquarters of the Royal Flying Corps, who placed an order for fifty. The problem was that the Sopwith factory's production capacity was at maximum capacity turning out the order for the Admiralty, so the War Office sought another manufacturer and selected Ruston, Proctor & Co., giving them the RFC's contract for fifty Sopwith 1½-Strutters.

No. 5 Wing, RNAS at Coudekerque was the first naval station to receive the new Sopwith 1½-Strutter, and they were in action the following day. Flight Sub-Lieutenants R. R. Soar and F. Potts were in their aircraft when they intercepted three German aircraft on a reconnaissance flight. After a great deal of diving, ducking and weaving, the navy pilot and his observer drove the enemy aircraft away.

The demand for the Sopwith 1½-Strutter was further highlighted when, on 21 February 1916, the German offensive began, resulting in the decimation of Allied troops at Verdun. The lack of air cover and reconnaissance for the troops on the ground had, it was felt, contributed in a small way as no information regarding German troop movements was available. The military hierarchy decided that the Allied offensive would take place in July, and they wanted aerial support. Trenchard, in an effort to assist, realised that the RFC's lack of squadrons was going to be a major stumbling block, so he approached the Admiralty for a loan of their aircraft. The Admiralty agreed, and immediately transferred forty Sopwith 1½-Strutters to the RFC, with a further thirty some months later.

The first batch of Sopwith 1½-Strutters arrived, but with no Vickers machine gun fitted for the pilot. Fortunately, the first of two synchronisation interruptor gears appeared, the Vickers-Challenger, which had been under development for some time. This was fitted to the Sopwith 1½-Strutter, making it the first two-seat fighter on the British market. The first squadron to receive the aircraft was No. 70 Squadron, RFC. The squadron was built up gradually and as each flight became equipped, it was shipped off to France. A and B Flights were sent to Fienvillers, followed by C Flight, which had been equipped with Sopwith 1½-Strutters from the RNAS. All the aircraft had been fitted with a fixed, forward-firing Vickers machine gun in front of the pilot and a Lewis machine gun mounted on a Scarff ring in the observer's cockpit. It soon became obvious that the Scarff ring was far superior to the Nieuport mounting that had been fitted in the aircraft up to this point. Trenchard was so impressed that he ordered that all Sopwith 1½-Strutters be fitted with the Scarff ring mounting.

Problems arose when it was discovered that at the high altitudes that the Sopwith 1½-Strutter could reach, the viscosity of the lubricating oils increased with the cold atmosphere. In addition to this, the rarefied atmosphere created a situation when it impaired the recoil energy required to activate the reloading cycle. The canvas webbing belts that held the ammunition for the Vickers gun absorbed moisture and when at height they had a tendency to freeze, causing stoppages.

The demand for the Sopwith 1½-Strutter caused a number of companies to be given contracts; among them were: Fairey Aviation Co.; Hooper & Co.; Morgan & Co.; Ruston, Proctor & Co.; and Vickers & Wells Aviation Co. The first Ruston, Proctor Sopwith 1½-Strutters were delivered to No. 45 Squadron, RFC in July 1916, but it was October before the squadron was fully up to strength and could be sent to France. It was found that in a fighter/reconnaissance role, the 1½-Strutter was outclassed by the latest German fighters that were being produced, so it was decided to fit bomb racks and use the aircraft in a bomber/reconnaissance role.

The first fifty Sopwith 1½-Strutters were delivered to No. 5 Wing, RNAS as fighters, but an additional order for 100 single-seat bomber versions was placed with Hooper & Co., with a provisional order for an additional 150. Thirty-one of the aircraft were built as bombers, and the aircraft was to carry either four 20-lb bombs or two 100-lb bombs and the Equal Distance Bomb Sight. A problem arose when it was discovered that the bombsight could not be fitted, and a report from an RFC evaluation stated:

It is considered impossible to design a satisfactory bombsight for this machine, and that if even moderate accuracy is needed in bombing with this machine, the bombs must be dropped from very low heights.

The bombers fitted with this sight never saw service with the RFC and were kept in aircraft parks until mid-1917, when they were handed over to the Russians. Six months later the Russians returned fifty of the aircraft, which were then assigned to training units and Home Defence squadrons. The existing squadrons that were still equipped with the Sopwith 1½-Strutter had them replaced with the Sopwith Camel (of which, more later).

The RNAS used both types in a bombing offensive along the German-held Belgian coast on 2 August. The Sopwith 1½-Strutters escorted ten Caudron G4s and one Farman to attack an ammunition dump and an airfield that was close by. The attack was a total success, with all aircraft returning safely. The Zeppelins were posing a threat, and attacks on them as they flew on bombing raids were not proving to be very successful. As the Zeppelin bases in Germany were, for the present, out of the reach of the Allies, it was decided to attack the German Army's airship sheds in Belgium and plans were drawn up for the attack. One week later, on 9 August 1916, two bombers flown by Flight Sub-Lieutenants R. H. Collet and D. E. Harkness from No. 5 Wing attacked the airship sheds at Berchem St Agathe and Evere. Both airship sites suffered serious damage, and both aircraft returned safely. Unfortunately there were no airships inside at the time, but what it did demonstrate was that nothing was outside the reach of the RNAS and the raid caused the Germans some concern about the vulnerability of their airships while on the ground.

There was another attack on the airship sheds at Cognolee, near Namur on 25 August, this time by three single-seat Sopwith 1½-Strutter bombers flown by Flight Lieutenant Wood, Flight Sub-Lieutenants C. W. Jamieson and R. H. Collet, the latter having flown on the previous mission. Halfway to the target, Flight Lieutenant Wood lost sight of the other two while in heavy cloud, and headed for the coast and returned. The remaining two pilots continued on and once over the target, despite heavy ground fire, dropped their bombs before heading back. Jamieson's aircraft was hit, but he managed to make it to Holland and landed there. The Dutch at the time were strictly neutral and impounded any aircraft that landed on their soil although they were slowly building themselves their own air arm. Flight Sub-Lieutenant Collet was the only one to have reached the target, released his bombs and returned. A number of other bombing and reconnaissance missions were carried out using the Sopwith 1½-Strutter but another Sopwith had appeared on the scene: the Sopwith Triplane.

Over 5,466 Sopwith 1½-Strutters were built: 4,200 by French aircraft companies; 246 built by the Sopwith Aviation Co.; 100 by Fairey Aviation; 150 by the Hooper Co.; 100 by the Morgan Co.; seventy-five by Mann Egerton Co.; 350 by Ruston, Proctor & Co.; 150 by Vickers; twenty by the Wells Co.; and seventy-five by Westland Aircraft Co.

Earlier in 1915, the Sopwith Admiralty Type 860 Seaplane appeared. Only eighteen were built, and they were used on anti-submarine patrols in home waters. Each carried an 810 lb, 14-inch torpedo together with machine guns, and was powered by a 225-hp Sunbeam engine. The aircraft had limited success, but suffice to say it was one of the seaplanes instrumental in keeping the U-boats at bay during the early part of the war.

Prior to this, a small scouting aircraft that had been designed by Harry Hawker appeared. The Sopwith Sparrow, as it was called, was an equal span, single-bay biplane powered by a 50-hp Gnome engine. Despite its frail appearance, it was capable of aerobatics and was subjected to a number of them when demonstrated by Harry Hawker. The original design was actually drawn full-size in chalk on the shop floor, although scale drawings were made later. Only four were built and none were purchased by the military, although some interest was shown.

What developed from the Sparrow was the Sopwith Pup. This was, in fact, a slightly enlarged version of the Sparrow and was designed as a single-seat fighter by Harry Hawker. It was powered by an 80-hp Le Rhône engine, and was fitted with a Vickers machine gun with a synchronised mechanism. Stronger supporting wing struts were fitted to support the wide-span centre section and ailerons replaced the wing warping.

At the time, Sopwith was contracted to supply the RNAS with aircraft, and a report on the Sopwith Pup sent to the Admiralty somehow found its way into Trenchard's hands. Trenchard was quick to realise the potential in the aircraft and immediately placed an initial order for fifty of the aircraft. The order was placed with the Standard Motor Co., who had been contracted to build aircraft for the Sopwith Aviation Co.

The first of the production aircraft were delivered to the RNAS in September 1916, followed three weeks later by the first of the Pups built by the Standard Motor Co. The first squadron to be equipped with the Sopwith Pup was No. 8 (Naval) Squadron, commanded by Squadron Commander G. R. Bromet. The squadron consisted of three flights: A Flight, which had Nieuport 17Bs, B Flight with Sopwith Pups and C Flight with Sopwith 1½-Strutters. The Sopwith Pup was a nimble little fighter very much favoured by the pilots, but it suffered from an ongoing problem with the engine and with the guns, which continually jammed. Despite this, the squadron scored sixteen 'kills', thirteen of which were shot down by the Sopwith Pup pilots.

Almost all the navy pilots who flew the Sopwith Pup were delighted with it, and in one incident Flight Lieutenant D. M. B. Galbraith, while flying alone on patrol, attacked six enemy aircraft; he shot down two of them and forced the remaining four to head back over their lines. For this, he was awarded a bar to his Distinguished Service Cross (DSC).

In October 1916, another order for 100 Sopwith Pups was awarded to Sopwith Aviation Company and was immediately given to the Whitehead Aircraft Co., Richmond, Surrey. At the beginning of January 1917 the first of the Whitehead-built Sopwith Pups rolled off the production line, a tremendous achievement in such a short period. Sopwith Pups were coming off the production line at the Standard Motor Co. at a steady pace, and by the end of December 1916 No. 54 Squadron RFC had been equipped with twenty of the aircraft. On 24 December, No. 54 Squadron, RFC, embarked for France complete with their Pups. As more and more of the Pups came off the production line, so No. 66 Squadron, RFC was refitted and on 12 March 1917, they too went to France.

One of the things that drew criticism from the pilots was the aircraft's lack of firepower. A number of attempts were made to try and increase the firepower, including an over-wing Lewis gun, but none were successful.

In an effort to increase the performance of the Sopwith Pup a 100-hp Gnome Monosoupape engine was fitted, but the improvement was negligible and those aircraft fitted with the engine were assigned to Home Defence squadrons. Even the fitting of a 110-hp Le Rhône 9J engine did nothing to improve the aircraft's performance. A total of 1,847 were built: ninety-seven by the Sopwith Company, the remainder by sub-contractors.

Slowly but surely, the Sopwith Pup was replaced by what was to become among the most famous fighter aircraft of the First World War, the Sopwith Triplane. Designed by Herbert Smith, it was simplicity itself. The rectangular fuselage was of conventional construction, using spruce longerons with spruce cross bracings. The three wings were of equal length but of narrow chord, and all the mainplanes had ailerons fitted to them. The circular engine cowl which covered the 110-hp Clerget rotary engine was faired into the fuselage, which had an additional fairing added to the top longeron, tapered to a knife edge, to which the rudder was hinged. The tail surfaces were identical to those of the Pup, but the tailplane could be adjusted by means of a wheel fitted in the cockpit. The undercarriage interplane struts were of the plank type and slightly longer than usual, and only had one pair of bracing wires.

A total of 1,847 Sopwith Pups were built; eighty by Beardmore Co., 850 by the Standard Co., 820 by the Whitehead Co. and ninety-seven by the Sopwith Aviation Co.

The first test flight was carried out on 30 May 1916 by Sopwith's company test pilot, Harry Hawker and so confident was he with the aircraft that he looped the Triplane just three minutes after taking off. The initial flight was carried out without any armament, but when it was sent to A Squadron at Furnes for evaluation, it was fitted with a Vickers fixed, forward-firing synchronised machine gun. Just fifteen minutes after landing, it was ordered into the air to intercept an enemy aircraft; it is not known whether or not it succeeded.

The aircraft was taken to various RNAS stations for testing, and almost all the reports that came back were extremely favourable. Among the criticisms, it was said that the engine was starved of fuel when put into a sudden turn, and that the seat should be adjustable. The aircraft immediately attracted the attention of the Royal Naval Air Service (RNAS) and the Royal Flying Corps (RFC). The first two prototypes were delivered to the RNAS for evaluation at the beginning of June 1916, and within a week forty Triplanes were ordered from Clayton & Shuttleworth, who were contracted by Sopwith to build their aircraft under licence. The first of these aircraft was delivered on 2 December 1916, and orders for the Sopwith 1½-Strutter from other manufacturers were cancelled and changed for the Sopwith Triplane. Such was the demand for the aircraft that at the end of January, a further order for 106 Sopwith Triplanes for the RFC was placed with Clayton & Shuttleworth.

It was around this time that the relationship between the War Office and the Admiralty was at an all-time low. There had been a 'them and us' situation between the two services for years, and the only thing that kept the peace between then as far as aviation was concerned was the Air Board. Their job was to place orders for aircraft and materials as requested by the two services and co-ordinate the supply of these items in an effort to prevent waste. Unfortunately, the Admiralty asserted their autonomous position and approached the Treasury for £3,000,000 to purchase their own aircraft and engines without going through the Air Board. This coincided with a letter from Haig to the Air Board asking for increased fighter squadrons to combat the threat of the continually increasing German Air Force.

The Air Board realised that something had to be done and called for a conference between the War Office and the Admiralty. The ongoing desperate situation in Europe forced both sides to put aside their rivalry and concentrate on the problems at hand. In order to increase the fighter squadrons, the Admiralty agreed to hand over half the SPADs currently being built under contract to them to the RFC. Later it was agreed that the Army would hand over all their Sopwith Triplanes to the RNAS, in exchange for all their French SPAD aircraft. In addition, the Admiralty agreed to lend the RFC four squadrons from the RNAS.

In fact, no Sopwith Triplanes were ever built for the RFC and the Clayton & Shuttleworth order was drastically reduced from a total of 166 to forty and an order from the Oakley Co. Ltd was reduced from twenty-five to three; in total, only ninety-eight of the aircraft were built.

There were some reports about the weakness of the wings in a power dive, but Air Vice-Marshal Raymond Collishaw said:

> It was all nonsense about a supposed weakness in the Sopwith Triplane. The problem was that there were three different manufacturers of the Sopwith Triplane, Sopwith themselves and two sub-contractors. For some unknown reason the sub-contractors reduced the sizes of the flying wires and landing wires substantially compared with the Sopwith Company. Naturally the structure of the aircraft was weakened when the aircraft was put into a dive while under full power because of the reduced size of the wires.

There were two disadvantages with the Sopwith Triplane: it was under-gunned and underpowered. Tommy Sopwith wanted to fit the Bentley rotary engine in the aircraft, but it was almost completely unavailable and the Admiralty was pressurising him to produce the Triplane. If the Bentley engine had been fitted, it had been intended to fit twin machine guns, but because they were restricted to the lower-powered Clerget engine, it was decided to just fit the one. If Tommy Sopwith had had his way, then there is no doubt that the Sopwith Triplane would have been a *tour de force* at the time.

A total of 152 Sopwith Triplanes were built, forty-six by the Clayton & Shuttleworth Co., three by the Oakley Co. and 103 by the Sopwith Aviation Co.

Without doubt the most famous British fighter aircraft of the First World War was the Sopwith Camel, which shot down more enemy aircraft than any other British fighter. The Camel developed out of a request from the Admiralty for an improved Baby floatplane. The Sopwith F.1 Camel was a single-bay biplane with wings of equal length, and the design that emerged produced an aircraft that bore a strong resemblance to the Pup, but had a deeper, squat fuselage, and the engine, weapons, fuel and pilot were all in close proximity to each other, giving the aircraft a humped appearance – hence the name Camel.

The fuselage was of conventional slab-sided, wire-braced, spruce wood box-girder construction, the top decking of the fuselage being slightly rounded. Only the sides of the fuselage were covered in plywood, the remaining sections were covered in fabric. Forward of the pilot, the engine bay was covered in aluminium sheet panelling. The wings and tail section were of a contemporary wooden structure covered in fabric. The upper wing was a single-piece assembly that had a small cut-out in the centre of the trailing edge to afford the pilot a very limited upward view. The whole wing was supported by struts mounted on the fuselage and interplane struts on the lower wing. Short ailerons were fitted to the wing, just outside where the interplane struts connected. The lower wing was built in two sections and given a five degree dihedral, which when compared with the straight upper wing, provided a very useful recognition reference point when seen from a distance. The one-piece upper wing only applied to the prototypes; the production models were constructed in three sections for ease of rigging.

A cowling that extended to the engine covered the Vickers machine guns that were mounted in front of the pilot. The reason behind this was that the lubricating oils on the guns became more viscose as the aircraft went higher and the air got colder. The hot air from the engine was channelled beneath the 'hump', keeping the guns and the hydraulic lines from the Kauper interruptor mechanism warm. One other problem with the standard Vickers machine gun was that the ammunition was fed from the right-hand side and the empty cartridge cases from the left. With two of these machine guns mounted side-by-side, one of them had to have a left-hand feed block and specially designed ammunition feed, and discharge chutes had to be made. The pilot's position, because of the humped arrangement, placed him under the trailing portion of the upper wing, affording him limited forward view and almost no upward view.

The Admiralty, having dealt with Sopwith from day one, placed an order at the beginning of January 1917 for fifty Sopwith F.1 Camels, even before the prototypes had flown. A further order for an additional fifty aircraft was cancelled soon after being placed and subsequent F.1 Camels for the RNAS were taken from the orders placed by the RFC. It wasn't until May 1917 that the RFC placed an order for 250 Sopwith F.1 Camels, and that was with one of the sub-contractors Ruston, Proctor & Co. of Lincoln. The following month, the War Office placed an order for an additional 200 from the Sopwith Company itself.

The first production model was flown from Dover to Dunkirk on 15 May 1917, where it took part in evaluation trials against the Sopwith Dolphin. The first squadron to be equipped with the new fighter was No. 4 Squadron, RNAS, although a small number were assigned to the Home Defence Wing after a number of air attacks had been made on London. This model was fitted with the 150-hp B.R.1 engine.

The Dolphin was a two bay, staggered wing, single-seat fighter powered by a 200-hp Hispano-Suiza engine, and during the prototype's initial test flight on 23 May 1917 it recorded a speed of 146 mph. This was a startling speed for an aircraft during this period, and it immediately drew the attention of Trenchard. The aircraft was delivered to Martlesham Heath for further testing, where the reports that came back complained that the aircraft was nose heavy. This had to be compensated by putting 20 lb of lead in the tail. It also had a tendency to go into a spin when carrying out a sharp turn to port, and because a strong left rudder had to be applied to correct it, it was found to be an extremely tiring aircraft to fly. The aircraft kept overheating, and it was impossible to enlarge the radiator without interfering with the wing bracings. A second prototype was built, taking the faults into consideration, and fitting the radiators on the top plane.

A third prototype was produced, but delays and problems with the new Hispano-Suiza engine and trials with different types of propeller caused the model to be used just as a test bed. This led to a fourth prototype being produced, and it was this one that was to be the forerunner for the production model. The first of the production models was sent to Martlesham Heath to be used for development work on a variety of engines, including the 200-hp Peugeot-built Hispano engine.

The full production model was fitted with a number of modifications, including a steel tailskid and cut-down decking. The fuselage was of the conventional rectangular design, albeit deeper than normal, and was constructed of spruce longerons with spruce and wire cross bracings and covered in fabric. The wings were of reversed stagger, the top wing being slightly behind the lower and with minimum clearance above the pilot's head. The armament consisted of two upward-firing Lewis machine guns mounted on the forward cross-wise member of the centre-section frame, in addition to the two fixed Vickers machine guns mounted on top of the engine cowling. The number of Lewis guns was reduced to one later, and this armament became standard arrangement for the Dolphin. The earlier problems with the radiators were resolved by mounting flank radiators either side of the engine. A re-designed fin and horn-balanced rudder improved the control and stability of the aircraft.

The first squadron to be equipped with the Sopwith Dolphin was No. 19 Squadron, RFC, who had their SPAD 7s replaced. There were one or two misgivings about the aircraft from the squadron pilots, the main one being that in the event of the aircraft overturning on landing, there was a possibility of serious injury because of the exposed position of the pilot's head. A number of quick release devices were tried and discarded, including an exit point in the starboard side of the aircraft. A number of the production models were fitted with this, but in practice it was found to be too impractical because of the top gun fitting and was moved to the port side. The other problem that was a cause for concern was the strengthening of the front main spars after one of the prototype aircraft had suffered a wing failure in flight. The strengthening had not been completed on the production models prior to them being sent to France.

Reports coming back from operational front-line pilots spoke very highly of the Sopwith Dolphin and left little doubt in anyone's mind that the aircraft was far superior to the S.E.5a, which was powered with the same engine, the 200-hp Hispano-Suiza 8Ba. The Sopwith Dolphin, like almost all the aircraft built during the First World War, suffered from problems with its engines. In the case of the Hispano-Suiza, it appeared that the main problem was with the faulty reduction gear. This was removed and the engines converted to direct-drive, which reduced the performance but increased the reliability considerably. The result was that all Dolphins were sent to France with un-geared, French-built Hispano-Suiza engines.

The final accolade came from the French themselves when they ordered a number of the aircraft and fitted them with the 300-hp Hispano-Suiza engine, but this version never saw action. A total of 1,559 Sopwith Dolphins were built: 300 by Darracq Co., 216 by Hooper Co., and the remaining 1,043 by the Sopwith Aviation Company itself.

While the development and construction of the Sopwith Dolphin was underway, the Sopwith F.1 Camel was also making its appearance and was entering into production. As more and more of the F.1 Camels reached France and entered into combat, enthusiastic reports were coming back from pilots about its effectiveness in combat situations despite the poor, almost non-existent upward vision and the problems clearing the guns. The British-built Clerget engines were also giving some cause for concern after it was found that the French-built Clerget was far superior in performance. This only applied to the F.1 Camels supplied to the RFC, as the ones supplied to No. 4 Squadron, RNAS and used later on operational duties with Naval squadrons, were fitted with the 150-hp Admiralty Rotary No.1 (AR.1) engine. Designed by W. O. Bentley, the engine had aluminium air-cooled cylinders. It was later renamed the Bentley Rotary No.1 (BR.1) engine.

Problems with the production models of the Sopwith F.1 Camel started to come to light after they had been assigned to RFC squadrons and flown in combat. It was not the design of the aircraft that was causing some concern but the manufacture of the aircraft, in particular those built by Ruston, Proctor & Co. Those built by Sopwith and other sub-contractors were found to be alright, but those built by Ruston, Proctor were found to be sluggish and heavy, in particular very tail-heavy. This was very apparent when compared to the other models built by other sub-contractors, as the main feature of the F.1 Camel was that the controls were highly sensitive, providing the instant response that in a combat situation was invaluable.

The one thing that affected all the Sopwith F.1 Camels was the reputation it had for going into a spin very easily. In the hands of the experienced pilot this wasn't a serious problem, but in the hands of the novice, it could be a fatal one. The problem lay in the concentration of weight in the nose: this, together with the sharp torque created by the rotary engine, caused the nose of the aircraft to drop when put into a right-hand turn. In a left-hand turn the nose came up. The drop in the nose of the aircraft could easily be counteracted if the coarse rudder was used quickly enough; if not, the aircraft went into an opposite spin. Records showed that over 200 crashes recorded against the Sopwith F.1 Camel were the result of the aircraft going into a spin.

The first recorded success of the Sopwith F.1 Camel was on 4 June 1917, when Flight Commander A. M. Shook, RN, intercepted and shot down a single-seat Fokker. The first F.1 Camel to be assigned to an RFC squadron arrived at No. 70 Squadron on 29 June 1917. The reason for the delay was that Ruston, Proctor & Co was way behind in its deliveries, possibly because of the pressure being put upon the company to improve the manufacture of the aircraft after numerous complaints had been received.

Besides its fighter and bomber escort duties, the Sopwith F.1 Camel was used extensively for strafing enemy trenches. But after a number of losses, modifications were made which incorporated the fitting of armour plating beneath the pilot's seat and around the engine, and the installation of downward-firing Lewis guns. This modified aircraft was not the success hoped for, and work was under way to produce a purpose-built aircraft which, when it arrived, was far too late to enter the war.

A small number of F.1 Camels were modified for use as night fighters in an attempt to intercept the Gotha bombers. Painted dark green with the roundel either painted over or partially obscured, the aircraft were fitted with both external and internal lights. One of the problems that initially affected the pilots was that the muzzle flashes from the twin Vickers machine guns would temporarily blind them. The problem was solved by fitting two over-wing Lewis machine guns on Foster mountings.

The Sopwith 2F.1 Camel, or Shipboard Camel as it was sometimes called, appeared late in 1917; it had been developed for operations aboard ships, and production of this aircraft was predominantly by the Beardmore Co. A number of Allied ships were equipped with launching platforms, usually over the forward gun turret. Some of the ships, like HMAS *Melbourne*, had a revolving platform, which meant that the platform could be moved around into the wind to save the ship from having to alter course. It also meant that an aircraft could be launched much quicker in the case of an emergency. Of course this was before the advent of the aircraft carrier, which meant that after the mission the aircraft had to ditch alongside its mother ship and hope to be picked up.

Trials were also carried out on lighters; these were barges covered with a wooden platform that were towed behind warships, the idea being that on reaching the right speed, the aircraft would take off, assisted by the wind created by the ship. The experiments were not very successful and the idea was not adopted. One of the problems was that it only seemed to work on calm days, but even then the wake created by the ship as it steamed forward caused the barge to pitch and roll. The reaction of the barge under these circumstances made it very unstable, and most of the time was spent keeping the aircraft from being thrown off into the sea. Commander Samson was one of the people who was involved in the experiments to a large extent, and he actually managed to take off from the lighter on a couple of occasions. He was a larger than life character who appeared to be involved in almost every aspect of experimental work concerning the Navy and aviation, in addition to being an excellent pilot himself. He was also one of the instigators of the development of the tank during the First World War.

The majority of complaints concerning the Sopwith F.1 Camel were about the engines, in particular the English-built 130-hp Clerget that had to be continually tuned. This complaint did not apply to the RNAS, as their Sopwith F.1 Camels were powered by the 150-hp B.R.1.

A number of other companies were sub-contracted to Sopwith to build the Sopwith F.1 Camel: Bolton & Paul (1,550); Portholme (300); British Caudron (100); Clayton & Shuttleworth (575); Hooper Co. (321); Marsh, Jones & Cribb (175); Nieuport & General (400); and Sopwith Aviation itself (503). It soon became obvious that the success the RNAS were enjoying was in the main due to the B.R.1 engines, and it wasn't until the engine was fitted into the F.1 Camels supplied to the RFC that they too started to recognise the improvement in the aircraft's performance.

A total of 5,497 Sopwith F.1 Camels and 250 Sopwith Shipboard Camels were built. The Shipboard Camels were built by Arrol Johnson (30); Beardmore Co. (140); Hooper Co. (30); and Sopwith Aviation Co. (50).

Another Sopwith aircraft destined for the Navy appeared in 1917: the Sopwith T.I or Sopwith Cuckoo, as it became known. This was the first aircraft capable of being operated from either a land base or from the deck of a ship. It was also the first aircraft ever to carry a torpedo and launch it successfully. The design of the aircraft was developed following a suggestion by Commodore Murray Sueter, who approached Sopwith with the idea. What came out of the Sopwith factory was a three-bay biplane powered by a 200-hp Sunbeam Arab engine. The fuselage was of the conventional slab-sided configuration with a rounded top. The three-bay wings had the capability of being folded just after the first bay section for ease of stowing aboard a ship. The split undercarriage was unusual inasmuch as each wheel was fitted independently of the other, unlike other aircraft where an axle between the two braced the wheels. They had to be mounted in such a way as to leave room for a torpedo to be fitted.

The prototype, powered by a 200-hp Hispano Suiza engine, made its first flight on 6 June and was passed by the Sopwith Experimental Department. It was sent to the Isle of Grain for tests by the Admiralty, and was so successful that an order was immediately placed for 100 of the aircraft. The prototype was returned to Sopwith for some modifications to be made before returning the aircraft to the Isle of Grain for torpedo tests to be carried out. The tests were carried out using a wooden box filled with lead shot, as it was thought that an actual torpedo was far too expensive to be used.

The first production Sopwith T.I Cuckoo was fitted with a 200-hp Sunbeam Arab engine, as were all subsequent models, but on arrival at the Isle of Grain it was discovered to have fractured the tubing on the starboard undercarriage on landing. This was before the aircraft had even had a torpedo installed. It was also discovered that the rudderpost and tailskid had broken, so urgent modifications were made to strengthen these faulty sections. One interesting development was the fitting of extensions to the exhaust pipes so that the hot air played over the torpedo mechanism to prevent it freezing at altitude.

The production models were sent to the newly created Torpedo Aeroplane School at East Fortune, where pilots were trained on the aircraft before being sent to operational squadrons. The Armistice intervened before any of the aircraft saw action. A total of 233 Sopwith T.I Cuckoos were built, 162 by the Blackburn Co., fifty by the Fairfield Co., twenty by the Pegler Co. and one, the prototype, by the Sopwith Aviation Co.

Another new aircraft appeared in the spring of 1917, the Sopwith 7F.1 Snipe. Based on the design of the F.1 Camel, the Snipe was a single bay biplane with wings of equal span and was powered by the 230-hp Bentley Rotary (B.R.) 2 engine, which gave the aircraft a top speed of over 200 mph when diving. Like the Camel, the Snipe was tail heavy when climbing and nose heavy when diving. The latter was because of the weight of the engine and the twin Vickers machine guns mounted on top of the engine. The prototype was fitted with the B.R.1 engine, which was considerably lighter than the B.R.2. It was discovered that when the pilot pulled out of a dive, it required less pressure to be exerted on the control stick.

Although this was a private venture by the Sopwith Company and not one commissioned by the War Office, the need for a new fighter was desperate and the Snipe fitted the criteria required by them. Six prototypes were ordered, and throughout the winter extensive trials were carried out to try and find all the problems that invariably were to be found with a newly designed and built aircraft. Inevitably it was compared with the Sopwith F.1 Camel because of its role as a fighter aircraft, and because of the similarity in design. The Snipe carried more fuel and ammunition than the Camel and, despite the extra weight, was faster and had a slightly higher rate of climb, but it lacked the manoeuvrability of the Camel. The aircraft was given to front-line pilots to fly, and the reports that came back were so favourable that the modifications that had been listed were rushed through. This included modifying the tailplane and elevators so as to increase the sensitivity of the controls and the longitudinal stability of the aircraft.

The second prototype was fitted with a 200-hp B.R.2 engine, and the narrow section in the middle of the upper wing was in fact an open frame supported by four vertical struts. Originally a celluloid panel covered the opening, but this had a tendency to blow out, so it was left open, giving the pilot a considerably better upward view than the pilot had in the Camel. The third prototype had a rounded fuselage, as compared with the slab-sided fuselage on the first two prototypes, and was a two-bay biplane with a Lewis machine gun mounted on the upper wing as well as the two fixed, forward-firing Vickers machine guns.

The first squadron to be equipped with the Sopwith 7F.1 Snipe was No. 43 Squadron, RFC, and on 23 September they carried out the first operational sortie with the aircraft. No. 4 Squadron AFC was the next to have their Camels replaced with the Snipe, and within days they had engaged the enemy. Nine Snipes were on patrol over Tournai when they came across fifteen Fokker D.VIIs. With the sun behind them, the nine Snipes swooped into the attack, scattering the German formation. The leader of the Australian flight, Captain C. R. Baker, shot down one of the Fokkers as it was about to shoot at one of his men. After the third Fokker had been shot down and a number of others damaged, the Germans headed back over their own lines to safety. The only casualty on the Australian side was one Snipe that had to make a forced landing due to the pilot being injured. The Snipe had acquitted itself very well against the very respected Fokker D.VII fighter.

One of the most outstanding and dramatic fights of the air war took place on 27 September 1918, when Major W. G. Barker went on patrol in his Sopwith Snipe with members of No. 201 Squadron, RAF in their Sopwith F.1 Camels. The flight came across a two-seat Aviatik over the Foret de Mormal, flying low on a reconnaissance mission. Major Barker dived and machine-gunned the aircraft, causing it to break up and crash. Ground-fire from the German trenches hit Major Barker's aircraft and one of the bullets hit him in the thigh. As he climbed away in great pain, he found himself in the middle of a formation of fifteen Fokkers. He immediately went into the offensive and attacked them; the third aircraft he attacked went down in flames, but he was wounded once again by another German fighter attacking him. He fainted momentarily and his aircraft spun out of control. He regained consciousness and brought his aircraft under control, only to find himself in the middle of the melee again. He shot down another fighter, and he was shot and wounded for the third time when a bullet shattered his right elbow. He fainted once more and again lost control of his aircraft, only to recover minutes later and head back into the fray. He then noticed smoke coming from his engine just as another German fighter crossed his path. He opened fire and sent it down in flames, and then decided that discretion was the better part of valour and dived to escape, only to be followed by three of the remaining German fighters. After dodging and weaving at low level, he managed to shake them off, but he was losing blood desperately and he crash-landed his aircraft just yards from a balloon company. He had managed to fly his aircraft with just one arm, as both his legs and other arm were disabled. For this heroic feat, Major Barker was awarded the Victoria Cross.

It soon became obvious that the Sopwith Snipe was better than anything the Germans had in the air, and the only complaint that could be levelled against it was the fact that had it arrived earlier in the war, there is no question that it could have made a significant difference.

The contribution made by the Sopwith Company to the war in the air is almost incalculable, and they were definitely instrumental in helping to bring the war to a conclusion.

SPECIFICATIONS

Sopwith Bat Boat I & II

Wing Span:	41 ft 0 in (12.4 m)
	55 ft 0 in (16.7 m) II
Length:	32 ft 1 in (9.7 m)
	30 ft 4 in (9.2 m) II
Height:	11 ft 5 in (3.5 m)
Weight Empty:	780 lb (353 kg)
Weight Loaded:	1,700 lb (771 kg)
Maximum Speed:	65 mph (104 km/h)
Engine:	One 100-hp Green
Armament:	None

Sopwith Tractor Biplane

Wing Span:	40 ft 0 in (12.1 m)
Length:	29 ft 0 in (8.8 m)
Height:	11 ft 5 in (3.4 m)
Weight Empty:	1,018 lb (461 kg)
Weight Loaded:	1,550 lb (703 kg)
Maximum Speed:	65 mph (104 km/h)
Engine:	One 100-hp Green
Armament:	None

Sopwith Tabloid

Wing Span:	25 ft 6 in (7.7 m)
Length:	20 ft 4 in (6.1 m)

Height:	8 ft 5 in (2.5 m)
Weight Empty:	730 lb (331 kg)
Weight Loaded:	1,120 lb (508 kg)
Maximum Speed:	93 mph (126 km/h)
Engine:	One 100-hp Gnome Monosoupape rotary
Armament:	Flechettes and revolver

Sopwith 1½-Strutter

Wing Span:	25 ft 6 in (7.7 m)
Length:	20 ft 4 in (6.1 m)
Height:	8 ft 5 in (2.5 m)
Weight Empty:	730 lb (331 kg)
Weight Loaded:	1,120 lb (508 kg)
Maximum Speed:	93 mph (126 km/h)
Engine:	One 100-hp Gnome Monosoupape rotary
Armament:	Flechettes and revolver

Sopwith Sparrow

Wing Span:	26 ft 9½ in (8.1 m)
Length:	19 ft 0 in (5.7 m)
Height:	8 ft 5 in (2.5 m)
Weight Empty:	Not known
Weight Loaded:	Not known
Maximum Speed:	63 mph (101 km/h)
Engine:	One 50-hp Gnome Monosoupape rotary
Armament:	None

Sopwith Pup

Wing Span:	26 ft 6 in (8.0 m)
Length:	19 ft 4 in (5.9 m)
Height:	9 ft 5 in (2.8 m)
Weight Empty:	787 lb (356 kg) (80-hp Le Rhône)
	856 lb (388 kg) (100 Monosoupape)
Weight Loaded:	1,225 lb (555 kg) (80-hp Le Rhône)
	1,297 lb (588 kg) (100-hp Monosoupape)
Maximum Speed:	115 mph (185 km/h)
Engine:	One 80-hp Le Rhône
	One 100-hp Gnome Monosoupape
Armament:	One forward firing Vickers machine gun

Sopwith Triplane

Wing Span:	26 ft 6 in (8.1 m)
Length:	18 ft 10 in (5.7 m)
Height:	10 ft 6 in (3.2 m)
Weight Empty:	1,103 lb (500 kg)
Weight Loaded:	1,543 lb (699 kg)
Maximum Speed:	95 mph (129 km/h)
Engine:	One 130-hp Clerget 9B rotary
Armament:	One fixed Vickers machine gun

Sopwith 1½-Strutter

Wing Span:	33 ft 6 in (10.2 m)
Length:	25 ft 3 in (7.6 m)
Height:	10 ft 3 in (3.1 m)
Weight Empty:	1,259 lb (671 kg)
Weight Loaded:	2,149 lb (974 kg)
Maximum Speed:	105 mph (168 km/h)
Engine:	One 110-hp Clerget 9Z
	One 130-hp Clerget 9B
Armament:	One forward firing Vickers machine gun
	One Lewis machine gun in observer's cockpit

Sopwith F.1 Camel

Wing Span:	28 ft 0 in (8.5 m)
Length:	18 ft 9 in (5.6 m)
Height:	8 ft 6 in (2.5 m)
Weight Empty:	962 lb (436 kg)
Weight Loaded:	1,482 lb (672 kg)
Maximum Speed:	108 mph (173 km/h)
Engine:	One 130-hp Clerget 9B rotary
	One 140-hp Clerget 9Bf
	One 110-hp Le Rhône
	One 100-hp Gnome Monosoupape
	One 150-hp Gnome Monosoupape
Armament:	Two fixed Vickers machine gun

Sopwith Dolphin

Wing Span:	32 ft 6 in (9.9 m)
Length:	22 ft 3 in (6.7 m)
Height:	8 ft 6 in (2.5 m)
Weight Empty:	1,350 lb (612 kg)
Weight Loaded:	2,003 lb (908 kg)
Maximum Speed:	128 mph (205 km/h)
Engine:	One 200-hp Hispano-Suiza 8Ba
	One 200-hp Hispano-Suiza 8Bc
Armament:	Two fixed Vickers machine guns
	One Lewis machine gun on mounting

Sopwith Snipe

Wing Span:	30 ft 0 in (9.1 m)
Length:	19 ft 2 in (5.7 m)
Height:	9 ft 6 in (2.8 m)
Weight Empty:	1,212 lb (549 kg)
Weight Loaded:	1,992 lb (903 kg)
Maximum Speed:	124 mph (200 km/h)
Engine:	One 230-hp Bentley B.R.2
Armament:	Two fixed forward-firing Vickers machine guns

SPAD (Société Anonyme pour l'Aviation et ses Dérivés)

SPAD was developed from a rather unusual source. When Armand Deperdussin, who owned the Société Provisoire des Aéroplanes, was jailed on fraud charges, a consortium, headed up by Louis Blériot, acquired the assets of the company. The company started producing Caudron G3 and G4 aircraft under licence and once production lines were under way, the chief engineer of the company, Louis Béchereau, began to produce aircraft under the company's new name, Société Anonyme pour l'Aviation et ses Dérivés.

A number of different variants appeared over the next three years, none of which attracted the attention of the British until the appearance of the SPAD 7.

The SA series of aircraft were of a basic conventional design, but the addition of a gunner's cockpit in front of the propeller gave the aircraft an unusual look. It gave the gunner, however, an interrupted forward view and a clear field of fire. The cockpit was hinged at the point on the undercarriage axle where the support struts were fixed, so as to give clear access to the engine. The engine could be started without having to move the cockpit forward, but it invariably was moved for safety reasons.

Powered by an 80-hp Le Rhône 9C, the first of these aircraft, the SA.1, appeared at the beginning of 1915. The aircraft was tested by the Aviation Militaire, who found that the engine overheated because of inadequate cooling caused by the nacelle in front of it. The gunner's cockpit also suffered badly from vibration. Despite the criticisms an order was placed, but only ten were built because of the arrival of the SA.2.

The SA.2 was an improved version of the SA.1 and fitted with a more powerful engine, the 110-hp Le Rhône 9J. A few minor modifications were made, and again the aircraft was tested by Aviation Militaire. Satisfied with the adjustments they had recommended, they ordered forty-two of the aircraft. The Russian Imperial Air Service had also seen the aircraft and placed an order for fifty-seven, but these were fitted with the 80-hp Le Rhône engine.

The crews never felt comfortable with the gunner's nacelle perched in the front of the aircraft. They felt vulnerable, and always worried that on landing, if the aircraft nosed over, they would be crushed by the engine right behind them. The forward view from the cockpit was very restricted, mainly because it was located in the middle of the fuselage and hampered by the gunner in front.

The SA.2 saw very limited service at the front, and was superseded by the SA.4. There was one SA.3 which had a crew of three, two gunners and a pilot, but it was the only one was built. The SA.4 consisted of an SA.2 airframe powered by an 80-hp Le Rhône engine. The wings were moved marginally backwards and the top wing was fitted with ailerons.

The first test flight took place on 22 February 1916 and was carried out by Aviation Militaire. They were not impressed and refused to order any, but the Russian Imperial Air Service was more approving and ordered ten.

The SA.4 was the last of the SA series of aircraft delivered to any combat service and were rapidly replaced, much to the relief of the aircrews. There were a number of other S series models built but none ever went into production.

The SPAD 7 was a single-seat, two-bay, equal-span biplane powered by a 150-hp Hispano-Suiza 8Ab engine. The first of the aircraft appeared at the beginning of 1916, and was immediately recognised by the RFC as having tremendous potential. Within a matter of days, the RFC had requested permission from the Directeur de l'Aéronautique Militaire to order three of the aircraft. The three aircraft arrived in September 1916 and were immediately sent to No. 60 Squadron for evaluation. The reports were excellent and prompted the RFC to place an order for another thirty. In order to support these orders, Blériot Aéronautique in England was given licence to build the additional orders, and the first came off the production line in November 1916.

The deliveries to the RFC squadrons were slow to start, but slowly and surely the production lines started to get into full swing, and by February 1917 most of the orders had been completed. The demand for the SPAD 7 was outstripping supply and when Trenchard asked for another fifty of them to be supplied to the RFC, the French transferred ten from their own Réserve Générale de l'Aviation. An order for 120 SPAD 7s plus spares was approved by the French in March 1917, and was built by the manufacturing company of Avionnerie Kellner et ses Fils.

The RNAS also saw the potential of the SPAD 7 and had ordered a substantial number of the aircraft from the Mann, Egerton Co. Ltd, who was also building the aircraft under licence. During the intense aerial battles over various fronts in October 1916, the RNAS were asked to release their quota to the RFC. A number of structural defects had, however, been discovered in the ones built by Mann, Egerton and Co. that needed serious modifications. It appears that none of these aircraft were ever sent to the front.

The Blériot Company supplied a further 100 to the RFC, and these were immediately assigned to Nos 30 and 63 Squadrons stationed in Mesopotamia and Palestine. During the Battle of Arras and the Third Battle of Ypres, it was discovered that the SPAD 7 was extremely effective when used in the ground attack role. Throughout the remainder of the war, the SPAD 7 served both in the front line as a ground attack aircraft and as a training aircraft. Although the majority of the SPAD 7s were replaced with Sopwith Dolphins, such was the respect for the aircraft that a number were retained and used on wireless interruption flights.

The number of countries which purchased the aircraft was twenty: Argentina (two), Belgium (twenty-two), Chile (one), Czechoslovakia (fifty), Estonia (two), Finland (one acquired from the Russians), Greece (sixteen), Italy (over 100), Japan (four), Netherlands (one interned after crash-landing); Peru (two); Poland (twenty); Portugal (seventeen), Romania (eight), Russia (forty-three bought – over 100 built under licence by Dux company), Serbia (eight), Siam (four), Ukraine (two), United Kingdom (over 100) and United States (167).

A number of other variations of the SPAD 7 appeared and the odd one was acquired by the RFC for evaluation, but none were ever purchased.

During this period, the SPAD 11 appeared. This was in fact an enlarged version of the SPAD 7, but with a positive stagger of the two-bay equal span wings. This was a two-seat, dual control aircraft armed with a fixed, forward-firing Vickers machine gun, with a Lewis machine gun mounted on a ring in the rear observer's cockpit. Extensive testing was carried out and the evaluation report was not good. It was found that the aircraft's performance was inadequate for its original purpose as a two-seat fighter, and that the Hispano-Suiza engine was unreliable.

Despite this damning report, production of the aircraft started in April 1917, mainly because there was nothing else available at the time and the aircraft situation was becoming desperate. In total over 1,000 of the aircraft were built, and this included a number of variants and different engines. One of the variants, a night fighter, was fitted with a searchlight that was mounted in front of the propeller.

In January 1918, the RFC acquired a SPAD 12 and subjected it to trials. It proved to be an extremely difficult aircraft to fly and crashed during a trial flight on the Isle of Grain. The problems with the SPAD 12 had been recognised by the manufacturers, and work started on finding a solution. What was developed was the SPAD 13. This was an aircraft that had been under development since the early part of 1917 and, after extensive tests, the only criticism that was any cause for concern was the limited view of the pilot from the cockpit. The SPAD 13 was almost an enlarged version of the SPAD 7. It retained the single-bay bracing with intermediate staggered struts, and the tail section, fin, rudder and tailplanes were more rounded. The armament was increased to twin 7.65 mm Vickers machine guns or, in some cases, four 25 lb Cooper bombs.

Disappointed as they were regarding the SPAD 12, the RFC examined one of the SPAD 13s and ordered one. It was subjected to stringent tests, and was found to be better that anything else that was presently available. An order for sixty of the aircraft was placed, the first being delivered in November 1917 and the last in March 1918. The majority of the SPAD 13s were assigned to No. 23 Squadron, RFC and saw action in some of the bitterest fighting during the Battle of Arras, the Third Battle of Ypres and Messines Ridge.

The Aviation Maritime, who depended on land-based fighter aircraft to provide escorts for their long-range reconnaissance seaplanes when required, put forward a proposal for one to be built. The result was the SPAD 14, which was based on the design of the SPAD 12. It was a two-bay biplane powered with a 220-hp Hispano-Suiza engine.

The prototype flew in November 1917, was an immediate success and an order was placed for thirty-nine more of the aircraft to be built by SPAD. It remained in service until well after the war. None were ever sold to other countries.

At the same time as the SPAD 14 made its appearance, an improved version of the SPAD 11, the SPAD 16, made its debut. This was a two-seat, two-bay biplane powered by a 240-hp Lorraine 8Bb engine, which, although it improved the aircraft's performance, still encountered the same design flaws that plagued the SPAD 11. The fabric-covered wings were constructed using spruce spars, with plywood ribs and a steel wire trailing edge and coated with 'Emaillite', a special enamel. The fuselage was constructed from four spruce longerons supported by piano wire and covered in fabric. It tapered down to the tail section, which consisted of a triangular fixed fin with a D-shaped rudder.

Over 1,000 SPAD 16 aircraft were built, but they still could not overcome the design faults that plagued both the SPAD 11 and 14.

The development of the SPAD 17 at the beginning of 1918 came as a result of a need for a more powerful fighter in order to maintain the air superiority that the Allies had gradually acquired. Based on the design of the SPAD 13, the SPAD 17 was fitted with a 300-hp Hispano-Suiza 8Fb engine. It was designed to be used as a fighter/reconnaissance aircraft, and as such was limited to carrying only one machine gun.

Twenty of the aircraft were built with the possibility of further orders to come later, but the Section Technical Aeronautique (STAé), who placed the orders for aircraft, decided that the improved Nieuport 29 would be better suited to carry out the role.

With the war in its fourth year, there was a need for a fast fighter/bomber. The Aviation Militaire asked for designs and tenders for such an aircraft, and SPAD produced the SPAD 20. Based on the design of the SPAD 18, the SPAD 20 was powered by a 300-hp Hispano-Suiza 8Fb engine. The fuselage was of a monocoque design made from moulded wood. The tail section was built in the same way as the fuselage, with large tail surfaces. This was a single-bay biplane, the upper wing having a slight sweepback and the lower wing being straight with ailerons. Constructed with spruce longerons and plywood ribs, the wings were covered in fabric.

One new innovation was that the engine mountings had been designed so as to make it quick and easy for the removal of the engine while in the field. Armament consisted of twin synchronised Vickers machine guns mounted on top of the engine fairing, and one 7.7 mm Lewis machine gun mounted in the rear gunner's cockpit.

Tests were carried out by military test pilots and a number of minor problems were discovered, but after these had been rectified an order for 300 of the aircraft was placed. The Armistice halted delivery of the aircraft and the order was reduced to 100, ninety-five of which actually ended up being delivered. This was the last SPAD aircraft to be built during the war, and the contribution made by the company was instrumental in bringing about the downfall of the German Air Service.

SPECIFICATIONS

SPAD SA.2

Wing Span:	31 ft 2 in (9.5 m)
Length:	25 ft 6 in (7.8 m)
Height:	8 ft 6 in (2.6 m)
Weight Empty:	912 lb (414 kg)
Weight Loaded:	1,486 lb (674 kg)
Maximum Speed:	86 mph (140 km/h)
Engine:	One 110-hp Le Rhône 9J
Armament:	One 7.7 mm Lewis machine gun mounted in gunner's cockpit

SPAD SA.4

Wing Span:	31 ft 2 in (9.5 m)
Length:	25 ft 6 in (7.8 m)
Height:	8 ft 6 in (2.6 m)
Weight Empty:	912 lb (414 kg)
Weight Loaded:	2,116 lb (960 kg)
Maximum Speed:	82 mph (135 km/h)
Engine:	One 110-hp Le Rhône 9J
Armament:	One 7.7 mm Lewis machine gun mounted in gunner's cockpit

SPAD 7

Wing Span Upper:	25 ft 8 in (7.8 m)
Wing Span Lower:	24 ft 10¼ in (7.5 m)
Length:	19 ft 11½ in (6.0 m)
Height:	7 ft 2½ in (2.2 m)
Weight Empty:	1,102 lb (500 kg)
Weight Loaded:	1,554 lb (705 kg)
Maximum Speed:	120 mph (193 km/h)
Engine:	One 150-hp Hispano-Suiza 8Ab
	One 180-hp Hispano-Suiza 8Ab
	One 150-hp Wolseley W.4A Python I
	One 180-hp Wolseley A.4A Python II.
Armament:	One fixed forward-firing Vickers machine gun
	Two 25 lb Cooper bombs

SPAD 11

Wing Span:	36 ft 8 in (11.2 m)
Length:	25 ft 6 in (7.8 m)
Height:	8 ft 6 in (2.6 m)
Weight Empty:	1,497 lb (679 kg)
Weight Loaded:	2,282 lb (1,035 kg)
Maximum Speed:	131 mph (211 km/h)
Engine:	One 220-hp Hispano-Suiza 8Bc
Armament:	One fixed forward-firing Vickers machine gun
	One 7.7 mm Lewis gun, mounted on a ring in observer's cockpit

SPAD 13

Wing Span:	26 ft 11 in (8.2 m)
Length:	20 ft 5 in (6.3 m)
Height:	8 ft 6 in (2.6 m)
Weight Empty:	1,325 lb (601 kg)
Weight Loaded:	1,887 lb (856 kg)
Maximum Speed:	131 mph (211 km/h)
Engine:	One 220-hp Hispano-Suiza 8Bc
Armament:	Two fixed forward-firing Vickers machine guns

SPAD 14

Wing Span:	32 ft 2 in (9.8 m)
Length:	24 ft 3 in (7.4 m)
Height:	13 ft 2 in (4.0 m)
Weight Empty:	1,697 lb (770 kg)
Weight Loaded:	2,337 lb (1,060 kg)
Maximum Speed:	127 mph (205 km/h)
Engine:	One 220-hp Hispano-Suiza 8Cb
Armament:	One fixed forward-firing Vickers machine gun

SPAD 16

Wing Span:	36 ft 9 in (11.2 m)
Length:	25 ft 6 in (7.8 m)
Height:	9 ft 2 in (2.8 m)
Weight Empty:	1,697 lb (770 kg)
Weight Loaded:	2,513 lb (1,140 kg)
Maximum Speed:	175 mph (108 km/h)
Engine:	One 240-hp Lorraine 8Bb
Armament:	One fixed forward-firing Vickers machine gun
	Two 7.7 mm Lewis machine guns mounted on a ring in observer's cockpit

SPAD 17

Wing Span:	26 ft 2 in (8.0 m)
Length:	20 ft 5 in (6.2 m)
Height:	8 ft 6 in (2.6 m)
Weight Empty:	1,514 lb (687 kg)

Weight Loaded: 2,077 lb (942 kg)
Maximum Speed: 134 mph (217 km/h)
Engine: One 300-hp Hispano-Suiza 8Fb
Armament: Two fixed forward-firing Vickers machine guns

SPAD 20

Wing Span: 32 ft 2 in (9.8 m)
Length: 23 ft 5 in (7.2 m)
Height: 8 ft 8 in (2.8 m)
Weight Empty: 1,911 lb (867 kg)
Weight Loaded: 2,438 lb (1,106 kg)
Maximum Speed: 150 mph (242 km/h)
Engine: One 300-hp Hispano-Suiza 8Fb
Armament: Two fixed forward-firing Vickers machine guns
One 7.7 mm Lewis machine gun in rear cockpit

Tellier

Alphonse Tellier designed and built his first aircraft, the T.1, in 1910. It was designed as a racing seaplane and was powered by a 35-hp Panhard-Levasseur engine and built specifically for a M. Dubonnet. Whether it was successful is not known, but Alphonse Tellier ceased making any more aircraft and turned his attention to building fast motor boats and hulls for other seaplane manufacturers.

Tellier returned to the manufacture of seaplanes in 1916, when he was paid 25,000 francs to design and build a two-seat patrol flying boat. Given the designation Tellier T.2, the aircraft was a joint venture: the Voisin Company built the wings, while Tellier designed and constructed the wooden hull. The T.2 was powered by a 200-hp Hispano-Suiza 8Ba engine.

The first test flight took place in June 1916, and was flown by Sgt Duyck, an Aviation Militaire pilot, with Alphonse Tellier as passenger. The series of test flights that followed were all very successful and, during one landing when the hull was damaged, the aircraft stayed afloat because of the watertight compartments inside the hull. The aircraft was later destroyed due to engine failure.

The success of the T.2 resulted in an order being placed for two more of the aircraft just one month after its demise. The T.3, as it was designated, was a two-bay, unequal span biplane where the lower wing was bolted on to the fuselage and the upper wing was attached to the four engine-mount struts. The wings were supported by metal struts mounted at oblique angles and intertwined metal cables. The ailerons were attached to the upper wing only. The aircraft was powered by a 200-hp Hispano-Suiza 8Ac pusher engine, which gave the T.3 a top speed of 135 km/h. The pilot sat directly in front of the engine, while the gunner/observer sat in the nose. The fuel tank was situated behind the engine inside the fuselage, while the oil reservoirs were mounted either side of the engine.

After the accident with the T.2, Alphonse Tellier had patented his seaplane design and incorporated the watertight compartments into the hull of the T.3. Flight tests were carried out by the Aviation Militaire and by the Navy, who then placed an order for ten of the aircraft to be built. It was then that the RNAS became interested and ordered two for evaluation purposes. After numerous tests, the two Tellier T.3s were given the designations N84 and N85 and taken to the Isle of Grain, where they were used for camouflage and gun trials. None were ever ordered, despite favourable reports from all the pilots who flew the aircraft.

The French Navy, although satisfied with the performance of the T.3, wanted a flying boat that could carry a larger payload. They issued a requirement for a flying boat that could carry 1,000 kg and have the same performance as that of the T.3. The Tellier Company produced two aircraft, the T.4 and T.5. The T.4 was fitted with the powerful 350-hp Sunbeam engine, and the T.5 was fitted with two 250-hp Hispano-Suiza engines mounted in tandem.

The T.4 had a re-designed bow, with a hull that had two steps and a strengthened fuselage which was constructed with two thicknesses of plywood. The unequal wings had spars made from metal tube, with ash/plywood ribs that were held in place with piano wire. The structure was covered in a linen fabric and coated with 'Emailite', a special enamel paint. Sixteen metal struts supported the wings with a tubular steel 'Y'shaped support that extended from the top leading edge of the wing to the top of the tail section.

After extensive tests the aircraft was accepted by the Navy, but modifications had to be made to the aircraft so that the wings folded back for ease of storage. A large number of the aircraft were ordered, but it is not known exactly how many were delivered.

The T.5 was developed to enable the Navy to mount a 47 mm cannon on the nose and be able to carry up to 300 kg of bombs. A biplane with an unequal span, the T.5 was considerably larger than the previous models. Carrying a crew of three, pilot and observer sitting side by side and a gunner in the nose, it had two 250-hp Hispano-Suiza engines mounted in tandem. Like the previous models, the wings had tubular steel spars with ash/plywood ribs that were supported by piano wire. The fuselage consisted of two steps and was covered in double thickness plywood.

After extensive tests and modifications so that the wings could be folded back, ten of the aircraft were ordered, the first being delivered in April 1918.

The limited success of the 47 mm cannon on ground-attack missions prompted the Navy to consider mounting the gun on a fighter. Tellier mounted one of the cannon in the nose of a T.3, but found that the weight of the gunner and cannon combined, caused the centre of gravity of the aircraft to be altered. To compensate for this, the fuselage was lengthened at the point of the second step. The new aircraft was designated the Tellier T.6 and was sent to the Navy for testing. Satisfied with the results, the Navy ordered fifty-five, but because of the earlier structural problems suffered by the T.3, the STAé ordered the fuselage to be strengthened. The T.6 was chiefly used in the Atlantic and the Mediterranean on anti-submarine patrols.

The Tellier Company built some of the French Navy's finest flying boats, several of which were still flying in the 1920s.

SPECIFICATIONS

Tellier T.3

Wing Span:	51 ft 1 in (15.6 m)
Length:	38 ft 9 in(11.8 m)
Height:	11 ft 7 in (3.6 m)
Weight Empty:	2,535 lb (1,150 kg)
Weight Loaded:	3,960 lb (1,796 kg)
Maximum Speed:	84 mph (135 km/h)
Engine:	One 200-hp Hispano-Suiza 8Ac
Armament:	One forward-firing Vickers machine gun in nose

Tellier T.4

Wing Span:	75 ft 5 in (23.0 m)
Length:	48 ft 3 in (14.7 m)
Height:	13 ft 3 in (4.1 m)
Weight Empty:	4,630 lb (2,100 kg)
Weight Loaded:	7,181 lb (3,257 kg)
Maximum Speed:	80 mph (128 km/h)

Engine: One 350-hp Sunbeam
Armament: One forward-firing 7.7 mm Vickers machine gun in nose
                          Four Corpet Lance bombs

Tellier T.5

Wing Span: 75 ft 4 in (22.9 m)
Length: 51 ft 10 in (15.8 m)
Height: 13 ft 3 in (4.1 m)
Weight Empty: 4,630 lb (2,100 kg)
Weight Loaded: 7,276 lb (3,300 kg)
Maximum Speed: 83 mph (135 km/h)
Engine: Two 250-hp Hispano-Suiza 8Bs
Armament: One 47 mm Hotchkiss cannon
                          Four 300 kg bombs

Tellier T.6

Wing Span: 51 ft 1 in (15.6 m)
Length: 41 ft 7 in (12.7 m)
Height: 11 ft 2 in (3.4 m)
Weight Empty: 2,668 lb (1,210 kg)
Weight Loaded: 5,887 lb (2,670 kg)
Maximum Speed: 78 mph (125 km/h)
Engine: One 200-hp Hispano-Suiza 8Ac
Armament: One 47 mm Hotchkiss cannon

Tellier T.7

Wing Span: 98 ft 5 in (30.0 m)
Length: 69 ft 9 in (21.3 m)
Height: 19 ft 5 in (5.9 m)
Weight Empty: 10,253 lb (4,650 kg)
Weight Loaded: 15,765 lb (7,150 kg)
Maximum Speed: 81 mph (130 km/h)
Engine: Three 250-hp Hispano-Suiza 8B
Armament: None

Vickers Aviation Ltd

The Vickers Company's first excursion into the field of aeronautics was in 1908, when they accepted a contract from the Admiralty to build a large rigid airship. The airship was the Naval Airship No. 1, or *Mayfly*, as she was called, and made her first appearance in 1911 when she left her floating hangar at Barrow and made the short journey to her mooring mast, which was on a pontoon. This was the first time any airship had actually tied up to a mooring mast and it wasn't until after the First World War, when the German *Graf Zeppelin* was flown, that it was used again. The *Mayfly* collapsed on leaving her hangar for her second flight, when she was caught by a sudden gust of wind. The damage was so extensive that it was beyond all economic repairs and so it was scrapped.

The company in the meantime had set up an aviation design and construction department with the intention of building their own aeroplanes. Their first aircraft were monoplanes and it wasn't until the advent of the First World War that they turned their attention to the design and construction of biplane fighter aircraft. A number of designs had been put forward, but the one selected was the Experimental Fighting Biplane (E.F.B) 1. This was a two-bay biplane fitted with an 80-hp Wolseley pusher engine mounted at the rear of the nacelles. The airframe was of a metal tube construction, with only the two cockpit nacelles being covered in duraluminium, and the staggered, equal wings were warped to obtain lateral control. The wings were braced, not with piano wire, which was the norm at the time, but with stranded steel wire. A single Vickers machine gun protruded from the front of the nacelle under the control of the observer/gunner who sat in the front cockpit.

The undercarriage consisted of two 'V's made of steel tubing extending outwards and downwards, and connected to a central hollow skid made of ash. Suspension consisted of strong rubber springs. The tail section consisted of a rectangular-shaped rudder to which the tailskid was attached. As the rudder was moved so was the tailskid, enabling the pilot to steer the aircraft while taxiing at low speeds. The top of the rudder was level with the top of the upper wing, and was attached to the top of the tubular steel tail outriggers.

The E.F.B.1 was shown at the Aero Show at Olympia in February 1913 and caused quite a stir, as it was the first aircraft ever to be shown equipped with a machine gun. Its appearance was short lived, as it crashed on its first test flight and was destroyed. However it laid the way open for the E.F.B.2 which, when it appeared, had unstaggered, unequal wings and large celluloid panels fitted into the sides of the cockpit nacelles. It was powered by a 100-hp Gnome Monosoupape rotary pusher engine. The aircraft carried out a number of trials that led to the appearance of the E.F.B.3 in December 1913. Almost identical to the E.F.B.2, the E.F.B.3 had the celluloid windows removed and ailerons fitted to replace the wing warping.

The Admiralty placed an order for six of the aircraft, but after an improved version was shown at the Olympia Aero Show in 1914, the contract was taken over by the War Office. What developed from this was the E.F.B.5 prototype that retained the semi-circular tailplane. The aircraft was put into production with a revised tail section that was rectangular and a different nacelle configuration, which incorporated another type of gun mounting which carried the Lewis machine gun instead of the Vickers. The production models had the prefix E dropped from its designation, and were given the unofficial name 'Gunbus'. The F.B.5 'Gunbus' fighter had arrived.

The first of three aircraft, built by the Crayford Works who had taken over production from Vickers, arrived at No. 6 Squadron, RFC, at Netheravon in November 1914. The following month two of the aircraft were sent to the small town of Joyce Green, near Dartford, Kent, as part of the Air Defence of London squadron, and almost immediately one of them was in action. On Christmas Day 1914, a German Taube monoplane was spotted flying over the coast and 2nd Lieutenant M. R. Chidson and his gunner/observer Corporal Martin took off to intercept it. Reports later stated that they shot the aircraft down, but this was never confirmed.

As more and more F.B.5s came off the production line, they were assigned to various squadrons and one of them, No. 2 Squadron, RFC, was posted to France, taking with them one of the F.B.5s. The aircraft was later transferred to No. 16 Squadron, RFC, but within days it had been forced down behind enemy lines, and into the hands of the German Air Service. In June 1915, No. 5 Squadron, RFC, was equipped with nine F.B.5s, but by the end of the month only three remained, the remainder having been shot down and destroyed.

On 7 November 1915, Lieutenant G. S. M. Insall of No. 11 Squadron, RFC, together with his observer/gunner, Airman T. H. Donald, was on patrol in an F.B.5 when they attacked an Aviatik over Arras. After forcing the aircraft down, they destroyed the aircraft by strafing it with machine gun fire and then proceeded to attack German trench positions. During this attack their aircraft was badly damaged, forcing them to make a forced landing near a wood just 500 yards from the German lines. Despite being subjected to intense shelling and small arms fire, the two men repaired their aircraft during the night and took off in the morning, successfully returning to their airfield at Bertangles. For their actions, Lieutenant Insall was awarded the Victoria Cross, and Aircraftsman Donald the Distinguished Conduct Medal.

As with the majority of aircraft that flew in the First World War, both Allied and German, one of the major problems that dogged them was the unreliability of the rotary engines, both in maintenance and repair. It has to be realised that the aero engine was still in its infancy at this time, and the experience and ability of mechanical engineers in the armed forces was not of the same standard that would be reached in later years. Both Vickers and Darracq & Co. built over 119 F.B.5s.

Vickers did develop an aircraft capable of carrying a one-pound quick-firing gun, the F.B.7. It was initially supposed to have been powered by two 100-hp Gnome Monosoupape rotary tractor engines, but because of the scarcity of them at the time, two 80-hp Renault engines were installed instead. The aircraft was considerably underpowered, but despite this the War Office ordered twelve of the aircraft, the contract being sub-contracted to the Darracq Co. There were problems with the aircraft from day one, and the prototype was taken to the Central Flying School (CFS) for evaluation. Those who flew that aircraft complained about the design, the handling, the power, in fact almost everything. The verdict was that it was operationally useless, so Vickers asked that the order be cancelled and only the one aircraft was built.

A modified F.B.5 was produced with a large upper wing that had a large overhang braced by pyramid kingposts. Given the designation F.B.6, only the one was produced, as the extended wing did not enhance the performance in any way, in fact quite the opposite.

Using the basic design of the F.B.5, the Vickers design department came up with the F.B.9. It had newly designed wings with rounded tips, a new tailplane and elevators, and a much simplified, but stronger undercarriage. All the external bracing wires were streamline-section Rafwires. It was powered by a 100-hp Gnome Monosoupape rotary engine.

The prototype was sent to the CFS for flight evaluation and the reports that came back were very encouraging. There was some criticism regarding the cramped conditions in the observer/gunner's cockpit and the Vickers No. 3 Mk I gun mounting, but despite this the aircraft was sent to France on 24 January 1916 for front line evaluation by pilots of No. 11 Squadron, RFC. All who flew the aircraft said that it was a great improvement on the F.B.5, but the observers criticised the gun mounting and had it replaced with one of their own.

On 2 April, Captain Champion de Crespigny, together with his observer/gunner 2nd Lieutenant Hughes-Chamberlain, was on patrol when they attacked five German fighters. One was shot down and another fled back to his own lines; the remaining three, however, fought desperately and forced de Crespigny to break off his attack. His rudder controls and propeller were shot away, forcing him to make a crash landing, fortunately within his own lines. The F.B.9 was damaged beyond repair and was scrapped, but it had proved itself to be a worthy adversary against the German fighter.

The results of the evaluation prompted the War Office to order seventy-five of the aircraft from Vickers, who immediately sub-contracted the Darracq Co. to start production of the F.B.9. Shortly after production started at Darracq, the machines that made the streamline-section Rafwires broke down. This inevitably delayed the production of the aircraft, and it wasn't until April 1916 that the first of the Darracq-built F.B.9s was delivered to No. 11 Squadron, RFC. It was immediately noticed that a cable had replaced one of the bracing wires, and the remaining wires were not braced properly. Vickers immediately sent over spare sets of wires, but when they arrived they were found to be the wrong size. Vickers replaced them with wires already swaged to their oval shape but not threaded, which meant that the Darracq Co. had to send men over to France to cut threads on the cables and provide the fittings. This of course caused considerable delays in the production of the aircraft, and it wasn't until June that a further four arrived for the squadron.

Some F.B.9s saw action during the Battle of the Somme that had started on 1 July 1916, however, but it was very limited.

In the meantime fifty of the aircraft contracted to be built by the Darracq Co. were transferred to the Wells Aviation Co. The delays caused by the various problems caused the aircraft to be withdrawn from front line service, and all the remaining F.B.9s were assigned to training duties. A total of ninety-five F.B.9s were built.

There was one aircraft that was built just after the war started which had been designed by Vickers' chief test pilot, Harold Barnwell: the Barnwell Bullet. It was a single-seat scout single-bay biplane of equal span, powered by a 100-hp Gnome Monosoupape engine. The fuselage was almost circular and portly in appearance. It is not clear whether or not the aircraft ever flew, but it was involved in an accident and was badly damaged. Either the undercarriage collapsed or it overturned while on taxiing trials, but the project was handed over to Rex Pierson in the Vickers drawing office to redesign the aircraft. The result was the Vickers E.S.1. It had new wings with rounded tips, and the ailerons had been lengthened.

On 6 November 1915, Harold Barnwell, the original designer, took the E.S.1 for its first test flight and carried out a series of loops (to the consternation of those below watching), such was confidence that he had in the aircraft. The E.S.1 was sent to Saint-Omer, France for evaluation by front-line pilots of the RFC. After a series of flights by different pilots, all of whom complained about the visibility from the cockpit, the aircraft crashed during a test after the engine caught fire. It was discovered that when the pilots choked the engine, filling the cowling with petrol, there was no gap in the bottom of the cowling to let it get away, so it immediately caught fire. In a letter to the Assistant Director of Military Aeronautics (ADMA) on 5 January 1916, Brooke-Popham wrote:

> The Vickers Scout (Bullet) with the Monosoupape engine has been tested out here. It has been decided that with the present engine, it is too dangerous to fly owing to the risk of fire and orders have been given for it not to be flown any more.

The aircraft was returned to England in a packing case and delivered back to the Vickers Company. Despite this major setback, the results that came back from the pilots as regards the aircraft's performance were encouraging, and the War Office ordered six to be built. Surprisingly, the complaint about the visibility from the cockpit was ignored and nothing was done about it.

There was one noticeable difference from the prototype, and that was the installation of a single Vickers machine gun mounted into a sunken section of the top decking. There were a number of other minor differences, including the replacing of the wires cables with streamlined Rafwires for the interplane bracing. Two different engines were tested in the E.S.1 at this time: the 110-hp Clerget and the 110-hp Le Rhône.

The first of the six E.S.1s ordered by the War Office was taken to No. 1 Aircraft Depot (A.D.) at Saint-Omer on 18 May 1916. From there it was assigned to No. 11 Squadron, RFC and used on a number of missions. It was returned to No. 2 A.D., minus its machine gun and interruptor gear and in a very sorry state. Two more of the six had also arrived in France, and within a few months they too were returned, as was the fourth. The remaining two were assigned to No. 50 Home Defence Squadron at Dover. The ones that were returned from France all had reports that the aircraft was no good for combat duty because of the difficulty in seeing out of the machine, a problem highlighted in the prototype but never addressed by the manufacturers. The second of the E.S.1s that had been returned had been modified by placing a small celluloid window in the centre section of the upper wing in an effort to improve the pilot's view. Re-designated the E.S.2 (E.S.1 Mk II), the aircraft was fitted with the 110-hp Clerget engine and the fairing was removed from the underside of the fuselage, enabling the surplus oil and petrol vapours to escape.

A second E.S.2 was made and used for trials with the Vickers-Challenger gun synchronising mechanism, which enabled the pilot to shoot through the arc of the propeller. With the tests completed, the aircraft was sent to France for operational trials with No. 11 Squadron, RFC. Despite having received good reports regarding performance, the same criticisms about the restrictive view from the cockpit prevailed. For some unknown reason, this problem failed to register with Vickers and nothing was ever done about it. However, in August 1916 an unstaggered version of the Vickers Bullet appeared as the F.B.19 Mk I, and later a staggered version known as the Mk II. Fifty Mk Is were built, and twelve Mk IIs, a number of the latter being sent to Russia after a demonstration of the Mk I. A few of the aircraft also saw service on the Western Front, Palestine and Macedonia.

Two other single-seat models were being evaluated at the time, the F.B.12 and the F.B.26. The F.B.12 was initially to have been fitted with the 150-hp Hart radial engine, but delay after delay resulted in the aircraft being fitted with an 80-hp Le Rhône. On the first test flight it became obvious that the aircraft was desperately underpowered, and so a 100-hp Gnome monosoupape engine was fitted. It was designated the F.B.12A, and although measurably better, it was still underpowered when compared with the D.H.2 and the F.E.8. Despite this, it was shipped to France in December 1916 for operational trials with the RFC. Two months later, the first of the aircraft fitted with the Hart radial engine appeared: the F.B.12B. During its second test flight, it crashed after the engine failed in flight. The contract with the Hart Company was cancelled.

In March 1917, a contract was given to the Wells Aviation Company of Chelsea to build eighteen F.B.12C models. Despite a number of different engines being tried, the aircraft was not a success and further contracts were cancelled.

Earlier in 1916 another model had appeared, the F.B.14, a single-engined tractor biplane designed specifically for general-purpose use. Based on the design of the F.B.11, the F.B.14 was a single-bay biplane with wings of unequal length and a steel-tube fuselage. Originally it had been intended to power the aircraft with the 200-hp B.H.P engine, but once again delays in obtaining it caused the aircraft to be fitted with a 160-hp Beardmore engine. The history of the unreliability of the later Beardmore engines caused the F.B.14 to be fitted with an older 120-hp Beardmore engine. Like many of the other models, it was desperately underpowered and out of 250 ordered, only 100 were actually built. A large number did see service in the Middle East, and seven were assigned to the Home Defence Squadrons; what happened to the remainder is not known. Three variants did emerge: the F.B.14A, which was fitted with a 150-hp Lorraine-Dietrich engine, the F.B.14D with a 250-hp Rolls-Royce engine, and the F.B.14F, fitted with a 150-hp R.A.F.4a engine of the sort which was fitted to the R.E.8 at the time.

While the development of the E.S.I and II was taking place, designers at Vickers were working on a model that would incorporate the Vickers-sponsored Hart radial engine. Designated the F.B.16 tractor, but also known as the Hart Scout, it was not the success hoped for and after numerous tests and a major redesign, the aircraft appeared as the F.B.16A, powered by the 150-hp Hispano-Suiza engine. A later model was fitted with the 200-hp Hispano-Suiza engine, and the aircraft was re-designated the F.B.16D.

The aircraft was subjected to a number of tests, and among them was one flown by one of Britain's top fighter aces, Major J. B. McCudden of 56 Squadron, RFC. McCudden was enthusiastic about the aircraft and flew it at almost every opportunity, and even made representation regarding taking the aircraft back to France with him. This was refused, despite being a highly decorated and distinguished airman, as it was not policy to allow pilots to have their own personal aircraft that differed from the ones flown by the squadron. This was unlike the practice in the German Army Air Service, where a number of their top pilots had sometimes two or even three personal aircraft. Despite the strong recommendations by McCudden and other pilots who flew the aircraft, it never went into production, as contracts had already been issued for the S.E.5a to be built by Vickers.

The development of the F.B.24, designed by test pilot Frank Barnwell, was another of those aircraft that looked good on the drawing board but in reality was not a success. A series of variants, F.B.24A, B, C, D, E, G, was identical in construction, the only difference being in the type of engine that was fitted. It was an ungainly-looking two-bay tractor aircraft with unequal wings and was very difficult to fly.

The design reverted back to the pusher-type with the development of the F.B.25, a two-seat night fighter. This was a development of the F.B.26, a single-seat pusher fighter, but only three were built. One was modified and re-designated the F.B.26A or Vampire Mk II, another was modified to become the F.B.25, and the other was fitted with a triple machine gun in an effort to increase the firepower. None were successful.

One aircraft that was built by Vickers and is deserving of a mention was the Vimy. Although it never flew operationally during the First World War, it started life in 1917 and was based on a design created in 1915. The design concerned was the E.F.B.8, a two-bay aircraft with unequal length wings into which were mounted two 100-hp Gnome Monosoupape engines. Only the one prototype was built, and that was seriously underpowered. Engine problems were to haunt Vickers and other manufacturers throughout the war years.

SPECIFICATIONS

E.F.B.8

Wing Span Upper:	38 ft 4 in (11.6 m)
Wing Span Lower:	36 ft 8 in (11.1 m)
Length:	28 ft 2 in (8.5 m)
Height:	9 ft 10 in (2.9 m)
Weight Empty:	1,840 lb (834 kg)
Weight Loaded:	2,610 lb (1,183 kg)
Maximum Speed:	98 mph (157 km/h)
Engine:	Two 100-hp Gnome Monosoupape Rotary
Armament:	One fixed forward-firing Lewis machine gun in nose

F.B.5

Wing Span:	36 ft 6 in (11.1 m)
Length:	27 ft 2 in (8.2 m)
Height:	11 ft 0 in (3.3 m)
Weight Empty:	1,220 lb (553 kg)
Weight Loaded:	2,050 lb (929 kg)
Maximum Speed:	70 mph (112 km/h)
Engine:	One 100-hp Gnome Monosoupape Rotary
Armament:	One fixed forward-firing Lewis machine gun

F.B.9

Wing Span:	33 ft 9 in (10.3 m)
Length:	28 ft 5½ in (8.6 m)
Height:	11 ft 6 in (3.5 m)
Weight Empty:	1,029 lb (466 kg)
Weight Loaded:	1,820 lb (825 kg)
Maximum Speed:	82 mph (131 km/h)
Engine:	One 100-hp Gnome Monosoupape Rotary
Armament:	One fixed forward-firing Lewis machine gun

E.S.1

Wing Span:	24 ft 5½ in (7.3 m)
Length:	20 ft 4 in (6.1 m)
Height:	8 ft 0 in (2.4 m)
Weight Empty:	1,052 lb (477 kg)
Weight Loaded:	1,600 lb (725 kg)
Maximum Speed:	118 mph (189 km/h)
Engine:	One 110-hp Le Rhône Rotary
Armament:	One fixed forward-firing Vickers machine gun

F.B.14

Wing Span Upper:	42 ft 0 in (12.8 m)
Wing Span Lower:	39 ft 6 in (12.1 m)
Length:	30 ft 8 in (9.3 m)
Height:	10 ft 3 in (3.1 m)
Weight Empty:	2,289 lb (1.038 kg)

Weight Loaded: 3,308 lb (1,500 kg)
Maximum Speed: 111 mph (178 km/h)
Engine: One 250-hp Rolls-Royce Eagle IV
Armament: Two Lewis and one Vickers machine gun

F.B.16

Wing Span Upper: 25 ft 0 in (7.6 m)
Wing Span Lower: 22 ft 4 in (6.7 m)
Length: 19 ft 6 in (5.9 m)
Height: 8 ft 9 in (2.6 m)
Weight Empty: 1,376 lb (624 kg)
Weight Loaded: 1,875 lb (850 kg)
Maximum Speed: 135 mph (217 km/h)
Engine: One 200-hp Hispano-Suiza
Armament: Two Lewis machine guns

F.B.25

Wing Span: 41 ft 6 in (12.6 m)
Length: 28 ft 1 in (8.5 m)
Height: 10 ft 10 in (3.3 m)
Weight Empty: 1,608 lb (729 kg)
Weight Loaded: 2,454 lb (1,113 kg)
Maximum Speed: 86 mph (138 km/h)
Engine: One 150-hp Hispano-Suiza
Armament: Two Vickers Crayford rocket guns

F.B.26

Wing Span Upper: 31 ft 6 in (9.6 m)
Wing Span Lower: 29 ft 0 in (8.8 m)
Length: 23 ft 5 in (7.1 m)
Height: 9 ft 5 in (2.8 m)
Weight Empty: 1,470 lb (666 kg)
Weight Loaded: 2,030 lb (920 kg)
Maximum Speed: 121 mph (193 km/h)
Engine: One 200-hp Hispano-Suiza
Armament: Two fixed forward-firing Lewis machine guns

Voisin

Gabriel Voisin was one of the most prolific French aircraft manufacturers of the First World War. In 1905, together with his brother Charles, Gabriel Voisin opened the first commercial aircraft factory in Europe, the Appareils d'Aviation Les Freres Voisin at Billancourt. In the years between 1907 and 1912, the company produced seventy-six aircraft and at the outbreak of war in 1914, two of the types built, the Voisin 1912 and 1913 Types were still in production. The French military carried out a number of trials with these two types, but it wasn't until the production of the Voisin 3 that the RFC became interested.

The Voisin 3 (LA) was a three-bay, equal span, two-seat biplane powered by a 130-hp Salmson M9 engine. The fuselage was constructed of metal and consisted of four booms, to which a single rudder with two elevators, one either side, were attached. The undercarriage was made up of four wheels that could be adjusted depending on the weight of the load being carried. The two rear wheels were fitted with brake drums, and were mounted directly beneath the engine and fuel tank. The front wheels were mounted just ahead of the nose of the aircraft, and were sometimes fitted with searchlights. All four struts of the undercarriage were fitted with spring shock absorbers. Armament consisted of a single Lewis machine gun mounted in the rear cockpit.

After obtaining two of the aircraft and subjecting them to various tests, the RFC placed an order for fifty of the aircraft to be manufactured in England under licence to the Dudbridge Iron Works. The Dudbridge Company already had the licence to build the Salmson Canton-Unné engines that were installed in the Voisin 3 aircraft, and it is almost certain that the construction of the airframe was sub-contracted out to Savages Ltd of Kings Lynn.

The first of the aircraft were assigned to No. 4 Squadron, RFC at the beginning of 1915. This was followed by deliveries to Nos 7 and 12 Squadrons, but by the end of the year all had been withdrawn from service. Not one had seen action in France, although those built in France saw action with No. 4 Squadron when the squadron was moved to the front. The Voisin 3 (LA)s that were remained were used for training purposes.

The Russians, however, were delighted with the aircraft, so much so in fact, that they purchased more than 800 Voisin 3s and built a further 400 under licence with five different factories – Anatra, Breshnev-Moller, Dux, Lebedev and Schetinin.

Even the Italians were persuaded to purchase two of the Voisin 3s and then, after extensive testing, decided to build the aircraft under licence. The S.I.T. (Societe-Italiana Transera) company acquired the rights and built over 100 between 1915 and 1917. Belgium and Romania also purchased a couple of the aircraft, but declined to build the aircraft under licence.

At the end of 1915, after seeing the results of tests from the RFC, the RNAS placed an order for thirty-six Voisin 3s, the first two arriving in Basra in January 1917. One of the Voisin 3 (LA.S) (the 'S' indicated the installation of a 140-hp Salmson engine) aircraft carried out more than eighty reconnaissance flights over the besieged city of Kut-al-Imara. When the RNAS withdrew from Mesopotamia in June 1916, the remaining Voisin 3 (LA.S) aircraft were transferred to the RFC. There is no record of exactly how many of the Voisin 3 aircraft were actually built for the RNAS, but it is believed that there were only a small number.

The Voisin 4 appeared in April 1915. This was a two-seat, equal span, three-bay, biplane powered by a 120-hp Salmson M9 engine. Armament consisted of a 37 mm cannon mounted in the extended nose and, to accommodate the recoil, the wings were moved back 40 cm. Otherwise, the dimensions of the aircraft were identical to those of the Voisin 3.

Tests were carried out successfully and a small number were ordered, but when tested under battle conditions, it was decided that the aircraft was too slow to be a fighter, and so was used for ground attack duties. One of the Voisin 4 aircraft was purchased by Argentina, a number were built by the Russian company Dux under licence, and the Netherlands acquired one when it landed on Dutch territory in error.

With the appearance of the triplane, the Voisin Company decided to produce a heavy bomber that was capable of attacking industrial targets in Germany using the triple wing. It was to be powered by four 270-hp Salmson radial engines mounted back-to-back, and had a wingspan of 124 ft 6 in (38 m). The workforce laboured night and day and in an incredible five weeks, the aircraft was rolled out for its first test flight – an unbelievable achievement. The landing gear consisted of three wheels mounted in tandem on either side of the fuselage, and a single large nosewheel that was slightly recessed in the fuselage. This was to prevent the huge aircraft from nosing over on landing.

The first flight, under the control of Voisin test pilot Joseph Frantz, was a complete success and the aircraft was then handed over to the military for further testing. The military immediately saw the one major problem that made the aircraft a liability – it was too slow. The maximum speed of the aircraft was just 86 mph (140 km/h), and that was without a maximum bomb load. The aircraft would be the perfect target for any anti-aircraft battery as it lumbered across the sky. It was rejected and returned to the factory.

Despite this setback, the company continued to design and produce more aircraft, and in August 1915 produced the Voisin 5. The Voisin 5 was in fact a Voisin 3 with a different engine, a strengthened fuselage and undercarriage. Powered by a 150-hp Salmson P9 engine, the Voisin 5 took to the air in September and the following month the first of the production models appeared at the front to replace the Voisin 3.

Although marginally faster that the 3, the new model carried almost the same payload and as such was no great improvement. Nevertheless, almost 300 of the aircraft were built and assigned to various Escadrilles.

In 1917, the RNAS purchased two Voisin 8Ca aircraft. These were aircraft capable of carrying a 37 mm Hotchkiss cannon together with 180 kg of bombs. The Voisin 8 had an enlarged fuselage capable of carrying three crewmembers, while the wings were set further back than those of the Voisin 3. The wingspan was also increased and a four-meter diameter propeller was fitted to the 220-hp Peugeot engine. The increased overall weight caused the undercarriage to be redesigned, the wheels being set further apart and the landing struts strengthened considerably. Six vertical tubes, three either side of the engine, carried the exhaust fumes over the top of the upper wing and prevented exhaust bubbles becoming trapped. The whole structure was made of steel, the fuselage covered in aluminium and the wings and tail section covered in fabric.

The two purchased by the RNAS were used in trials against submarines, but proved to be ineffective so no more were purchased. The two they had bought were then used for training purposes.

The Peugeot engine was the primary cause of all the problems with the Voisin 8, and despite attempts to rectify the problems it was finally replaced with the 280-hp Renault engine.

Within weeks of reaching the front line and engaging the Germans, it was quickly realised that it was no match for their faster and more manoeuvrable fighters. It was decided that the aircraft would be more suitable as a night-bomber. As it turned out the aircraft was ideal for this role, and throughout the next six months, the Voisin 8 was used extensively in successful bombing attacks against German airfields, train stations and enemy convoys of troops and materials.

The fitting of the 280-hp Renault 12 Fe engine made a significant difference to the Voisin aircraft and the development of the next model, the Voisin 10, which was identical in size to the 8, prompted the STAé to order 300 of the aircraft to be built. As time went by and problems with Farman and Caudron production lines caused delays, further orders were placed for the Voisin 10 and eventually a total of 900 of the aircraft were built. There was even an experiment to adapt one of the 10s to be converted into a flying ambulance, but although viable it was not completed until after the war.

The Voisin 10 was in fact the last of the military aircraft built by Voisin to go into full production. There were a number of other models built, including flying boats, but they never reached the production stage.

SPECIFICATIONS

Voisin 3 (LA)

Wing Span:	48 ft 4 in (14.7 m)
Length:	31 ft 2 in (9.5 m)
Height:	9 ft 8 in (2.9 m)
Weight Empty:	2,094 lb (950 kg)
Weight Loaded:	2,976 lb (1,350 kg)
Maximum Speed:	65 mph (105 km/h)
Engine:	One 130-hp Salmson Canton-Unné M9 (LA)
	One 140-hp Salmson Canton-Unné B9 (LA.S)
Armament:	One Lewis machine gun mounted in observer's cockpit
	200 lb of bombs

Voisin 4

Wing Span:	48 ft 4 in (14.7 m)
Length:	31 ft 2 in (9.5 m)
Height:	9 ft 8 in (2.9 m)
Weight Empty:	2,315 lb (1,050 kg)
Weight Loaded:	3,417 lb (1,550 kg)
Maximum Speed:	65 mph (105 km/h)
Engine:	One 120-hp Salmson M9
Armament:	One 37 mm cannon mounted in forward cockpit

Voisin 5

Wing Span:	48 ft 4 in (14.7 m)
Length:	33 ft 5 in (10.2 m)
Height:	12 ft 5 in (3.8 m)
Weight Empty:	2,149 lb (975 kg)

Weight Loaded:	3,197 lb (1,450 kg)
Maximum Speed:	74 mph (120 km/h)
Engine:	One 150-hp Salmson P9
Armament:	300 kg bombs

Voisin 8 CA

Wing Span:	59 ft 0 in (18.0 m)
Length:	33 ft 8 in (10.3 m)
Height:	12 ft 8 in (3.9 m)
Weight Empty:	2,888 lb (1,310 kg)
Weight Loaded:	4,101 lb (1,860 kg)
Maximum Speed:	73 mph (118 km/h)
Engine:	One 220-hp Peugeot 8Aa
Armament:	One 37 mm Hotchkiss cannon
	400 lb of bombs

Voisin 10

Wing Span:	59 ft 0 in (18.0 m)
Length:	33 ft 8 in (10.3 m)
Height:	12 ft 8 in (3.9 m)
Weight Empty:	3,087 lb (1,400 kg)
Weight Loaded:	4,851 lb (2,200 kg)
Maximum Speed:	80 mph (130 km/h)
Engine:	One 280-hp Renault 12Fe
Armament:	One 37 mm Hotchkiss cannon
	660 lb (300 kg) bombs

J. Samuel Wight & Co.

One of the least known of the British aircraft manufacturers was Samuel Wight from the Isle of Wight. One of their first aircraft, a pusher seaplane, made its appearance at Olympia in 1913. This large aircraft, the Wight Pusher Seaplane, was a five-bay, unequal span biplane, with a twin rudder and single top elevator that was attached by means of four booms. The upper two booms were attached to the upper wings, while the two lower booms were part of the undercarriage assembly. At the beginning of the First World War a military version was made with folding wings, which enabled the aircraft to be carried aboard seaplane-carriers like HMS *Ark Royal*. During this period, two of the eleven built for the RNAS saw service aboard HMS *Ark Royal* in the Dardanelles and carried out a number of reconnaissance sorties over Turkish lines.

With the desperate need for a torpedo-carrying seaplane high on the agenda for the Admiralty, the Wight Company produced the Wight Twin Seaplane. This was a two-seat, five-bay biplane powered by two 200-hp Salmson radial tractor engines. It had been initially designed and built as a landplane bomber, but had crashed during trials. The Wight Twin Seaplane had two fuselages which were fixed to the lower wing, and to which the engines and floats were connected. Two additional cylindrical-shaped floats were fitted to the lower wing tips to help support the aircraft. The crew was carried in a nacelle that was situated between the two fuselages; however, this was later discarded and the crew's positions were moved onto the two fuselages. Two prototypes with the new crew positions were built and re-designated the Wight Twin AD 100. They were seriously underpowered, as was discovered when they tried unsuccessfully to leave the water with a full fuel load and armed with a torpedo. They never reached their potential, and after numerous trials, were rejected by the RNAS.

But what did develop from these prototypes was the Wight Admiralty Type 840 Seaplane. The requirements were the same as those stipulated for the Short Type 184, and trials were carried out with the aircraft carrying a single 810 lb 14-inch torpedo. The aircraft was a two-seat, three-bay, equal span, tractor biplane powered by a 225-hp Sunbeam engine, which was cooled by means of twin radiators mounted on either side of the engine. The fuselage was of a simple box-shaped construction, with the two main floats attached to the fuselage by a complex series of struts with arched cross braces to accommodate the torpedo that was slung beneath the fuselage in between the floats.

The RNAS ordered seventy of the aircraft, forty-five of which were built by the Wight Company, the remainder by the William Beardmore Co. in Scotland and Portholme Aerodrome Co., Huntingdon. They were used on anti-submarine patrols in both Scapa Flow and Gibraltar, but there is no record of them using a torpedo during this period.

A landplane version was constructed using a tricycle undercarriage very much like the one used on the Graham-White Type 18, but only the one prototype was built.

Also in 1915, a new type of seaplane appeared, built under Admiralty requirements for a seaplane that could operate as a long-range bomber or torpedo carrier. The aircraft was known as the AD Seaplane Type 1000. The twin-fuselage, equal span biplane was powered by three 310-hp Sunbeam engines, two tractor, one in the nose of each fuselage and the other, a pusher, fitted at the rear of the central nacelle which held the crew of two. The Type 1000 had a wingspan of 155 feet, the largest of any aircraft built by the British at the time, and a tail section that consisted of rounded twin rudders and fins situated at the end of each fuselage. Twin floats at the front and the rear of this massive aircraft supported the aircraft on the water. Trials with the aircraft proved to be disastrous due to problems with lack of power and manoeuvrability. The project was abandoned and only the one aircraft was built.

In 1916, the Wight Company produced a single-engine bomber that was rejected by the RNAS, but when it was represented as a converted seaplane some months later, it was accepted and orders for fifty of the aircraft were placed. Only thirty-seven were actually built as the Short 184 production was increased and replaced many of the seaplanes.

A 322-hp Rolls-Royce Eagle VI engine powered the two-seat, unequal span three-bay biplane. The pilot and observer sat in tandem, the pilot in front and observer behind. A single Lewis machine gun mounted on a Scarff ring was the aircraft's only defence, but it carried four 100 lb bombs or 112 lb bombs beneath the wings.

The aircraft were used primarily on anti-submarine duties and on 22 September 1917, while on patrol in the English Channel, a Wight 'Converted' seaplane flown by Flt Sub-Lt C. S. Mossop and Air Mechanic A. E. Ingledew operating out of RNAS Cherbourg, came across U-boat UB-32, commanded by Kapitänleutnant Ditfurth, on the surface. Diving into attack they dropped a 100 lb bomb on the U-boat, scoring a direct hit and sank it with the loss of all hands. This was the first U-boat to be sunk by a direct attack from the air.

A second submarine was sunk in the English Channel on 5 May 1918, when Wight 'Converted' Seaplane No. 9850 operating from Portland, flown by Captain N. C. Harrison and Corporal Argent, RM, attacked the UB-70, commanded by Oberleutnant Remy. Three 100 lb bombs and one 65 lb bomb scored direct hits as it was diving. Wreckage from the submarine was later found by a trawler.

Throughout the remainder of the war the Wight 'Converted' Seaplane carried out patrols in the English Channel, but by the Armistice only seven of the original thirty-seven were still flying.

SPECIFICATIONS

Wight 'Converted' Seaplane

Wing Span:	65 ft 6 in (19.9 m)
Length:	44 ft 8 in (13.6 m)
Height:	16 ft 0 in (4.8 m)
Weight Empty:	3,758 lb (1,704 kg)
Weight Loaded:	5,556 lb (2,520 kg)
Maximum Speed:	85 mph (136 km/h)
Engine:	One 332-hp Rolls-Royce Eagle VI
Armament:	One Lewis machine gun mounted on a Scarff ring
	400 lb of bombs

Wight Pusher Seaplane

Wing Span:	63 ft 0 in (19.2 m)
Length:	44 ft 8 in (13.6 m)
Height:	16 ft 0 in (4.8 m)
Weight Empty:	1,758 lb (797 kg)
Weight Loaded:	3,500 lb (1,587 kg)
Maximum Speed:	72 mph (116 km/h)
Engine:	One 200-hp Salmson radial
Armament:	One Lewis machine gun
	400 lb of bombs

Wight Admiralty Type 840 Seaplane

Wing Span:	61 ft 0 in (18.5 m)
Length:	41 ft 0 in (12.4 m)
Height:	15 ft 3 in (4.6 m)
Weight Empty:	3,158 lb (1,432 kg)
Weight Loaded:	4,453 lb (2,019 kg)
Maximum Speed:	81 mph (130 km/h)
Engine:	One 225-hp Sunbeam
Armament:	One Lewis machine gun mounted on a Scarff ring
	One 810 lb 14-inch torpedo
	400 lb of bombs

The majority of British companies that produced aircraft in the First World War either faded away or were absorbed by other companies. Those that did survive led the world in aviation for decades to come, and encouraged other countries to contribute to aviation both in the military and civil fields.

ALSO AVAILABLE FROM AMBERLEY PUBLISHING

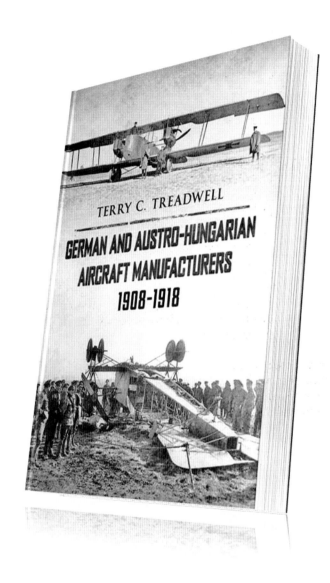

German and Austro-Hungarian
Aircraft Manufacturers
1908-1918
Terry C. Treadwell
ISBN 978-1-4456-0102-1

ALSO AVAILABLE FROM AMBERLEY PUBLISHING

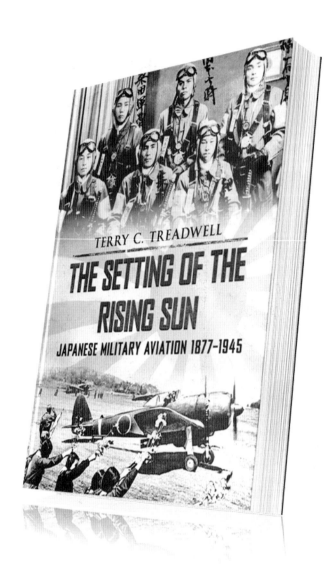

The Setting of the Rising Sun
Japanese Military Aviation 1877-1945
Terry C. Treadwell
ISBN 978-1-4456-0226-4

ALSO AVAILABLE FROM AMBERLEY PUBLISHING

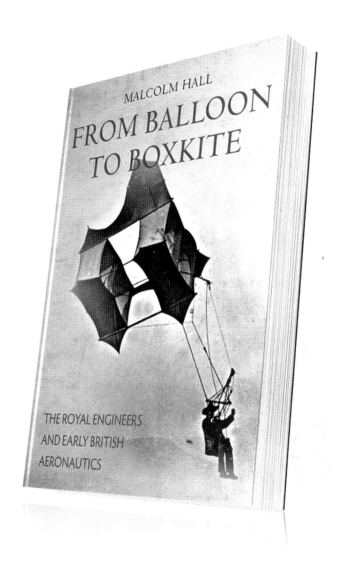

From Balloon to Boxkite
The Royal Engineers and early British
Aeronautics
Malcolm Hall
ISBN 978-1-4868-992-3

ALSO AVAILABLE FROM AMBERLEY PUBLISHING

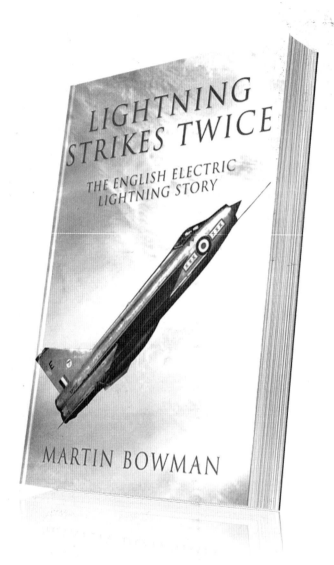

Lightning Strikes Twice
The English Electric Lightning Story
Martin Bowman
ISBN 978-1-84868-493-5